Selected Readings in Psychology
心理学专业英语教程

沈德灿　沈政　选

张华　注

北京大学出版社
北　京

图书在版编目(CIP)数据

心理学专业英语教程/张华编注.—北京：北京大学出版社，2001.8

(大学专业英语系列教程)

ISBN 978-7-301-05045-3

Ⅰ.心… Ⅱ.张… Ⅲ.心理学-英语-高等学校-教材 Ⅳ.H31

中国版本图书馆 CIP 数据核字(2001)第 034701 号

书　　　名：心理学专业英语教程
著作责任者：张　华　沈德灿　沈　政
著　作　编　辑：朱丽娜
标　准　书　号：ISBN 978-7-301-05045-3/H・0628
出　版　发　行：北京大学出版社
地　　　址：北京市海淀区成府路 205 号　100871
网　　　址：http://www.pup.cn
电　　　话：邮购部 62752015　发行部 62750672　编辑部 62767347
　　　　　　出版部 62754962
电　子　邮　箱：zpup@pup.pku.edu.cn
印　刷　者：北京虎彩文化传播有限公司
经　销　者：新华书店
　　　　　　850 毫米×1168 毫米　32 开本　9.25 印张　235 千字
　　　　　　2001 年 8 月第 1 版　2021 年 3 月第 10 次印刷
定　　　价：36.00 元

未经许可,不得以任何方式复制或抄袭本书之部分或全部内容。
版权所有,侵权必究　举报电话：010－62752024
　　　　　　电子邮箱：fd@pup.pku.edu.cn

大学专业英语系列教程

北京大学英语系大学英语教研室
北京大学文学文化与翻译研究会

顾问：李赋宁
主编：辜正坤
编委会：安美华　黄必康　石春祯　沙露茵　索玉柱
　　　　　范　红　赵白生　林庆新　何　姝　汪海涛
　　　　　付国英　张　华　张　政　余苏凌　孟凡君
专家委员会：
胡壮麟（北京大学）
刘意青（北京大学）
申　丹（北京大学）
沈　虹（北京大学）
袁可嘉（社科院）
李文俊（社科院）
何其莘（北京外国语大学）
裘克安（外交部）
方　平（上海译文出版社）
程慕胜（清华大学）
彭镜禧（台湾大学）
刘士聪（南开大学）
黄新渠（四川师范大学）
University of Chicago：Bevington David
State University of New York：Michelle Tsao
Graduate School of City University of New York：Tanya Viger

总　　序

辜正坤

　　西学东渐给东方的外语出版界造成一种奇特的景观:在相当短的时间内,外语出版物的数量扶摇直上,使它种民族语出版物相对汗颜,这是可以理解的。日本明治维新之后,就出现过类似的情形,外语(尤其是英语)原著注释读物动辄一套就是数百本,洋洋大观。毫无疑问,这对推进日本的外语教学起到了非常重要的作用。时至今日,其效应已经明显昭示出来:当今的中国各大学发表的论文为 SCI 所收录者,最多者一年达 500 篇,而东京大学一年就达 40000 篇,两者相距 80 倍! 如果以为日本的论文数量必与其科学水平成正比,因而中国大学的科学研究水平就落后了东大 80 倍的话,恐怕是一种很大的误解。其中的奥妙之一,就在于日本学者的英语水平普遍较高,许多论文是直接用英文写成,因此容易被世界各地的媒体注意到,其入选 SCI 的机会也就相对增多。反观中国学者的论文,绝大多数用汉语写成,少量靠懂英语的学者翻译,只有极少量的学者能够自己用英文直接写作。因此,大多数的中国论文是难以进入西方学者的视野的。当然入选 SCI 的机会也就相对少得多了。当然,这并非是说,中国的科研水平就反过来比日本高,而是说,由于中国学者英语写作水平普遍偏低的原因,其实际的科研水平未能在英语世界的文献中充分显示出来。由此可以明白,提高中国学者的英语能力(尤其是阅读文献与用英语写作的能力)是一件非常迫切的事。

　　然而,改革开放二十多年来的英语学习大潮虽然使许多中国人在英语学习方面获得了较高的造诣,上了一个较为理想的台阶,但是有更多的人却老在一个水平上徘徊不前:要学的教材已经学了,该考的科目已经通过了,但是,面对英语的殿堂,人们并没有登堂入室的感觉。听说能力未能应付裕如或者情有可原,因为学习者可以抱怨没有相应的可以一试身手的客观条件,但是在阅读方面,例如阅读文史哲数理化的专业文献方面,却仍是磕磕绊绊、跋前疐后,字典不离手,冷汗不离身。这种处于瓶颈地带,欲罢不可、欲进不能的促迫感,源于一个关键的原因:缺乏专业外语文献阅读训练。学校里使用的基础英语教材编得再好,也只能解决基础问题,不能解决超过基础的专业阅读问题。正如要做游泳健儿的人只在游泳池里按照游泳要领奋力拨拉了一阵池水,自觉亦有劈波斩浪之感,但与真正的河涛海潮相比,终究属于两重洞天。

于是,就产生了这一整套专业英语阅读教程。

它的目标非常明确,无非是要把英语知识与技能的培训和高层次系统知识的灌输二者有机结合起来,达到既学语言又学知识的目的;既温故,又知新。照我看来,这是最有效率的学习与巩固方略。

如前所述可以明白,这套教程不只是对一般想要提高英语实际水平的人有用,对于专家学者或研究人员,也有很大的好处。一个人无论多么博学多才,也不太可能对各个专业的英语经典文献和地道表达都了然于胸,因此,当需要在尽可以短的时间内对某专业的英语经典文献或概念有所把握时,这一整套书无疑不会使人们失望。

这套书的编选思路最初萌发于1991年,当时称作《注释本英文世界文化简明百科文库》。编者当时曾会同北京大学英语系大学英语教研室教师和北京大学出版社若干编辑共商过具体编选事宜,并由北京大学出版社出版。尔后还进行过多次类似的讨论。文库分上、中、下三编,每编含精选名著一百种左右。在编选思路上,力求达到雅俗共赏,深入浅出,系统全面。在系统性方面,注意参照《大英百科全书》和《中国大百科全书》的知识框架,用英文把更为完备的知识系统介绍给读者。在实用性方面,亦注意选材的内容与词汇量与现行的英语教材、实际英语教学水平相呼应。

本编为上编,除可供大学英语分科专业阅读选用教材之用外,亦可供社会上一般读者提高英语水平、直接经由阅读原著而掌握某一专业知识之用。基本的编辑方针是 1)选目必须系统、广泛,尽可能把大学的重要专业都包容进去(包括人文社会科学和理工科专业);2)选目可大致分三类:A. 简史类;B. 名篇、名著类;C. 比较规范的或经典的西方专业教材类;3)每册书的字数最好在 20 万字上下(个别可以例外)。至于其他具体事项,则随书说明。

教育部在 1999 年亦强调大学英语教学不能停留在基础英语教学上,而要逐步过渡到教授专业分科英语,使学生尽可能进入阅读专业英语文献的水平。因此这套教材的产生是适得其时的。

当然,它的具体效果如何,还有待检验。好在这套教材的编注与出版都是一个较长的过程,这期间可望获得有关方面的建议与批评,以期使它精益求精,日臻完善。

是为序。

2001 年于北京大学英语系

出版说明

《心理学专业英语教程》精选十九世纪末期和二十世纪的17位世界著名心理学家的代表作品。17篇心理学名著反映了心理学及其流派的发展,为心理学专业的研究生、本科生、心理学爱好者以及需要扩大知识范围,培养交叉学科研究能力和构建跨学科知识框架的学生提供学习英语的文献,也是为学习心理学专业英语的学生编写的教材。

在每篇名著注释后面,我们编有练习题及答案,以便更好地帮助大家理解每篇文章的主要观点。练习除问答题、判断正误以外,还将作品中一些较难较长的句子挑选出来,要求译成中文,其目的是对复杂句子的结构有清楚的理解。阅读心理学家的名篇不仅帮助大家对某一学科历史的发展有明确了解,更重要的是通过阅读原著提高英语水平和能力。在所选文章中,有大量的短语、习语及词汇,为了帮助大家有效地掌握它们,我们还设计了选词填空题,希望提高语言的语用能力。

我们热诚希望得到各界专家、学者和广大读者的批评、指导和支持。

编注者
1999 年 9 月 27 日

CONTENTS

1. The Association of Ideas ·············· J. Mill(1)
   观念的联合 ································· 穆勒
2. The Composition of Mind ············ H. Spencer(15)
   心的构成 ···································· 斯宾塞
3. Habit ························· W. James(29)
   习惯 ·· 詹姆士
4. Adolescence ····················· G. S. Hall(42)
   青春期 ······································ 霍尔
5. Early Empiricism, Naturalism, Materialism
   ······························ J. M. Baldwin(55)
   早期经验主义,自然主义,唯物主义 ·········· 鲍尔温
6. The Postulates of a Structural Psychology
   ······························ E. B. Titchener(67)
   构造心理学公设 ···························· 铁钦纳
7. The Reflex Arc Concept in Psychology ········ J. Dewey(79)
   心理学中的反射弧概念 ···················· 杜威
8. General Characteristics of Original Tendencies
   ······························ E. L. Thorndike(91)
   原本趋向的普遍特征 ······················ 桑代克
9. Unlearned Behavior:"Emotion" ········ J. B Watson(105)
   非习得的行为:情绪 ························ 华生
10. The Principal Instincts and the Primary Emotion
    of Man ························· W. McDougall(116)
    人类的主要本能和原始情绪 ·············· 麦独孤

1

11. The Uses of Intelligence Tests ············ D. M. Terman(128)
    智力测验的功用 ·· 特曼
12. The Interpretation of Dreams ·············· S. Freud(140)
    梦的解析 ·· 弗洛伊德
13. Attention in Cognitive Neuroscience:
    An Overview ······························· M. I. Posner(153)
    认知神经科学中的注意:总论 ························ 波斯纳
14. Attention, Intelligence, and the
    Frontal Lobes ······························ J. Duncan(169)
    注意,智力和额叶 ······································ 敦坎
15. Implicit Memory: A New Frontier
    for Cognitive Neuroscience ············ D. L. Schacter(184)
    内隐记忆:认知神经科学的一个新领域 ············· 夏克特
16. Mental Models, Deductive Reasoning,
    and the Brain ···················· P. N. Johnson-Laird(198)
    心理模型,演绎推理和脑 ······················ 约翰逊-莱尔德
17. Models of Consciousness: Serial
    or Parallel in the Brain? ·········· M. Kinsbourne(218)
    意识的模型:脑内是串行的还是并行的? ·········· 肯斯伯尼
词汇表·· (236)
练习参考答案··· (253)

1. The Association of Ideas

James Mill

詹姆士·穆勒(James Mill 1773—1836)是苏格兰联想主义心理学家。他在心理学方面最重要的贡献是完成《人心现象的分析》一书。他继承了英吉利联想主义传统。早期他的联想主义包含机械论的观点,认为简单观念由于机械的结合,造成复杂观念并把机械观的联想主义推演到极端的地步。穆勒认为一切心理现象源于感觉,心理状态是由感觉与观念决定的,观念是感觉的摹本和影象,观念互相联合即产生更复杂的观念。他在观念感觉、意识的看法上表现了极端联想主义者的片面性。

《观念的联合》(The Association of Ideas)是詹姆士·穆勒的代表作品《人心现象的分析》中的第三章。此文发表于1829年。当时的新启蒙运动对心理学发展具有重要意义,主要表现为功利主义和联想主义这两种学说的紧密联系。功利主义的动机学说代表边沁(Jeremy Bentham, 1748—1832)对功利主义的享乐主义作了有力的表述。他认为个体应该选择那些将使人得到最大快乐和最小痛苦的行动来安排他或她的生活。快乐和痛苦的值由相应感觉的强度延续性、确定性和接近性来决定。近代不可知论的代表休谟(David Hume, 1711—1776)把心理内容区别为印象和观念并提出三条联想律,即相似律、时空接近律和因果律。穆勒热心解释边沁的享乐主义,同时追随休谟的区别感觉与它们的复本—观念学说,力图把所有心理活动归结为联想,把因果关系归结为固定的联想链。

"To have a clear view of the phenomena of the mind, as mere affections or states of it, existing successively, and in a certain series, which we are able, therefore, to predict, in consequence of[①] our knowledge of the past, is, I conceive, to have made the most important acquisition which the intellectual inquirer can make.[②]"

Brown,[③] *Lectures*, i. 544.

1

THOUGHT succeeds thought; idea follows idea, incessantly. If our senses are awake, we are continually receiving sensation④, of the eye, the ear, the touch, and so forth; but not sensations alone. After sensations, ideas are perpetually excited of sensations formerly received; after those ideas, other ideas; and during the whole of our lives, a series of those two states of consciousness, called sensations, and ideas, is constantly going on⑤. I see a horse: that is a sensation. Immediately I think of his master: that is an idea. The idea of his master makes me think of his office; he is a minister of state: that is another idea. The idea of a minister of state makes me think of public affairs; and I am led into a train of political ideas; when I am summoned to dinner. This is a new sensation, followed by the idea of dinner, and of the company with whom I am to partake it. The sight of the company and of the food are other sensations; these suggest ideas without end; other sensations perpetually intervene, suggesting other ideas: and so the process goes on.

In contemplating this train of feelings, of which our lives consist, it first of all strikes the contemplator, as of importance to ascertain, whether they occur casually and irregularly, or according to a certain order.

With respect to⑥ the SENSATIONS, it is obvious enough that they occur, according to the order established among what we call the objects of nature, whatever those objects are; to ascertain more and more of which order is the business of physical philosophy in all its branches.

Of the order established among the objects of nature, by which we mean the objects of our senses, two remarkable cases are all which here we are called upon to notice; the SYNCHRONOUS ORDER and the SUCCESSIVE ORDER⑦. The synchronous order, or order of simultaneous existence, is the order in space; the successive order, or order of antecedent and consequent existence, is the order in time. Thus the various objects in my room, the chairs, the tables, the books, have the synchronous order, or order in space. The falling of the spark, and the explosion of the gunpowder, have the successive order, or order in time.

According to this order, in the objects of sense, there is a synchronous, and a successive, order of our sensation. I have SYNCHRONICALLY, or at the same instant, the sight of a great variety of objects; touch of all the objects with which my body is in contact; hearing of all the sounds which are reaching my ears; smelling of all the smells which are reaching my nostrils; taste of the apple which I am eating; the sensation of resistance both from the apple which is in my mouth, and the ground on which I stand; with the sensation of motion from the act of walking. I have SUCCESSIVELY the sight of the flash from the mortar fired at a distance, the hearing of the report, the sight of the bomb, and of its motion in the air, the sight of its fall, the sight and hearing of its explosion, and lastly, the sight of all the effects of that explosion.

Among the objects which I have thus observed synchronically, or successively; that is, from which I have had synchronical or successive sensations; there are some which I have so observed frequently; others which I have so observed not frequently; in other words, of my sensations some have been frequently synchronical, others not frequently; some frequently successive, others not frequently. Thus, my sight of roast beef and my taste of roast beef, have been frequently SYNCHRONICAL; my smell of a rose, and my sight and touch of a rose, have been frequently synchronical; my sight of a stone, and my sensations of its hardness, and weight, have been frequently synchronical. Others of my sensations have not been frequently synchronical: my sight of a lion, and the hearing of his roar; my sight of a knife, and its stabbing a man. My sight of the flash of lightning, and my hearing of the thunder, have been often SUCCESSIVE; the pain of cold, and the pleasure of heat, have been often successive; the sight of a trumpet, and the sound of a trumpet, have been often successive. On the other hand, my sight of hemlock, and my taste of hemlock, have not been often successive; and so on.

It so happens, that, of the objects from which we derive the greatest part of our sensations, most of those which are observed synchronically, are frequently observed synchronically; most of those which are observed successively, are frequently observed successively. In other words, most of our synchronical sensations, have been frequently synchronical; most of our successive sensations, have been frequently successive. Thus, most of our synchronical sensations are derived from the objects around us, the objects which we have the most frequent occasion to hear and see; the members of our family; the furniture of our houses; our food; the instruments of our occupations or amusements. In like manner[8], of those sensations which we have had in succession; we have had the greatest number repeatedly in succession[9]; the sight of fire, and its warmth; the touch of snow, and its cold; the sight of food, and its taste.

Thus much with regard to[10] the order of SENSATIONS; next with regard to the order of IDEAS.

As ideas are not derived from objects, we should not expect their order to be derived from the order of objects; but as they are derived from sensations, we might by analogy expect, that they would derive their order from that of the sensations; and this to a great extent is the case[11].

Our ideas spring up, or exist, in the order in which the sensations existed, of which they are the copies[12].

This is the general law of the "Association of Ideas"; by which term, let it be remembered, nothing is here meant to be expressed, but the order of occurrence.

In this law, the following things are to be carefully observed.

1. Of those sensations which occurred synchronically, the ideas also spring up synchronically. I have seen a violin, and heard the tones of the violin, synchronically. If I think of the tones of the violin, the visible appearance of the violin at the same time occurs to me. I have seen the sun, and the sky in which it is placed, synchronically. If I think of the one, I think of the other at the same time.

One of the cases of synchronical sensation, which deserves the most particular attention, is, that of the several sensations derived from one and the same object; a stone, for example, a flower, a table, a chair, a horse, a man.

From a stone I have had, synchronically, the sensation of colour, the sensation of hardness, the sensations of shape, and size, the sensation of weight. When the idea of one of these sensations occurs the ideas of all of them occur. They exist in my mind synchronically; and their synchronical existence is called the idea of the stone; which, it is thus plain, is not a single idea, but a number of ideas in a particular state of combination.

Thus, again, I have smelt a rose, and looked at, and handled a rose, synchronically; accordingly the name rose suggests to me all those ideas synchronically; and this combination of those simple ideas is called my idea of the rose.

My idea of an animal is still more complex. The word thrush, for example, not only suggests an idea of a particular colour and shape, and size, but of song, and flight, and nestling, and eggs, and callow young, and others.

My idea of a man is the most complex of all; including not only colour, and shape, and voice, but the whole class of events in which I have observed him either the agent or the patient.

2. As the ideas of the sensations which occurred synchronically, rise synchronically, so the ideas of the sensations which occurred successively, rise successively.

Of this important case of association, or of the successive order of our ideas, many remarkable instances might be adduced. Of these none seems better adapted to the learner[13] than the repetition of any passage, or words; the Lord's Prayer[14], for example, committed to memory. In learning the passage, we repeat it; that is we pronounce the words, in successive order, from the beginning to the end. The order of the sensations is successive. When we proceed to repeat the passage, the ideas of the words also rise in succession, the preceding always suggesting the succeeding, and no other. *Our* suggests *Father*, *Father* suggests *which*, *which* suggests *art*; and so on, to the end[15]. How remarkably this is the case, any one may convince himself, by trying to repeat backwards[16], even a passage with which he is as familiar as the Lord's Prayer. The case is the same with numbers. A man can go on with the numbers in the progressive order, one, two, three, &c. scarcely thinking of his act; and though it is possible for him to repeat them backward, because he is accustomed to subtraction of numbers[17], he cannot do so without an effort.

Of witnesses in courts of justice it has been remarked, that eye-witnesses, and ear-witnesses, always tell their story in the chronological order; in other words, the ideas occur to them in the order in which the sensations occurred; on the other hand, that witnesses, who are inventing, rarely adhere to[18] the chronological order.

3. A far greater number of our sensations are received in the successive, than in the synchronical order. Of our ideas, also, the number is infinitely greater that rise in the successive than the synchronical order.

4. In the successive order of ideas, that which precedes, is sometimes called the suggesting, that which succeeds, the suggested-idea[19]; not that any power is supposed to reside in the antecedent over the consequent[20]; suggesting, and suggested, mean only antecedent and consequent, with the additional idea, that such order is not casual but, to a certain degree, permanent.

5. Of the antecedent and consequent feelings, or the suggesting, and suggested; the antecedent may be either sensations or ideas; the consequent are always ideas. An idea may be excited either by a sensation or an idea. The sight of the dog of my friend is a sensation, and it excites the idea of my friend. The idea of Professor Dugald Stewart delivering a lecture, recalls the idea of the delight with which I heard him; that, the idea of the studies in which it engaged me; that, the trains of thought which succeeded; and each epoch of my mental history[21], the succeeding one, till the present moment; in which I am endeavouring to present to others what appears to me valuable among the innumerable ideas of which this lengthened train has been composed[22].

6. As there are degrees in sensations, and degrees in ideas; for one sensation is more vivid than another sensation, one idea more vivid than another idea; so there are degrees in association. One association, we say, is stronger than another: First, when it is more permanent than another; Secondly, when it is performed with more certainty; Thirdly, when it is performed with more facility.

It is well known, that some associations are very transient, others very permanent. The case which we formerly mentioned, that of repeating words committed to memory, affords an apt illustration㉓. In some cases, we can perform the repetition, when a few hours, or a few days have elapsed; but not after a longer period. In others, we can perform it after the lapse of many years㉔. There are few children in whose minds some association has not been formed between darkness and ghosts. In some this association is soon dissolved; in some it continues for life.

In some cases the association takes place with less, in some with greater certainty㉕. Thus, in repeating words, I am not sure that I shall not commit mistakes㉖, if they are imperfectly got; and I may at one trial repeat them right, at another wrong: I am sure of always repeating those correctly, which I have got perfectly. Thus, in my native language, the association between the name and the thing is certain; in a language with which I am imperfectly acquainted, not certain. In expressing myself in my own language, the idea of the thing suggests the idea of the name with certainty. In speaking a language with which I am imperfectly acquainted, the idea of the thing does not with certainty suggest the idea of the name; at one time it may, at another not.

That ideas are associated in some cases with more, in some with less facility, is strikingly illustrated by the same instance, of a language with which we are well, and a language with which we are imperfectly, acquainted. In speaking our own language, we are not conscious of any effort; the associations between the words and the ideas appear spontaneous. In endeavouring to㉗ speak a language with which we are imperfectly acquainted, we are sensible of a painful effort: the associations between the words and ideas being not ready, or immediate.

(From *Analysis of the Phenomena of the Human Mind*, Chapter 3)

注　释

① in consequence of　由于……缘故,等于 as a consequence of。例如:In consequence of your bad behavior I am forced to dismiss you. 由于你行为不轨,我只得解雇你。

② ... to have made the most important acquisition which the intellectual inquirer can make.　此句中 which 引导一个定语从句,译为:……就是从事理智探究的人所能收到的最重要的心得了。the intellectual inquirer 指从事理性研究工作的人。

③ Brown(Thomas Brown, 1778—1820)　托马斯·布朗是苏格兰学派代表人。他强调心灵的主动性。他用提示(suggestion)一词代替联想概念,提出九条联想副律,说明联想得以实现的具体条件。布朗心理学代表著作是《关于人心的哲学讲演》。

④ sensation 指从感觉器官(耳、眼等)获得到的感觉,而 sense 是指感官即感觉器官。

⑤ ... a series of those two states of consciousness, called sensations, and ideas, is constantly going on. 在这句中, states of consciousness 指意识处于某种状态。全句译为:这种叫做感觉和观念的意识状态,连成一串,永久延续着。

⑥ with respect to　至于,关于。

⑦ the SYNCHRONOUS ORDER and the SUCCESSIVE ORDER：同时的秩序和继起的秩序。指秩序的发生和变化有其先后顺序。

⑧ in like manner　同样地。

⑨ in succession　连续地。如 Reports of victory came in quick succession. 捷报频传。

⑩ with regard to＝in regard to　关于……的问题。如:With(In) regard to your request for a refund, we have referred the matter to our main office.关于你要求退款一事,我们已转给总公司办理。

⑪ ...but as they are derived from sensations, we might by analogy expect, that they would derive their order from that of the sensations; and this to a great extent is the case.　可是观念是从感觉中产生的,以此类推,我们可以预期观念的秩序是由感觉秩序产生的;实际情形大体如此。

⑫ Our ideas spring up, or exist, in the order in which the sensations existed, of which they are the copies.　我们的观念是我们感觉的摹写,所以观念存在的秩序是依照感觉存在的秩序。

⑬ ...better adapted to the learners...　此句中,adapt to 表示适合于。例如:the calling best adapted to one's taste.译为最适合某人的职业。

⑭ the Lord's Prayer　指主的祈祷文。

⑮ *Our* suggests *Father*, *Father* suggests *which*, *which* suggests *art*; and so on, to the end. 这是祈祷文的开始:"我们在天上的父"。"我"引起"们","们"引起"在","在"引起"天","天"引起"上";这样一直到背完为止。

⑯ ...repeat backwards　这里指将数字倒背。

⑰ subtraction of numbers　减去

⑱ adhere to　指坚持。如:He adheres too closely to the regulation. 他拘泥规则。

⑲ In the successive order of ideas, that which precedes, is sometimes called the suggesting, that which succeeds, the suggested idea.　此句中,the suggesting idea 指能引的观念,the suggested idea 指所引的观念。人的观念的获得更多情况下是先后得来的。先获得的观念是能引观念,后来得到的是所引观念。

⑳ ...not that any power is supposed to reside in the antecedent over the consequent　此句中 reside...over...表示(某种权利)属于或强加于。全句译为:这并不是以为前观念对于后观念有什么控制力量。

㉑ ...and each epoch of my mental history　我思想发展的每一时

期。

㉒ ...in which I am endeavouring to present to others what appears to me valuable among the innumerable ideas of which this lengthened train has been composed. 这一长串的无数观念，其中有些在我看来像有价值的，我此刻正想呈献于读者。

㉓ The case which we formerly mentioned, that of repeating words committed to memory, affords an apt illustration. 上文提到的背诵文字的过程是一个适宜的例证。

㉔ after the lapse of many years 过了好多年。a lapse of 指时间流逝，间隔，如：with the lapse of time 时间流逝。

㉕ In some cases the association takes place with less, in some with greater certainty. 在此句中，有部分成分被省略。全句为：In some cases the association takes place with less (certainty), in some (cases the association takes place) with greater certainty. 此句译为：在有些事例中，联想不那么确定会出现；在其他地方，联想的出现比较可靠。

㉖ commit mistakes 犯错误。

㉗ in endeavouring to 指努力去做某事。

练　习

1. 回答问题

(1) What are the meanings of sensation and idea? What are the relations between these two terms? Please take an example to state them.

(2) What are the three characteristics of association? What are the causes of strength in association?

(3) What are the two remarkable cases which we are called upon to notice?

(4) What do the suggesting idea and the suggested idea refer to?

2. 判断正误
(1) The synchronous order is the order in time.
(2) Most of our synchronical sensations are derived from the objects around us, the objects which we have the most frequent occasion to hear and see.
(3) My idea of a man is simple, just like that of a stone. From a stone I have had, synchronically, the sensation of color, the sensation of hardness, the sensations of shape, and size, the sensation of weight.
(4) In my native language, the association between the name and the thing is certain; in a language with which I am imperfectly acquainted, not certain.
(5) In learning a foreign language, we are sensible of a painful effort: the association between the words and ideas being not ready, or immediate.

3. 选词填空
Fill in the blanks with the words or expressions given below
apt, lengthen, commit, with regard to, precede, successive, by analogy, endeavor
(1) Historically there should be no letter I in the word could, it was inserted _____ with would.
(2) They have _____ many horrible crimes against the American people.
(3) His _____ reply to the question showed that he had understood it very quickly.
(4) Mother has to _____ my coat because it is too short for me.
(5) She was always in perfect sympathy with me _____ my love of nature.
(6) We should all _____ to be more considerate of others.

(7) The singer who is _____ the pop group in the program is very good.

(8) The moon progresses through its _____ phases.

4. 句型模拟

Model: make up a sentence with "given"

Given the high success rate of acupuncture treatment, Jack is sure to get well.

(1) to a great extent
(2) in consequence of

5. 英译汉

(1) With respect to the SENSATION, it is obvious enough that they occur, according to the order established among what we call the objects of nature, whatever those objects are; to ascertain more and more of which order is the business of physical philosophy in all its branches.

(2) The ideas are associated in some cases with more, in some with less facility, is strikingly illustrated by the same instance, of a language with which we are well, and a language with which we are imperfectly, acquainted.

(3) In some cases the association takes place with less, in some with greater certainty.

6. 汉译英

Model:

如果证据能证实指控的话,这个人将被判有罪。(bear out)

If the evidence bears out the charge, the man will be convicted.

(1) 乡村许多地方仍坚持使用旧历。(adhere to)
(2) 我们必须把这所房子改得适合老人们的需要。(adapt to)

(3) 我从他的忠告中得到很多益处。(derive from)
(4) 灾厄频仍。(in succession)
(5) 到处杂草丛生。(spring up)

7. 写作指导

In the last paragraph of the article, the author says: That ideas are associated in some cases with more, in some with less facility, is strikingly illustrated by the same instance, of a language with which we are well, and a language with which we are imperfectly, acquainted. In speaking our own language, we are not conscious of any effort, the associations between the words and the ideas appear spontaneous. In endeavoring to speak a language with which we are imperfectly acquainted, we are sensible of a painful effort: the association between the words and ideas being not ready, or immediate.

In order to have a better understanding of these above words, you are encouraged to share with your experience both in learning English and speaking your native language of Chinese with examples illustrated. The following language points taken from the article may serve as a good means of expressing yourself well.

——commit mistakes
——afford an apt illustration
——perform the repetition
——elapse
——after the lapse of many years
——form some association in minds

2. The Composition of Mind

Herbert Spencer

赫伯特·斯宾塞(Herbert Spencer, 1880—1903)是英国哲学家、教育家、社会学家和心理学家。他用生物学规律解释社会现象,是个进化论者。早在1859年达尔文(Charles Darwin, 1809—1882)发表《物种起源》之前,他就把进化论和英国的联想主义心理学结合起来,发表了穆勒父子的理论,成为进化的联想主义心理学家。他认为心理的元素,不仅有感觉和情绪,而且还存在着各种关系,他还探讨有机体的心理对环境适应的问题,并认为这才是研究心理学的主要目的。

《心的构成》(The Composition of Mind)节选自《心理学原理》(1885)。此书是赫伯特·斯宾塞的代表著作,是他《综合哲学》全书的一部分。斯宾塞强调用科学方法来研究社会现象。哲学是各学科基本原理的综合。他将自然科学及社会科学知识总结为一个综合的哲学体系。《心理学原理》是在斯宾塞这种思想指导下完成的。

§64. In the last chapter we incidentally encroached on the topic to which this chapter is to be devoted. Certain apparently-simple feelings were shown to be compounded of units of feeling; whence it was inferred that possibly, if not probably, feelings of other classes are similarly compounded. And thus treating of the composition of feelings, we, by implication, treated of the composition of Mind, of which feelings are themselves components.

Here, however, leaving speculations about the ultimate composition of Mind[①], we pass to observations on its proximate composition[②]. Accepting as really simple those constituents of Mind which are not decomposable by introspection[③], we have to consider what are their fundamental distinctive characters, and what are the essential principles of arrangement among them.

§ 65. The proximate components of Mind are of two broadly-contrasted kinds — Feelings and the Relations between feelings. Among the members of each group there exist multitudinous unlikenesses[4], many of which are extremely strong; but such unlikenesses are small compared with those which distinguish members of the one group from members of the other. Let us, in the first place, consider what are the characters which all Feelings have in common[5], and what are the characters which Relations between feelings have in common.

Each feeling, as we here define it, is any portion of consciousness which occupies a place sufficiently large to give it a perceivable individuality[6]; which has its individuality marked off[7] from adjacent portions[8] of consciousness by qualitative contrasts[9]; and which, when introspectively contemplated, appears to be homogeneous. These are the essentials. Obviously if under introspection, a state of consciousness is decomposable, into unlike parts that exist either simultaneously or successively, it is not one feeling but two or more. Obviously if it is indistinguishable from an adjacent portion of consciousness, it forms one with that portion — is not an individual feeling but part of one. And obviously if it does not occupy in consciousness an appreciable area, or an appreciable duration[10], it cannot be known as a feeling.

A relation between feelings is, on the contrary, characterized by occupying no appreciable part of consciousness. Take away the terms it unites, and it disappears along with them; having no independent place — no individuality of its own. It is true, that, under an ultimate analysis, what we call a relation proves to be itself a kind of feeling — the momentary feeling accompanying the transition from one conspicuous feeling to an adjacent conspicuous feeling. And it is true that, notwithstanding its extreme brevity, its qualitative character is appreciable; for relations are (as we shall hereafter see) distinguishable from one another only by the unlikenesses of the feelings which accompany the momentary transitions[11]. Each relational feeling may, in fact, be regarded as one of those nervous shocks[12] which we suspect to be the units of composition of feelings; and, though instantaneous, it is known as of greater or less strength and as taking place with greater or less facility. But the contrast between these relational feelings and what we ordinarily call feelings, is so strong that we must class them apart. Their extreme brevity, their small variety, and their dependence on the terms they unite, differentiate them in an unmistakable way[13].

Perhaps it will be well to recognize more fully the truth that this distinction cannot be absolute. Besides admitting that, as an element of consciousness, a relation is a momentary feeling, we must also admit that just as a relation can have no existence apart from the feelings which form its terms, so a feeling can exist only by relations to other feelings which limit it in space or time or both. Strictly speaking, neither a feeling nor a relation is an independent element of consciousness[14]: there is throughout a dependence such that the appreciable areas of consciousness occupied by feelings, can no more possess individualities apart from the relations which link them, than these relations can possess individualities apart from the feelings they link. The essential distinction between the two, then, appears to be that whereas a relational feeling is a portion of consciousness inseparable into parts[15], a feeling ordinarily so-called, is a portion of consciousness that admits imaginary division into like parts[16] which are related to one another in sequence or coexistence. A feeling proper[17] is either made up of like parts that occupy time, or it is made up of like parts that occupy space, or both. In any case, a feeling proper is an aggregate of[18] related like parts, while a relational feeling is undecomposable[19]. And this is exactly the contrast between the two which must result if, as we have inferred, feelings are composed of units of feeling, or shocks.

§ 66. Simple feelings as above defined, are of various kinds. To say anything here about the classification of them, involves some forestalling of a future chapter. This breach of order, however, is unavoidable; for until certain provisional groupings have been made[20], further exposition is scarcely practicable.

Limiting our attention to seemingly-homogeneous feelings as primarily experienced, they may be divided into the feelings which are centrally initiated and the feelings which are peripherally initiated[21]— emotions and sensations[22]. These have widely unlike characters. Towards the close of this volume evidence will be found that while the sensations are relatively simple, the emotions, though seeming to be simple are extremely compound; and that a marked contrast of character between them hence results. But without referring to any essential unlikeness of composition, we shall shortly see that between the centrally-initiated feelings and the peripherally-initiated feelings, fundamental distinctions may be established by introspective comparison.

A subdivision has to be made. The peripherally-initiated feelings, or sensations, may be grouped into those which, caused by disturbances at the ends of nerves distributed on the outer surface, are taken to imply outer agencies[23], and those which, caused by disturbances at the ends of nerves distributed within the body, are not taken to imply outer agencies; which last, though not peripherally initiated in the ordinary sense, are so in the physiological sense. But as between the exterior of the body and its interior, there are all gradations of depth㉔, it results that this distinction is a broadly marked one, rather than a sharply marked one. We shall, however, find that certain differential characters among the sensations accompany this difference of distribution of the nerves in which they arise; and that they are decided in proportion to㉕ the relative superficiality or centrality of these nerves.

In contrast with this class of primary or real feelings㉖, thus divided and subdivided, has to be set the complementary class of secondary or ideal feelings㉗, similarly divided and subdivided. Speaking generally, the two classes differ greatly in intensity㉘. While the primary or originally-produced feelings are relatively vivid, the secondary or reproduced feelings㉙ are relatively faint. It should be added that the vivid feelings are taken to imply objective exciting agents㉚ then and there acting on the periphery of the nervous system; while the faint feelings, though taken to imply objective exciting agents which thus acted at a past time, are not taken to imply their present action.

We are thus obliged to carry with us a classification based on structure and a classification based on function. The division into centrally-initiated feelings, called emotions, and peripherally-initiated feelings, called sensations; and the subdivision of these last into sensations that arise on the exterior of the body and sensations that arise in its interior; respectively refer to differences among the parts in action. Whereas the division into vivid or real feelings and faint or ideal feelings, cutting across the other divisions at right angles as we may say, refers to difference of amount in the actions of these parts. The first classification has in view㉛ unlikenesses of kind among the feelings; and the second, a marked unlikeness of degree, common to all the kinds.

§ 67. From the classes of simple feelings we pass to the classes of simple relations between feelings, respecting which also, something must be said before we can proceed. In default of^㉜ an ultimate analysis, which cannot be made at present, certain brief general statements must suffice.

As already said, the requisite to the existence of a relation is the existence of two feelings between which it is the link. The requisite to the existence of two feelings is some difference. And therefore the requisite to the existence of a relation is the occurrence of a change — the passage from one apparently-uniform state^㉝ to another apparently-uniform state, implying the momentary shock produced by the commencement of a new state.

It follows that the degree of the change or shock, constituting in other words the consciousness of the degree of difference between the adjacent states, is the ultimate basis of the distinctions among relations. Hence the fundamental division of them into relations between feelings that are equal, or those of likeness (which however must be divided by some portion of consciousness that is unlike them), and relations between feelings that are unequal, or those of unlikeness. These last fall into what we may distinguish as relations of descending intensity and relations of ascending intensity, according as the transition is to a greater or to a less amount of feeling. And they are further distinguishable into relations of quantitative unlikeness, or those occurring between feelings of the same nature but different in degree, and relations of qualitative unlikeness, or those occurring between feelings not of the same nature.

Relations thus contemplated simply as changes, and grouped according to the degree of change or the kind of change, severally belong to one or other of two great categories which take no account of the terms as like or unlike in nature or amount, but which take account only of their order of occurrence, as either simultaneous or successive. This fundamental division of relations into those of co-existence and those of sequence④, is, however, itself dependent on the preceding division into relations of equality between feelings and relations of inequality between them. For relations themselves have to be classed as of like or unlike kinds by comparing the momentary feelings that attend the establishment of them, and observing whether these are like or unlike, and, as we shall hereafter see, the relations of co-existence and sequence are distinguished from one another only by process of this kind.

§ 68. Having defined simple feelings and simple relations, and having provisionally classified the leading kinds of each, we may now go on to observe how Mind㉟ is made up of these elements, and how different portions of it are characterized by different modes of combination of them.

Tracts of consciousness㊱ formed of feelings that are centrally initiated, are widely unlike tracts of consciousness formed of feelings that are peripherally initiated; and of the tracts of consciousness formed of peripherally-initiated feelings, those parts occupied by feelings that take their rise in the interior of the body are widely unlike those parts occupied by feelings that take their rise on the exterior of the body㊲. The marked unlikenesses are in both cases due to the greater or smaller proportions of the relational elements that are present. Whereas among centrally-initiated feelings, the mutual limitations, both simultaneous and successive, are vague and far between; and whereas among peripherally-initiated feelings caused by internal disturbances, some are extremely indefinite, and few or none definite in a high degree; feelings caused by external disturbances are mostly related quite clearly, alike by co-existence and sequence, and among the highest of them the mutual limitations in space or time or both, are extremely sharp. These broad contrasts, dependent on the extent to which the elements of feeling are compounded with the elements of relation, cannot be understood, and their importance perceived, without illustrations. We will begin with those parts of Mind distinguished by predominance of the relational elements[38].

Remembering that the lenses of the eye[39] form a nonsentient optical apparatus[40] that casts images on the retina, we may fairly say that the retina is brought more directly into contact with the external agent[41] acting on it than is any other peripheral expansion of the nervous system. And it is in the tracts of consciousness produced by the various lights reflected from objects around and concentrated on the retina, that we find the elements of feeling most intimately woven up with[42] the elements of relation. The multitudinous states of consciousness yielded by vision, are above all others sharp in their mutual limitations; the differences that occur between adjacent ones are extremely definite. It is further to be noted that the relational element is here dominant under both of its fundamental forms. Some of the feelings simultaneously limit one another with great distinctness, and some of them with equal distinctness successively limit one another. The feelings caused by actions on the general surface of the body are marked off clearly, though by no means so clearly as those which arise in the retina. Sensations of touch initiated at points on the skin very near one another, form parts of consciousness that are separate though adjacent; and these are distinguishable not only as co-existing in close promixity, but also as distinct from kindred sensations immediately preceding or immediately succeeding them. Moreover the definiteness of their mutual limitations, in space if not in time, is greatest among the sensations of touch proceeding from parts of the surface which have, in a sense, the greatest externality — the parts which, like the tips of the fingers and the tip of the tongue, have the most frequent and varied converse with outer objects[43]. Next in the definiteness of their mutual limitations come the auditory feelings[44]. Among such of these as occur together, the relations are marked with imperfect clearness. Received through uncultivated ears, only a few simultaneous sounds are vaguely separable in consciousness; though received through the ears of a musician, many such sounds may be distinguished and identified. But among successive sounds the relational components of mind are conspicuous. Differences between tones that follow one another, even very rapidly, are clearly perceived. But the demarcations are less decided than those between contrasted sensations in the field of vision[45].

(From *The Principles of Psychology*, Part II, Chapter II)

注 释

① the ultimate composition of Mind　指心的最底层的构成形式。
② the proximate composition　指心的最表层的构成形式。
③ introspection　这是心理学术语,指内省,即自我观察,是指把经验回忆起来加以观察。
④ multitudinous unlikenesses　众多的不同性
⑤ in common　共有
⑥ a perceivable individuality　可以感觉出的个性。
⑦ mark off　分开
⑧ adjacent portions　指(意识)中的邻接部分。
⑨ qualitative contrasts　性质对比
⑩ an appreciable duration　指觉察出的时间持续。
⑪ the momentary transitions　指瞬间的过渡。
⑫ nervous shocks　神经震荡
⑬ Their extreme brevity, their small variety, and their dependence

on the terms they unite, differentiate them in an unmistakable way. 此句中 differentiate 是 vt. 有区分,区别的意思。比如 They differentiate one variety from another. 他们区别品种。全句译为:(关系的自我体验)是极端短促的,很少变化,依靠被联系的事项。这些性质使它们自成一类,绝不会被错误地认为与其他自我体验同类。

⑭ an independent element of consciousness 指意识的独立元素。
⑮ ...inseparable into parts 不能再分成小部分
⑯ like parts 相同部分
⑰ a feeling proper 指狭义的感觉体验。
⑱ an aggregate of 一集合体
⑲ undecomposable 不可分
⑳ ...for until certain provisional groupings have been made,... 在这句中,provisional 指临时性的,如 a provisional contract 临时契约。groupings 指编组。如 tactical groupings 战斗编组,provisional groupings 指暂用的分类。作者先将下一章内容提前说明。
㉑ ...they may be divided into the feelings which are centrally initiated and the feelings which are peripherally initiated. 这里的 centrally initiated 及 peripherally initiated 分别指中枢产生的及末梢产生的。
㉒ sensations 指任何因感觉器官、感觉神经或大脑感觉区受刺激而形成的具体的、有意识的经验,译为感觉。feeling 对体内自我的知觉,译为体验。
㉓ outer agencies 指外部力量。
㉔ gradations of depth 指深度的许多等级
㉕ in proportion to 意思是与……成比例。如:His expenditure is not in proportion to his means, 他的支出与他的收入不相称。
㉖ primary or real feeling 原始的或确实的感觉体验
㉗ secondary or ideal feelings 后起的或理想的感觉体验

㉘ intensity   强度
㉙ reproduced feelings   复现的感觉体验
㉚ objective exciting agents   指客观的刺激物。
㉛ in view   指被考虑，被注意。We have in view a new hospital for seamen. 我们计划为海员新建一座医疗。
㉜ in default of   因没有，缺少。如 In default of paying the fine, he will be imprisoned for a further period of 80 days. 因未付罚款，他将再受为期 80 天的监禁。
㉝ one apparently-uniform state   指似乎单一的状态。
㉞ This fundamental division of relations into those of coexistence and those of sequence. 在这里 coexistence 指并存的关系，sequence 指继起的关系。
㉟ Mind   译为心
㊱ tracts of consciousness   指意识的部分
㊲ ... those parts occupied by feelings that take their rise in the interior of the body are widely unlike those parts occupied by feelings that take their rise on the exterior of the body. 在此句中，take one's rise in (on) 表示发源于，起源于。比如：The river takes its rise among the hills. 这条河发源于群山之中。全句译为：在后一类意识中，起源于身体内部的体验所占的那些部分与起源于身体外部的体验所占的那些部分大不相同。
㊳ We will begin with those parts of Mind distinguished by predominance of the relational elements. 我们从那些由于相关元素的突出而被区分出来的心灵元素谈起。
㊴ the lenses of the eye   眼睛的晶状体
㊵ optical apparatus   光学仪器
㊶ the external agent   指外界刺激物。
㊷ woven up with   与……结合
㊸ ... like the tips of the fingers and the tip of the tongue, have the most frequent and varied converse with outer objects. 在此句中

converse with 原本表示交谈，这里表示与外界客观物质的接触。作者的意思是舌头是个很灵活的触觉器官，舌头的触觉不限于咀嚼食物的感觉，嘴面也是舌头感受的外物范围。
㊹ the auditory feelings 听觉
㊺ But the demarcations are less decided than those between contrasted sensations in the field of vision. 可是这些界限不如互相对比的视觉之间的界限那么明显清楚。

练　习

1．回答问题
（1）What are two kinds of the proximate components of Mind?
（2）What characters of each feeling are regarded as the essentials?
（3）What do sensations and emotions refer to?

2．判断正误
（1）This fundamental division of relations into those of co-existence and those of sequence, is itself dependent on the preceding division into relations of equality between feelings and relations of inequality between them.
（2）The marked unlikenesses are in both cases due to the greater or smaller proportions of the relational elements that are present.
（3）The multitudinous states of consciousness yielded by sensations, are above all others sharp in their mutual limitations.

3．选词填空
Fill in the blanks with the words or expressions given below
sensation, feeling, intensity, in common, unite, mark off, provisional, inseparable
（1）The blind and his dog are _____.
（2）The _____ of the light depends on the wattage of the bulb.

(3) The swimming pool is used _____ by all the children in the neighborhood.
(4) Mustard gas creates a painful _____ in the throat and lungs.
(5) The new opera did not cause the least _____ in the capital.
(6) A _____ government was formed in the following year.
(7) An area at the end of the site was _____ off as a future playground.
(8) His policy was therefore to see that his enemies did not _____ _.

4. 英译汉
(1) Take away the terms it unites, and it disappears along with them; having no independent place — no individuality of its own. It is true, that, under an ultimate analysis, what we call a relation proves to be itself a kind of feeling — the momentary feeling to an adjacent conspicuous feeling.
(2) There is throughout a dependence such that the appreciable area of consciousness occupied by feelings, can no more possesses individualities apart from the relations which link them, than these relations can possess individualities apart from the feelings they link.
(3) We shall, however, find that certain differential characters among the sensations accompany this difference of distribution of the nerves in which they arise; and that they are decided in proportion to the relative superficiality or centrality of these nerves.
(4) It follows that the degree of the change or shock, constituting in other words the consciousness of the degree of difference between the adjacent states, is the ultimate basis of the distinctions among relations.

5. 汉译英
(1) 根据家庭背景来区别对待小学生是荒谬的。(differentiate)
(2) 他比你聪明,这与他比你年龄大成比例。(in proportion to)
(3) 该党的政见稳健。(in view)
(4) 他无可推诿,只好哑口无言。(in default of)

3. Habit

William James

威廉·詹姆士(William James, 1842—1910)是美国心理学家,唯心主义哲学家和实用主义的主要代表之一。1890年他出版《心理学原理》(The Pinciples of Psychology)总结了实验心理学的主要研究成果,具有从经验的、思辨的心理学向实验心理学过渡的特点。詹姆士的心理学含有实用主义色彩,对美国机能心理学发展有直接影响。他的其他著作有《心理学简编》(1892),《对教师讲心理学及对学生讲生活理想》(1899)。

《习惯》(Habit)是威廉·詹姆士《心理学原理》(1890)的第四章。美国心理学发展为一门独立的科学,主要受德国冯特(Wilhelm Wundt, 1832—1920)的影响,向着机能主义方向发展。强调实验方法的研究,注重心理现象在人对环境的适应过程中的作用,从而注重个人间的心理能力的差异。美国的心理学发展正值美国资本主义发展上升时期。资本家利用研究如何应付环境的方法攫取利润。达尔文生物进化的理论对美国机能心理学的发展也起了重要作用。詹姆士心理学的实用主义思想在《心理学原理》中有充分的体现,也促进了美国心理机能主义的发展。

The first result of it is that *habit simplifies the movements required to achieve a given result, makes them more accurate and diminishes fatigue*[①]..

"The beginner at the piano not only moves his finger up and down[②] in order to depress the key, he moves the whole hand, the forearm and even the entire body, especially moving its least rigid part, the head, as if he would press down the key with that organ too. Often a contraction of the abdominal muscles[③] occurs as well. Principally, however, the impulse is determined to the motion of the hand and of the single finger. This is, in the first place, because the movement of the finger is the movement *thought of*, and, in the second place, because its movement and that of the key are the movements we try to *perceive*, along with the results of the latter on the ear. The more often the process is repeated, the more easily the movement follows, on account of the increase in permeability of the nerves engaged[4].

"But the more easily the movement occurs, the slighter is the stimulus required to set it up; and the slighter the stimulus is, the more its effect is confined to the fingers alone.

"Thus, an impulse which originally spread its effects over the whole body, or at least over many of its movable parts, is gradually determined to a single definite organ, in which it effects the contraction of a few limited muscles. In this change the thoughts and perceptions which start the impulse acquire more and more intimate causal relations with a particular group of motor nerves.

"To recur to a simile, at least partially apt[5], imagine the nervous system to represent a drainage-system[6], inclining, on the whole, toward certain muscles, but with the escape thither somewhat clogged. Then streams of water will, on the whole, tend most to fill the drains that go towards these muscles and to wash out the escape. In case of a sudden 'flushing', however, the whole system of channels will fill itself, and the water overflow everywhere before it escapes. But a moderate quantity of water invading the system will flow through the proper escape alone[7].

"Just so with the piano-player. As soon as his impulse, which has gradually learned to confine itself to single muscles, grows extreme, it overflows into larger muscular regions. He usually plays with his fingers, his body being at rest. But no sooner does he get excited than his whole body becomes 'animated', and he moves his head and trunk, in particular, as if these also were organs with which he meant to belabor the keys."⑧

Man is born with a tendency to do more things than he has ready-made arrangements for in his nerve-centres⑨. Most of the performances of other animals are automatic. But in him the number of them is so enormous, that most of them must be the fruit of painful study. If practice did not make perfect, nor habit economize the expense of nervous and muscular energy, he would therefore be in a sorry plight. As Dr. Maudsley says⑩:

"If an act became no easier after being done several times, if the careful direction of consciousness were necessary to its accomplishment on each occasion, it is evident that the whole activity of a lifetime might be confined to one or two deeds—that no progress could take place in development. A man might be occupied all day in dressing and undressing himself; the attitude of his body would absorb all his attention and energy; the washing of his hands or the fastening of a button would be as difficult to him on each occasion as to the child on its first trial; and he would, furthermore, be completely exhausted by his exertions. Think of the pains necessary to teach a child to stand, of the many efforts which it must make, and of the ease with which it at last stands, unconscious of any effort. For while secondarily automatic acts are accomplished with comparatively little weariness—in this regard approaching the organic movements, or the original reflex movements—the conscious effort of the will soon produces exhaustion. A spinal cord without ... memory would simply be an idiotic spinal cord.... It is impossible for an individual to realize how much he owes to its automatic agency until disease has impaired its functions."⑪

The next result is that *habit diminishes the conscious attention with which our acts are performed*.

One may state this abstractly thus: If an act requires for its execution a chain, A, B, C, D, E, F, G, etc., of successive nervous events[12], then in the first performances of the action the conscious will must choose each of these events from a number of wrong alternatives that tend to present themselves; but habit soon brings it about that each event calls up its own appropriate successor without any alternative offering itself, and without any reference to the conscious will[13], until at last the whole chain, A, B, C, D, E, F, G, rattles itself off as soon as A occurs, just as if A and the rest of the chain were fused into a continuous stream. When we are learning to walk, to ride, to swim, skate, fence, write, play, or sing, we interrupt ourselves at every step by unnecessary movements and false notes. When we are proficients, on the contrary, the results not only follow with the very minimum of muscular action requisite to bring them forth, they also follow from a single instantaneous 'cue'.[14] The marksman sees the bird, and, before he knows it, he has aimed and shot. A gleam in his adversary's eye, a momentary pressure from his rapier, and the fencer finds that he has instantly made the right parry and return. A glance at the musical hieroglyphics[15], and the pianist's fingers have rippled through a cataract of notes[16]. And not only is it the right thing at the right time that we thus involuntarily do, but the wrong thing also, if it be an habitual thing. Who is there that has never wound up his watch on taking off his waistcoat in the daytime, or taken his latchkey out on arriving at the door-step of friend? Very absent-minded persons in going to their bedroom to dress for dinner have been known to take off one garment after another and finally to get into bed, merely because that was the habitual issue of the first few movements when performed at a later hour. The writer well remembers how, on revisiting Paris after ten years' absence, and, finding himself in the street in which for one winter he had attended school, he lost himself in a brown study, from which he was awakened by finding himself upon the stairs which led to the apartment in a house many streets away in which he had lived during that earlier time, and to which his steps from the school had then habitually led. We all of us have a definite routine manner of performing certain daily offices connected with the toilet, with the opening and shutting of familiar cupboards, and the like. Our lower centres know the order of these movements, and show their knowledge by their 'surprise' if the objects are altered so as to oblige the movement to be made in a different way. But our higher thought-centres know hardly anything about the matter. Few men can tell off-hand which sock, shoe, or trousers-leg they put on first. They must first mentally rehearse the act; and even that is often insufficient—the act must be *performed*[17]. So of the questions, Which valve of my double door opens first? Which way does my door swing? etc. I cannot *tell* the answer; yet my *hand* never makes a mistake. No one can *describe* the order in which he brushes his hair or teeth; yet it is likely that the order is a pretty fixed one in all of us.

These results may be expressed as follows:

In action grown habitual, what instigates each new muscular contraction to take place in its appointed order is not a thought or a perception, but the *sensation occasioned by the muscular contraction just finished*[18]. A strictly voluntary act[19] has to be guided by idea, perception, and volition, throughout its whole course. In an habitual action, mere sensation is a sufficient guide, and the upper regions of brain and mind are set comparatively free. A diagram will make the matter clear:

Let A, B, C, D, E, F, G represent an habitual chain of muscular contractions, and let a, b, c, d, e, f stand for the respective sensations which these contractions excite in us when they are successively performed. Such sensations will usually be of the muscles,

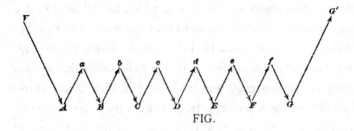

FIG.

skin, or joints of the parts moved, but they may also be effects of the movement upon the eye or the ear. Through them, and through them alone, we are made aware whether the contraction has or has not occurred. When the series, A, B, C, D, E, F, G, is being learned, each of these sensations becomes the object of a separate perception by the mind. By it we test each movement, to see if it be right before advancing to the next. We hesitate, compare, choose, revoke, reject, etc., by intellectual means; and the order by which the next movement is discharged is an express order from the ideational centres[20] after this deliberation has been gone through.

In habitual action, on the contrary, the only impulse which the centres of idea or perception need send down is the initial impulse[21], the command to *start*. This is represented in the diagram by V; it may be a thought of the first movement or of the last result, or a mere perception of some of the habitual conditions of the chain, the presence, e. g., of the keyboard near the hand. In the present case, no sooner has the conscious thought or volition instigated movement A, than A, through the sensation a of its own occurrence, awakens B reflexly[22], B then excites C through b, and so on till the chain is ended, when the intellect generally takes cognizance of the final result. The process, in fact, resembles the passage of a wave of 'peristaltic' motion[23] down the bowels. The intellectual perception at the end is indicated in the diagram by the effect of G being represented, at G', in the ideational centres above the merely sensational line. The sensational impressions, a, b, c, d, e, f, are all supposed to have their seat below the ideational lines. That our ideational centres, if involved at all by a, b, c, d, e, f, are involved in a minimal degree, is shown by the fact that the attention may be wholly absorbed elsewhere. We may say our prayers, or repeat the alphabet, with our attention far away.

"A musical performer will play a piece which has become familiar by repetition while carrying on an animated conversation[24], or while continuously engrossed by some train of deeply interesting thought; the accustomed sequence of movements being directly prompted by the *sight* of the notes, or by the remembered succession of the *sounds* (if the piece is played from memory), aided in both cases by the guiding sensations derived from the muscles themselves. But, further, a higher degree of the same 'training' (acting on an organism specially fitted to profit by it) enables an accomplished pianist[25] to play a difficult piece of music at sight; the movements of the hands and fingers following so immediately upon the sight of the notes that it seems impossible to believe that any but the very shortest and most direct track can be the channel of the nervous communication through which they are called forth[26]. The following curious example of the same class of *acquired aptitudes*[27], which differ from instincts only in being prompted to action by the will, is furnished by Robert Houdin:

"'With a view of cultivating the rapidity of visual and tactile perception, and the precision of respondent movements[28], which are necessary for success in every kind of prestidigitation[29], Houdin early practised the art of juggling with balls in the air; and having, after a month's practice, become thorough master of the art of keeping up *four* balls at once, he placed a book before him, and, while the balls were in the air, accustomed himself to read without hesitation. 'This,' he says, 'will probably seem to my readers very extraordinary; but I shall surprise them still more when I say that I have just amused myself with repeating this curious experiment. Though thirty years have elapsed since the time I was writing, and though I have scarcely once touched the balls during that period, I can still manage to read with ease while keeping *three* balls up.'"[30] (Autobiography, p. 26.)

We have called a, b, c, d, e, f, the antecedents of the successive muscular attractions, by the name of sensations. Some authors seem to deny that they are even this. If not even this, they can only be centripetal nerve-currents, not sufficient to arouse feeling, but sufficient to arouse motor response[31]. It may be at once admitted that they are not distinct *volitions*. The will, if any will be present, limits itself to a *permission* that they exert their motor effects. Dr. Carpenter[32] writes:

"There may still be metaphysicians who maintain that actions which were originally prompted by the will with a distinct intention, and which are still entirely under its control, can never cease to be volitional; and that either an infinitesimally small amount of will [33] is required to sustain them when they have been once set going, or that the will is in a sort of pendulum-like oscillation[34] between the two actions — the maintenance of the train of *thought*, and the maintenance of the train of *movement*. But if only an infinitesimally small amount of will is necessary to sustain them, is not this tantamount to saying that they go on by a force of their own? And does not the experience of the *perfect continuity* of our train of thought during the performance of movements that have become habitual, entirely negative the hypothesis of oscillation? Besides, if such an oscillation existed, there must be *intervals* in which each action goes on *of itself*; so that its essentially automatic character is virtually admitted. The physiological explanation, that the mechanism of locomotion㉟, as of other habitual movements, *grows to* the mode in which it is early exercised, and that it then works automatically under the general control and direction of the will, can scarcely be put down by any assumption of an hypothetical necessity, which rests only on the basis of ignorance of one side of our composite nature."㊱

(From *The Principles of Psychology*, Chapter IV)

注　释

① diminish fatigue　减少疲劳
② ...move his finger up and down　手指上下移动
③ contraction of the abdominal muscles　腹部肌肉的收缩
④ on account of the increase in permeability of the nerves engaged　指因为使用的神经更容易让神经冲动通过。
⑤ at least partially apt　至少是比较恰当的(比喻)
⑥ a drainage-system　排水系统(比喻神经系统)
⑦ But a moderate quantity of water invading the system will flow through the proper escape alone. 指注进中等的水量,水就会只从那个应走的出水口流出去。
⑧ 詹姆士引用排水沟的比喻,是译自施耐德(Kurt Schneider)的《人的意志》(Der Menschliche Wille)(1882),第 417—419 页。施耐德是德国心理学家。同时在斯宾塞(Spencer)《心理学原理》(Principles of Psychology)第五篇第八章中也有相应内容。
⑨ ...he has ready-made arrangements for in his nerve-centres　指他想做的事情比他神经中枢已有现成准备的事情还多。

37

⑩Dr. Maudsley 的话见《心的生理学》(Physiology of Mind)第 155 页。

⑪disease has impaired its function　疾病损害了脊髓的功能。

⑫...of successive nervous events　一串先后的神经变化

⑬...and without any reference to the conscious will　用不着自觉的意志

⑭a single instantaneous 'cue'　指单独的立刻的"记号"。

⑮...the musical hieroglyphics　乐谱

⑯a cataract of notes　瀑布似的琴音

⑰They must first mentally rehearse the act; and even that is often insufficient——the act must be performed. 他们必须先在心里排演一遍那个动作，即使这样往往还不够，他们必须实际做一遍那个动作。

⑱the sensation occasioned by the muscular contraction just finished　指刚才终了的肌肉收缩所引起的感觉。

⑲A strictly voluntary act　确实有意的行为

⑳ideational centers　指观念作用中枢。

㉑the initial impulse　第一个冲动

㉒...awakens B reflexly　指(A)又由于反射作用引起动作 B。

㉓a wave of 'peristaltic' motion　上下蠕动的波

㉔an animated conversation　活跃的谈话

㉕an accomplished pianist　有成就的钢琴家

㉖called forth　引起

㉗the same class of acquired aptitudes　这类学来的能力

㉘and the precision of respondent movements　反应动作的准确性

㉙in every kind of prestidigitation　在任何一种要求灵活手法的活动中

㉚此引文见 Robert Houdin(侯玎)的自传第 26 页。

㉛motor response　指运动的反应。见哈特门(Von Hartmann, 1842—1906)的《无意识哲学》(*Philosophy of the Unconscious-*

ness)。

㉜Carpenter 卡彭特《心理的生理》(1874)第217页。
㉝...an infinitesimally small amount of will 无限少的意志
㉞a sort of pendulum-like oscillation 像钟摆似地(在下列两件事之间)摆动
㉟the mechanism of locomotion 行走的机制
㊱见《心理的生理》第20页。

练　习

1. 回答问题
(1) What is gradually determined to a single definite organ in which it effects the contraction of a few limited muscles?
(2) According to Dr. Maudsley, what produces exhaustion?
(3) Why can no one describe the order in which he brushes his hair or teeth?

2. 判断正误
(1) The more easily the movement occurs, the heavier is the stimulus required to set it up.
(2) Principally, the impulse is limited to the motion of the hand and of the single finger.
(3) It is easy for a man to realize how much he owes to its automatic agency until disease has impaired its functions.
(4) Habit diminishes the conscious attention with which our acts are performed.
(5) Our lower centers fail to show knowledge by their "surprise" if the objects are altered so as to oblige the movements to be made in a different way.

3. 选词填空

Fill in the following blanks with the verbs given below:
impair, instigate, diminish, rehearse, economize, occasion, awaken, overflow

(1) Mr. Otis was _____ by a curious noise in the corridor.
(2) His constant attempts to _____ his colleagues' achievements eventually caused his dismissal.
(3) Being a poor schoolmaster I have to _____.
(4) His work is _____ by stupid mistakes.
(5) The plot to overthrow the government was _____ by the military.
(6) The boy's return _____ great rejoicing.
(7) If you get into a bath full of water come of the water will _____ on to the floor.
(8) He said the didn't think he'd have time to _____ a play.

4. 句型模拟
(1) No sooner had ... than ...
(2) if only

5. 英译汉
(1) Habit simplifies the movements required to achieve a given result, makes them more accurate and diminishes fatigue.
(2) Man is born with a tendency to do more things than he has ready-made arrangements for in his nerve-centers.
(3) The process, in fact, resembles the passage of a wave "peristaltic" motion down the bowels.

6. 汉译英
(1) 由于天气原因,比赛延期。(on account of)
(2) 她是一个才华出众的歌唱家。(accomplished)

(3) 从因果两个方面对这个局势作了考查。(with a view of = with a view to)
(4) 果断是指挥员必须具备的品质。(requisite)
(5) 为了防洪,沿河筑堤。(in case of)

7. 写作指导

You are required to write a composition based on the topic Practice Makes Perfect. The following expressions taken from the text are for your reference.

——economize energy
——absorb all one's attention and energy
——the conscious effort of the will
——produce exhaustion
——impair the functions
——the habitual issue of

4. Adolescence

Granville Stanley Hall

葛朗危勒·斯坦利·霍尔(Granville Stanley Hall, 1844—1924)是美国心理学家、教育家,也是美国发展心理学的先驱。霍尔的发展心理学思想受达尔文进化论的影响,重视心理机能。他与詹姆斯同为美国机能主义心理学的前辈。霍尔是德国心理学家冯特(Wilhelm Wundt, 1832—1920)的第一个美国学生。他接受冯特心理学思想,但不满足于内省分析,他重视个体如何发展以及如何适应环境的问题。霍尔关于心理活动的观点是美国心理学的一般机能主义的表现。1887年他创办《美国心理学杂志》,1891年创设《教育学讨论》及《应用心理学杂志》。其他著作有:《衰老》(1922),《一个心理学家的生平和自由》(1923)。

《青春期》(Adolescence)节选于霍尔《青少年:它的心理学及其与生理学、人类学、社会学、性、犯罪、宗教和教育的关系》(1904)。在研究方法方面,他用问卷法研究儿童的心理内容。在此书中,霍尔提出了复演说,认为儿童的个体发展重复了种系的生活历史,即人类进化的过程;胎儿在胎内的发展复演了动物进化的过程。因此霍尔曾被认为是"心理学中的达尔文"。

Youth loves intense states of mind and is passionately fond of excitement. Tranquil, mild enjoyments are not its forte. The heart and arteries are, as we have seen, rapidly increasing in size, and perhaps heightened blood pressure is necessary to cause the expansion normal at this stage. Nutritive activities are greatly increased; the temperature of the body is probably a trifle higher. After its period of most rapid growth, the heart walls are a little weak, and peripheral circulation is liable to slight stagnation[①], so that in the interests of proper irrigation of the tissues after the vascular growth[②] has begun, tension seems necessary. Although we do not know precisely the relation between blood pressure and the strong instinct to tingle and glow[3], some correlation may safely be postulated. It is the age of erectile diathesis[4], and the erethism, that is now so increased in the sexual parts is probably more or less so in nearly every organ and tissue. The whole psycho-physic organism is expanding, stretching out, and proper elasticity that relaxes and contracts and gives vaso-motor range is coordinated with the instinct for calenture or warming up, which is shown in phenomena of second breath in both physical and mental activity[5]. In savage life this period is marked by epochs of orgasm and carousal, which is perhaps one expression of nature's effort to secure a proper and ready reflex range of elasticity in the circulatory apparatus[6]. The "teens" are emotionally unstable and pathic. It is the age of natural inebriation[7] without the need of intoxicants, which made Plato[8] define youth as spiritual drunkenness. It is a natural impulse to experience hot and perfervid psychic states[9], and is characterized by emotionalism. This gives a sense of vitality and the hunger for more and fuller life. This desire to feel and to be very much alive, and the horror of inertness and apathy, is, as we saw in Chapter V, one of the chief features which incline youth to intoxicants. Indeed, everything men strive for—fame, wealth, knowledge, power, love—are only specialized forms of the will to attain and to feel the maximum of vitality. Hence comes the proclivity to superlativeness, to high, lurid color and fast life, because youth must have excitement[10], and if this be not at hand in the form of moral and intellectual enthusiasms, it is more prone, on the principle of kinetic equivalents, to be sought for in sex or in drink[11]. Athletic enthusiasm, the disposition of high school and college youth to yell and paint the town, to laugh, become boisterous and convivial, are better than sensuality and reduce temptation to it[12]. Better that a few of the most promising youth should be maimed or even killed on the gridiron or in college rushes, or lose standing in their devotion to teams⁽¹³⁾ and to emotional culture, than that they should find excesses, some forms of which seem necessary now, in the lower life of sinful indulgence⁽¹⁴⁾, which is so prone to stunt and arrest the precious last stages of growth in mind and body. More or less of this erethic diathesis is necessary and inevitable, and one of the chief problems of education is to prevent its lower forms and give it ever higher vents and fields. Interest in and devotion to all that is good, beautiful, and true is its loftiest expression, but it is often best cultivated on a lower plane⁽¹⁵⁾, to be applied later on the higher.

We here see the instability and fluctuation now so characteristic⁽¹⁶⁾. The emotions develop by contrast and reaction into the opposite. We will specify a few of its antithetic impulses⁽¹⁷⁾ now so marked.

1. There are hours, days, weeks, and perhaps months of over-energetic action. The young man trains with ardor⁽¹⁸⁾; perhaps breaks a record; sleep may be reduced; he studies all night in a persistent cram⁽¹⁹⁾; is swept away by some new fad; is exalted and hilarious and then reacts; is limp, languid, inert, indifferent, fatigued, apathetic, sleepy, lazy; feels the lack of motive power, and from overwork and excessive effort, when he goaded himself to do or die⁽²⁰⁾, he relapses to a dull state of relaxation and doubts whether anything is really worth while in the world. Thus youth now is really and easily overworked; is never so fresh or more rested as when at the top of its condition, but very easily wearied and exhausted with the languor due to overtraining. We have seen that early adolescent years⁽²¹⁾ are prone to be sickly, although the death rate is now lowest, and this is closely connected with the changes from overefficiency to low tension so frequent. Sometimes the stage of torpor comes first or predominates⁽²²⁾ and causes friends to be anxious. Many great men, as we

saw in Chapter VIII, loitered in their development, dawdled in their work and seemed to all about them entirely unpromising[22]; but later woke up, went to work, made up for lost time, and outstripped their fellows[24]. These changes are perhaps in slight degree modified by weather[25], like moods, and have no doubt a physiological basis. Sometimes it is as if anemia and hyperemia[26] followed each other with extreme sloth and then almost convulsive activity of motor centers[27]. There are periods when one can do easily twice the ordinary task without fatigue. Girls of fifteen or sixteen would often like to sleep or rest a week, and seem incapable of putting forth real effort, and then there are fevers of craving hard and even disagreeable work. Many returns[28] show that in the spring there is very often great loathing to exert one's self[29], but this is occasionally broken by hours, days, or even weeks of supernormal activity, when stints are not only completed, but extra and self-imposed tasks are done with alacrity and satisfaction. Often there is a periodicity of activity in young men that suggests a monthly and sometimes a seasonal rhythm. The regular changes of day and night do not suffice, but this is complicated by some larger cycle of alternating recuperative and energetic periods of latent and patent, or inner and outer work. This, like so much else, suggests an atavistic trace of savage life[30], more controlled by moon and tides and warm and cold seasons. Indeed, diurnal regularity of work, play, food, and sleep is a recent thing in the develpment-history of man, is hard to establish, and in the vagrant, criminal, vicious, and pauper class is often never reached. But spells of[31] overactivity, alternating with those of sluggishness and inertness, still seem in these years like neural echoes[32] of ancient hunts and feasts, fasts and famines, migration and stagnation. Now at least nature pushes on her work of growth by alternation, now centering[33] her energies upon function, now upon increase in size of organs, and perhaps by this method of economy attains a higher level than would be reached by too much poise, balance, and steadiness. It is as if the momentum of growth energies[34] had to overcome obstacles at every point, by removing now this, now that hindrance, where if its energies had been applied to all simultaneously they would have been less effective.

2. Closely connected with this are the oscillations between pleasure and pain—the two poles of life, its sovereign masters[35]. The fluctuations of mood in children are rapid and incessant. Tears and laughter are in close juxtaposition[36]. Their emotional responses to impressions are immediate. They live in the present and reflect all its changes, and their feelings are little affected by the past or the future[37]. With the dawn of adolescence, the fluctuations are slower and often for a time more extreme, and recovery from elation and especially from depression is retarded. The past, and still more the future, is involved, and as the mental life widens, either tendency acquires more momentum. Youth can not be temperate, in the philosophical sense. Now it is prone to laughter, hearty and perhaps almost convulsive, and is abandoned to pleasure, the field of which ought gradually to widen with perhaps the pain field, although more. There is gaiety, irrepressible levity, and euphoria that overflows in every absurd manifestation of excess of animal spirits[38], that can not be repressed, that danger and affliction, appeals to responsibility and to the future, can not daunt nor temper. To have a good time is felt to be an inalienable right. The joys of life are never felt with so keen a relish; youth lives for pleasure, whether of an epicurean or an esthetic type. It must and ought to enjoy life without alloy. Every day seems to bring passionate love of just being alive, and the genius for extracting pleasure and gratification from everything is never so great.

But this, too, reacts into pain and disphoria, as surely as the thesis of the Hegelian logic passes over to its antithesis[39]. Young people weep and sigh, they know not why; depressive are almost as characteristic as expansive states of consciousness. The sad Thanatopsis mood of gloom paints the world in black[40]. Far-off anticipations of death come in a foreboding way, as it is dimly felt, though not realized, that life is not all joy and that the individual must be subordinated and eventually die. Hence statistics show, as we have seen, a strange rise in the percentage of suicides. Now there is gloom and anon spontaneous exuberance[41]. In 766 of Lancaster's returns, thirteen had thought seriously of suicide, although only three had successfully attempted it. Perhaps elation precedes and depression comes as a reaction in the majority of cases, although this is not yet clear. Some feel despondent on awakening, at school time, or at noon, suggesting nutritive changes. "The curve of despondency starts at eleven, rises steadily and rapidly till fifteen, culminates at seventeen, then falls steadily till twenty three." Young people are often unaccountably pleased with every trifle. They can shout for joy from the very fact of being alive. The far-off destiny of senescence looms up[42], and in fatigue the atrabiliar psychic basis of pessimism clouds life[43] for a time and brings into dominance a new set of associations like another personality. Youth fears inadequacy of its powers to cope with the world. How this is connected with the alternating extremes of sexual tension, we have seen, although this by no means explains all. Sometimes the tears are from no assignable cause, and often from factitious motives[44]. Suspicion of being disliked by friends, of having faults of person or character that can not be overcome; the fancy of being a supposititious child of their parents, of having unwittingly caused calamity to others, of hopeless love; failure in some special effort; a sense of the necessity of a life of work and hardship—these bring moods that may be more or less extreme according to environment, heredity, temperament, and other causes, may succeed each other with greater or less frequency, and may threaten to issue in brooding, depression, and melancholy, or in a careless and blind instinct to live for the day; but these, too, are due to the fact that the range of pleasure and pain is increased, so that there are new motives to each, and perhaps a long period with occasional special dangers must elapse before a final adjustment.

This is the age of giggling, especially with girls, who are at this stage of life farthest from Vassey's view[45] that man is not originally a laughing animal and that the gentleman and lady should never laugh, but only smile. If convulsive laughter is an epilepsy[46], it is one that begins in the highest regions and passes down the meristic levels[47]. Goethe well says, that nothing is more significant of men's character than what they find laughable. The adolescent perhaps is most hilarious over caricature of nationalities, teachers, freshmen, the other sex, etc., who are mimicked, burlesqued, and satirized. Ridicule is now a powerful weapon of propriety[48]. Again, the wit of the ephebos sometimes provokes a mental ticklishness[49] about certain sacred and sometimes sexual topics, which may make jocularity and waggishness[50] almost a plague. Another of the chief butts of adolescent fun[51] is what is naive and unconscious; the blunders of the greeny, the unsophisticated way not only of the freshman, but of the countryman, the emigrant, and the *Bachfisch* girl now abound, while the simple idea of disaster or misfortune, which constitutes the humor of nine-tenths of the professional joke-makers, is rare. The horror of old or even once-told jests is never so intense, nor the appreciation for novelty so keen.

(From *Adolescence*, Chapter I)

注　释

① and peripheral circulation is liable to slight stagnation. 外周的循环容易有轻微的迟滞。
② the vascular growth 血管的增长发展。
③ the relation between blood pressure and the strong instinct 血压同强烈的本能二者的关系。
④ The age of erectile diathesis 出现勃起的年龄。
⑤ The whole psycho-physic organism is expanding, stretching out and proper elasticity that relaxes and contracts and gives vaso-motor range is coordinated with the instinct for calenture or warming up, which is shown in phenomena of second breath in both physical and mental activity. 整个心身有机体不断在伸延、扩展，有适当伸缩的弹性，给血管的舒缩留有余地，这与整个有机体天生的炽热和激动是协调的。这些都表现在身心活动的第二次高峰期。
⑥ the circulatory apparatus 循环系统
⑦ the age of natural inebriation 自然陶醉时期
⑧ Plato 柏拉图(约公元前428—348)，是古希腊三大哲学家之一，和苏格拉底、亚里斯多德共同奠定西方文化的哲学基础。
⑨ to experience hot and perfervid psychic states 要体验炽烈和热情的心理状态
⑩ Hence comes the proclivity to superlativeness, to high, lurid color and fast life, because youth must have excitement... 因而出现极端性的倾向，追求色彩鲜艳、奢侈放荡的快节奏的生活，因为青少年需要兴奋……
⑪ ...it is more prone, on the principle of kinetic equivalents, to be sought for in sex or in drink. 在此句中，on the principle of 是按照……原则。distribute on the principle of equal pay for equal work. 按照同工同酬的原则进行分配。全句译为：如果这种兴

49

奋不表现为道德热情和理智热情的形式，那么根据动态等值原则，他们就比较容易在酒色中寻找欢乐。

⑫...are better than sensuality and reduce temptation to it. 比耽于声色好，并会减少声色的诱惑。

⑬...on the gridiron or in college rushes, or lose standing in their devotion to teams... 指在橄榄球场上或在大学比武中，或在献身于球队上失败。

⑭in the lower life of sinful indulgence 不道德的下流生活

⑮...but it is often best cultivated on a lower plane... 最好先在较低水平上加以培养。

⑯We here see the instability and fluctuation now so characteristic. 我们看到作为其特征的动摇和起伏。

⑰antithetic impulses 互相对立的冲动。

⑱The young man trains with ardor. 男青年热衷于训练。

⑲...he studies all night in a persistent cram 指在学习上通宵开夜车，死记硬背。

⑳when he goaded himself to do 当他鼓励自己拼命干时

㉑early adolescent years 青年早期

㉒the stage of torpor comes first or predominates 迟钝阶段首先出现或占有优势。

㉓...dawdled in their work and seemed to all about them entirely unpromising 指在工作中虚度年华，似乎完全没有出息。

㉔outstripped their fellows 指超过他们的同伴。

㉕...in slight degree modified by weather 轻微地受到天气变化的影响。

㉖anemia and hyperemia 贫血和充血

㉗...and then almost convulsive activity of motor centers 指运动中枢几乎是痉挛性活动。

㉘return 指报告。

㉙...there is very often great loathing to exert one's self 指一个

人十分懒于振奋自己。

㉚This, like so much else, suggests an atavistic trace of savage life. 这和其他方面一样,暗示着野蛮人生活的一种返祖现象的遗迹。

㉛spells of 一段时间

㉜like neural echoes 在神经上的回响一般

㉝...now centering... 一时致力于……

㉞the momentum of growth energies 指成长能量的总量。

㉟its sovereign masters 生活的最高统治者

㊱Tears and laughter are in close juxtaposition. juxtaposition 是同时发生的意思,这里指儿童的眼泪和欢笑是无常的。

㊲此段话见德国心理学家 Karl Just 的 Die Gefuhle des Frohsinns und her Heiterkeit und der Wechsel der Stimmung im Gemuthsleben des Kindes 一书。

㊳in every absurd manifestation of excess of animal spirits 在每一种带着动物般激情的荒唐行径中

㊴...the Hegelian logic passes over to its antithesis. 黑格尔逻辑命题肯定走向自己的反面。

㊵The sad Thanatopsis mood of gloom paints the world in black. 指悲哀的,死一般的忧郁心境把世界涂抹成漆黑一团。

㊶Now there is gloom and anon spontaneous exuberance. 现在充满忧郁,不久以后又自发地热情洋溢了。

㊷The far-off destiny of senescence looms up... 指遥远的、要衰老的命运朦胧地出现了。

㊸...the atrabiliar psychic basis of pessimism clouds life... 厌世主义的抑郁心境使生活暗淡无光……

㊹factitious motives 虚构的动机

㊺此段见维塞(Vassey)的书《大笑与微笑的哲学》(The Philosophy of Laughing and Smiling, 1877)第 194 页。

㊻If convulsive laughter is an epilepsy... 假如痉挛式的狂笑是一

种癫痫……

㊼. . . it is one that begins in the highest regions and passes down the meristic levels 癫痫从身体最高部分开始，下降到身体各部分。

㊽Ridicule is now a powerful weapon of propriety. 嘲笑已是一种正当有力的武器。

㊾a mental ticklishness 指逗得人心痒难挨。

㊿jocularity and waggishness 诙谐和恶作剧

(51)adolescent fun 青春期的玩笑

练 习

1. 回答问题

(1) Why is heightened blood pressure necessary to cause the expansion normal at the stage of adolescence?

(2) Why are the teens regarded as emotionally unstable and pathic?

(3) Why does the author believe that pleasure and pain——the two roles of life should be the oscillations?

2. 判断正误

(1) Because we have known precisely the relation between blood pressure and the strong instinct to tingle and glow, some correlation may safely be postulated.

(2) One of the main problems of education, according to Hall in this essay, is to prevent its lower forms and give it even higher vents and fields.

(3) There is a periodicity of activity in young men that suggests a monthly and sometimes a seasonal rhythm.

(4) Youth cannot be temperate, in the philosophical sense.

(5) Statistics show that elation precedes and depression comes as a reaction in the majority of cases.

(6) Youth never fear inadequacy of its power to cope with the world.

2. 选词填空

Fill in the blanks with the words given below:

 hilarious, despondency, prone convivial, exuberance, elation, melancholy, factitious

(1) Ruth was filled with _____ at winning the prize.
(2) There is an _____ of fancy in him.
(3) This small road is _____ to accidents.
(4) In his _____ the old man retired to his farm and led a hermit's life.
(5) The _____ celebrators of the victory sang their college songs.
(6) All at once I fell into a state of profound _____.
(7) The party got quite _____ after they brought more wine.
(8) A _____ demand for sugar was caused by false stories that there would be a lack of it.

4. 汉译英

(1) 人人都可能犯错。(be liable to)
(2) 这个公司的分配是按照同工同酬的原则。(on the principle of)
(3) 合同规定屋顶用红瓦,并非石板瓦。(specify)
(4) 相识已经发展成为友谊。(develop into)
(5) 我被他的无礼激怒了。(provoke)

5. 写作指导

Write a composition based on the topic Youth Is Treasure. The following sentences taken from the text are useful to you in compiling this composition.

Youth loves intense states of mind.
Youth is passionately fond of excitement.
The teens are emotionally unstable and pathic.
Youth must have excitement.
The young man trains with ardor.
The oscillations between pleasure and pain—the two poles of life...
The fluctuations of mood are rapid and incessant.
Tears and laughter are in close juxtaposition.
They live in the present and reflect all its changes.
Youth can not be temperate in the philosophical sense.
To have a good time is felt to be an inalienable right.
The joys of life are never felt with so keen a relish.
Youth lives for pleasure.
Every day seems to bring passionate love of just being alive.
Youth fears inadequacy of its powers to cope with the world.
Nothing is more significant of men's character than what they find laughable.
Ridicule is now a powerful weapon of propriety.

5. Early Empiricism, Naturalism, Materialism

James Mark Baldwin

詹姆斯·马克·鲍尔温(James Mark Baldwin, 1861—1934)是美国心理学家,他的理论强调感觉性反应与运动性反应是由于个人间的差异造成的。注意个人差异是美国机能主义总倾向的较早表现。主要著作《心理学史》(1913)。1894 年鲍尔温与卡特尔共同创办《心理学评论》、《心理学索引》和《心理学专刊》。

《早期经验主义,自然主义,唯物主义》(Early Empiricism, Naturalism, Materialism)节选于鲍尔温的《心理学史》(History of Psychology)。鲍尔温心理学思想受德国冯特和达尔文进化论的影响,在《心理学史》中提出了人类心理发展的阶段与个人心理发展阶段的顺序大体相同的看法。这种看法是机能主义思想的反应。

Psychology as Empirical Theory of Knowledge. —— in *John Locke*(1632—1704)[①] the full empirical point of view revealed itself. Locke limits the problem to the events of the inner life; and uses the method of observation and induction. He attempts to treat of the actual sources of knowledge by a scientific method, as proposed by Francis Bacon[②].

Moreover, he transferred the problem of the origin of knowledge, of all knowledge, from metaphysics to fact; from theories of divine illumination, pre-established harmony, and innate ideas, to hypotheses based on children, animals, and primitive men. Passing from this examination of actual knowledge, he proceeds to the more critical and epistemological questions of its validity and applications.

Pursuing what he describes as this "sober method of investigating the origin and connection of our ideas," Locke distinguishes between "simple" and "complex ideas". Simple ideas, which are those of immediate perception, and distinguished as coming either through the "external sense"—and belonging to the external world—or through the "internal sense", and belonging to the inner world of the mind itself. This latter, the sphere of the internal sense, is that of "thought" as defined in the system of Descartes[3]; the external corresponds to the system of nature or "extension".

In this conception of simple, underived, original elements or data of consciousness, the basis is laid for the work of qualitative and analytic psychology, one of the problems of which has remained that of determining these original elements.

In this general position, certain other problems were raised. The mind is conceived of as having certain "powers" native to it. But there is only the one agent or person, who has ideas through the use of all the powers or faculties. These latter are simply its ways of acting. It may be aroused in the way of sensation and perception, in the way of memory, of imagination, of will, etc. This is Locke's refutation of the "faculty psychology" of Scholasticism, afterwards continued by Wolff[4].

Judged by their internal characters, the simple ideas of the external sense show different marks. They have "primary" and "secondary qualities",[5] both attributed to the external object. The primary qualities are those which reproduce essentially external conditions—extension, resistance, movement, etc. These are the qualities by reason of which the external object is what it is, as independent of perception. The secondary qualities, on the other hand, are those in which the process of perception itself has a part—such as colour, taste, position. In the primary qualities the reality of the "extension" of Descartes is vindicated. In the secondary, the variations arise which produce relativity and illusion.

Locke does not stop, with Hobbes, at a mechanical view of the play of ideas. He finds a further and higher power of the mind: that of "reflecting upon the course of ideas ". Beyond ideation there is reflection. Ideas are the "objects of the understanding *when it thinks*."

Reflection is the source of a new series of ideas—general, abstract, universal—which involve relations between and among simpler ideas. Such are the ideas of cause, substance, relation itself. Locke's distinction between sensation and reflection reminds us of that of Leibnitz[6] between perception and apperception; and it is likely that the latter is a revision of the former, for Leibnitz kept Locke's *Essay*[7] constantly in mind.

The ideas of reflection are not innate; there are no innate ideas. This Locke argues with great wealth of inductive proof; but by innate ideas he generally means actual conscious presentations or images. He shows that children lack innate ideas in this sense. This Leibnitz was able to meet by postulating "unconscious presentations " which slumber in obscure form and in the undeveloped psychic modes, but are still essentially innate. The admission by Locke of certain inherent "powers" or functions would seem to leave open the door for the later critical distinction between the *a posteriori* or experiential content, and the *a priori* or native form[8], in the structure of knowledge.

The motive of Locke is clear, however: it is the general refutation of rationalism[9]. For to all rationalism it is essential that the reason be not dependent upon purely sensational or empirical data, either in its origin or in its products. Locke's aim was to establish empiricism.

To Locke, further, reflection was largely a passive power; it was reflection *upon* the course or flow of our ideas, not reflection as itself determining this flow or course to be what it is. Reflection is an "inner sense". The actual flow of ideas is due to the laws of association, a term first used, though in a special reference, by Locke. So while the mind reserved the power of thought or reflection, still and other contents, together with the laws of organisation of these contents in complex ideas, were due to sensations and their interaction. As over against rationalism, the programme of a mental mechanics, a pure "presentationism", was suggested in anticipation; and at the hands of Hume and the Associationists[10], this programme was to be speedily realised.

Locke's *Essay* contains a wealth of sound psychological observation. His analysis of the ideas of reflection, the categories, is the first of its sort: analytic, empirical, psychological. He accepts the certainty of the existence of the mind, immediately given, as Descartes declared. The existence of the external world, on the contrary, was derived; it depended upon the character of "liveliness" attaching to certain sensations.

The active powers, feeling and will, have scant notice. They have not the importance that cognition has in a polemic against rationalism[11]. Pleasure and pain are simple ideas or sensations. Will is an original movement of the mind, an effort motived by "uneasiness". Both feelings and conations[12], or efforts, like other simple ideas, are involved in the processes of association.

Locke focused certain problems by means of experiment also. His proof of the relativity of temperature is classical: he pointed out that the two hands feel the same water as of different temperatures when they themselves are. He also demonstrated the limited area or span of consciousness, by showing the inability of the attention to take in more than a certain number of items or units exposed simultaneously to the eye.

Locke's significance for psychology, in sum, resides primarily in the empiricism of his point of view. This made possible an analytical method[13], as expounders of Locke generally recognise. But it is not so generally remarked that Locke's research was one of origins also. He aimed to show the nature and validity of ideas[14] as dependent upon their origin and development. This is the point of view, in so far, of modern genetic psychology[15]. The analytical empiricism of Locke was taken up and carried forward by his successors; but the genetic factor remained undeveloped until the theory of evolution came to reveal its true value.

Sensationalism and Associationism.—David Hume (1711—1776), the greatest of the Scottish philosophers, developed Locke's position in the two directions in which empiricism still retained rationalistic features.

First, the distinction between sensation and reflection, sense and reason, was abolished; even in the functional form of it that Locke's theory of mental "powers" had retained. Second, a thorough-going "associationism", essentially mechanical in character, took the place of Locke's Cartesian theory of self-consciousness[16]. The synthetic activity of the mind[17] was replaced by the association of ideas.

Hume entirely denied any effective rôle to mental function or process as such. He distinguished in mental contents two grades, "impressions" and "ideas". But he distinguished among impressions, the first data of experience, "inner" and "outer" impressions. Inner impressions were those of the inner sphere itself, such as pleasures, pains, efforts, etc; and outer impressions were those received by the senses and having the imprint of externality. All possible materials of knowledge, of experience throughout, arise in impressions; and since the term sensation is commonly used for such first data of knowledge, "sensationalism" became the term applied to the resulting theory of knowledge. Rationalism asserts the originality of reason, and explains away or ignores sensation; sensationalism asserts the originality of sensation, and explains away or derives the reason.

The term "idea" is confined by Hume to the derivatives or revived contents of mind in which impressions reappear. They take on various forms of revival and composition. In general, the "idea" of Hume corresponds to the "complex idea" of Locke, and "impression" to Locke's "simple idea". In the use of the term impression itself, the passivity of the mind, its mere impressiveness, is emphasised. As a *tabula rasa*[18], it receives or suffers impressions.

Ideas, the contents of imagination, differ from impressions, the contents of sensation, in vividness or intensity. According to Hume the most vivid idea is less so than the least vivid impression. This difference is, therefore, the distinguishing one.

The course of ideas—their flow, connection, composition—was ruled by the principle of association. In this, a mental principle was substituted for the material inertia of the brain[19], postulated by Hobbes. It also replaced, as we have already seen, the active principle of thought of Descartes. For the first time, a psychological mode of organisation was suggested to justify a naturalistic view of conscious process. Association came to be recognised by a great school of thinkers as the one principle of mental change and movement, somewhat as attraction was found to be in the domain of the physical[20].

Hume recognised three cases of association, generalised in laws: the cases of "resemblance", "contiguity" in space and time, and "cause and effect".[21] As compared with Aristotle's[22] classification, this omits "contrast", and includes in new case of "cause and effect". In the tracing out, the detection as it were, of association in the more complex and synthetic products of the mental life—such as the ideas of the self, the external world, etc.—Hume showed his analytical ability and consistency. He was the first, and remains one of the greatest, of those psychological naturalists who have consistently applied a positive method. Association seemed to supply the hint to the process of progressive mental accommodation, as natural selection subsequently supplied the hint to that of organic adaptation. It gave to naturalism a positive weapon, to mental process a positive lawfulness. And it remains the resort of all those psychologists who find in apperception, mental causation, subjective synthesis, etc., the resort to new modes of obscurantism[23], such as the natural selectionist finds in the newer modifications of vitalism. It was not until the conception of a structural psychology, based upon the analogy of the mechanical processes of physics, was succeeded by that of a functional and truly genetic psychology, to which mechanism was not the last word, that association was finally assigned a more modest rôle. The "mechanics of ideas" of Herbart[24] and the radical "composition theory" of mind of Spencer were first to have their development, both based upon the principle of association.

Hume worked out, in detail, association theories of the higher ideas or concepts of thought, classed by him under the terms "relations", "modes", and "substances". The "self" became a "bundle" of associated ideas; in this the "presentation" theories were anticipated, which were later on brought into direct opposition to "activity" theories. The belief in reality, both external and internal, is ascribed to the vividness of certain impressions, whose force is transferred to associated ideas or memories; these latter are thus distinguished from mere ideas of fancy. Judgments of reality involve a similar reference to impressions. The grounds of belief in reality are in this way carried back to the characters or coefficients of sense impressions. The persistent character of external reality[25] looked upon as having continuing existence apart from perception—is due to the imagination, which connects recurrent impressions in an experience equivalent to that of an identical persistent object[26]. The logical relations, so-called, such as that involved in the universal, are also brought under association. The quality white, for example, is not a logical universal, but an "abstract idea", due to the association by resemblance of many white objects. In this procedure, Hume foreshadows the development of what is known as "psychologism" in logic[27].

(From *History of Psychology*,
Part Ⅳ, Modern Psychology, Chapter Ⅰ)

注　释

① John Locke(1632—1704)约翰·洛克是英国哲学家和教育家,联想主义心理学的先驱。洛克在认识论上继承和发展了培根和霍布斯的唯物主义经验论。霍布斯(Thomas Hobbes, 1588—1679)是英国机械唯物主义哲学家,他提出"白板说",认为人的一切观念都来自经验,根本就没有什么天赋。洛克在心理学上的贡献是第一次提出联想的概念,为联想主义心理学奠定了基础。他认为感觉和反省得来的观念最初都是简单观念,很多复杂观念都是人心使用自己的力量来联合简单观念而获得的。主要著作《人类理性论》(1698)、《人类知性论》(1690)。

② He attempts to treat of the actual sources of knowledge by a scientific method, as proposed by Francis Bacon. 此话见洛克的文章 An Essay Concerning Human Understanding(1690)。

③ Descartes (René Descartes, 1596—1650)　笛卡尔。

④ Wolff(Christian von Baron Wolff, 1679—1754) 沃尔夫是德国哲学家,也是德国康德以前的哲学和心理学权威。沃尔夫同时也是唯理论者,主张宗教教条必须符合理性。主要著作《经验的心理学》(1732),《理论的心理学》(1734)。

⑤ …primary and secondary qualities 引自克莱门(Klemm)的 The History of the Distinction 一书中 the distinction of the terms between primary and secondary qualities(第28页)

⑥ Leibnitz (Gottfried Wilhelm von Leibnitz, 1646—1716) 莱布尼茨是德国数学家和自然科学家,也是德国近代第一个哲学家和心理学家。在科学方面,他独立发明了微积分学。主要著作有《单子论》(1714)、《人类悟性新论》(1704)。

⑦ Locke's Essay 指洛克的文章《人类悟性论》(1690)。在此文中,洛克把心理现象分析为简单成分,然后再把这些成分合成复杂的观念。洛克的思想就是后来的联想主义。他最先用"联想"这个词语,即观念的联结(association of ideas)。

⑧ … between the *a posteriori* or experiential content, and the *a priori* or native form 在其后或经验的内容方面与先前或天然形式方面之间

⑨ the general refutation of rationalism 对理性主义的普遍反驳。

⑩ Hume and the Associationists 休谟与联想主义者。

⑪ in a polemic against rationalism 在反对理性主义的争论方面。

⑫ conations 心理学的意动。

⑬ an analytical method 分析方法。

⑭ validity of ideas 观念的有效性或效度。

⑮ modern genetic psychology 当代发生心理学。

⑯ Locke's Cartesian theory of self-consciousness 洛克的笛卡尔式自我意识理论。这里的 Cartesian 是德文英译 René Descartes。

⑰ the synthetic activity of the mind 心灵的综合活动。

⑱ a tabula rasa 白板(拉丁文)。

⑲ the material inertia of the brain 脑的物质性迟钝。

⑳ in the domain of the physical 在自然物质领域中。
㉑ ... the cases of "resemblance", "contiguity" in space and time and "cause and effect". 休谟在《人类理性研究》中提到观念之间的联系只有三个规律：相似律，时空接近律和因果律。
㉒ Aristotle 亚里斯多德(公元前384—公元前322)，古希腊哲学家。
㉓ resort to new modes of obscurantism 此短语中 resort to 凭借、诉诸 obscurantism 指蒙昧主义。
㉔ Herbart (Hohann Friedrich Herbart, 1776—1841) 赫尔巴特，德国哲学家，教育家和心理学思想家。他的心理学思想受康德和莱布尼茨的影响。他第一次宣称心理学是一门科学，而且是建立在经验之上的。主要著作《心理学教科书》(1816)和《作为科学的心理学》(1824)。
㉕ the persistence character of external reality 外在现实的一贯特点
㉖ ... recurrent impressions in an experience equivalent to that of an identical persistent object. 休谟这一思想见他的书 *Thought and Things* 第一卷第十章。后来的思想家们多次引用休谟的这一思想。
㉗ ..."psychologism" in logic 指在逻辑中对心理因素的注重。

练　习

1. 回答问题
(1) What methods does Locke use in this essay?
(2) What do the primary and secondary qualities suggest?
(3) To Locke, what was reflection?
(4) Who first used the term "the laws of association"?
(5) David Hume, the great Scottish philosopher, developed Locke's position in the two directions in which empiricism still retained rationalistic features. What are the two directions?

(6) What does inner impression suggest?

2. 判断正误
(1) Pursuing what he describes as this "sober method of investigating the origin and connection of our ideas", Hume distinguishes between "simple" and "complex ideas".
(2) Reflection is the source of a new series of ideas which involve relations between and among simpler ideas.
(3) The ideas of reflection are innate.
(4) The course of ideas—their flow, connection, composition—was ruled by the principle of inner impressions.
(5) To Locke, the "self" became a "bundle" of associated ideas.

3. 选词填空
Fill in the blanks with the words given below:
   reveal, transfer, proceed, vindicate, abolish, substitute, slumber, pursue
(1) I hope to _____ my client and return him to society as a free man.
(2) I was _____ soundly when the alarm rang.
(3) There are many bad customs and laws that ought to be _____.
(4) The family _____ their prejudice when they refused to associate with their new neighbor.
(5) He _____ to give hall a vivid description of his grotesque guest.
(6) The poet has _____ fame all his life, but has never experienced it.
(7) The government has _____ primary education to the local councils.

(8) Her brother _____ as host while her husband was away.

4．句型模拟
(1) It is essential that...
(2) Judged by...

5．汉译英
(1) 每次发言者均有时间限制一两分钟。(limit...to...)
(2) 这句话一向被认为是孔子说的。(ascribe to)
(3) 他始终坚持他有分享那笔钱的权利。(assert)
(4) 大家认为两个教皇都死于心脏病发作。(attribute to)
(5) 想象不出更好的东西了。(conceive of)
(6) 我并不愿意怀疑你的诚意。(reflect on)

6. The Postulates of a Structural Psychology

Edward Bradford Titchener

爱德华·波瑞佛德·铁钦纳(Edward Bradford Titchener, 1867—1927)是英国心理学家,构造主义心理学的主要代表。他试图从经验的构造方面去说明人的整个心理。他认为人的心理可以用内省法分析成为元素,即感觉、意象、情感等。这些元素各有属性(质量、强度、持续性等)。元素在时间和空间上混合(或联想)而形成知觉、观念、感觉、情感、情绪等心理过程。他的主要著作有《心理学教科书》(1909—1910)、《实验心理学》(1905)。

《构造主义心理学公设》(The Postulates of a Structural Psychology)节选于《心理学评论》(1898年)第七卷第449—465页,十九世纪九十年代和二十世纪头十年,由于内容心理学(以心理内容为研究对象)和机能主义心理学都有了发展和变化,因此两种心理学的对立明显起来。此时在美国出现了构造主义心理学与机能主义心理学的争论。这两种心理学作为互相对立的名称是铁钦纳于1898年利用詹姆斯的用语而提出的。此后就成了流行名称。构造主义心理学是冯特的内容心理的极端化。

构造主义心理学是十九世纪心理学成为一门独立的实验科学以后出现于欧美的第一个心理学流派,与机能主义心理学对立,代表人物为冯特和铁钦纳。构造主义心理学认为心理学研究对象是意识经验,主张采用实验内省法分析意识的内容和构造,并找出意识的组成部分以及它们连接成各种复杂心理过程的规律。

机能主义心理学(Functional Psychology)是十九世纪末二十世纪初出现于美国的心理学流派。代表美国心理学的主流。这个学派受达尔文进化论的影响和詹姆斯实用主义思想推动,主张心理学的研究对象是具有适应性的心理活动。强调意识活动在人类需要和环境之间的重要中介作用。创始人为杜威,代表人物为安吉尔和卡尔。

BIOLOGY, defined in its widest sense as the science of life and of living things, falls into three parts[1], or may be approached from any one of three points of view. We may enquire into the structure of an organism, without regard to function[2],—by analysis determining its component parts, and by synthesis exhibiting the mode of its formation from the parts[3]. Or we may enquire into the function of the various structures which our analysis has revealed, and into the manner of their interrelation as functional organs. Or, again, we may enquire into the changes of form and function that accompany the persistence of the organism in time, the phenomena of growth and of decay. Biology, the science of living things, comprises the three mutually interdependent sciences of morphology, physiology, and ontogeny[4].

This account is, however, incomplete. The life which forms the subject matter of science is not merely the life of an individual; it is species life[5], collective life, as well. Corresponding to morphology, we have taxonomy or systematic zoölogy[6], the science of classification. The whole world of living things is here the organism, and species and sub-species and races[7] are its parts. Corresponding to physiology[8], we have that department of biology—it has been termed 'œcology'[9]—which deals with questions of geographical distribution, of the function of species in the general economy of nature[10]. Corresponding to ontogeny we have the science of phylogeny[11] (in Cope's sense): the biology of evolution, with its problems of descent and of transmission[12].

We may accept this scheme as a 'working' classification of the biological sciences. It is indifferent, for my present purpose, whether or not the classification is exhaustive, as it is indifferent whether the reader regards psychology as a subdivision of biology or as a separate province of knowledge. The point which I wish now to make is this: that, employing the same principle of division, we can represent modern psychology as the exact counterpart of modern biology. There are three ways of approaching the one, as there are the three ways of approaching the other; and the subject matter in every case may be individual or general. A little consideration will make this clear[13].

1. We find a parallel to morphology in a very large portion of 'experimental' psychology[14]. The primary aim of the experimental psychologist has been to analyze the structure of mind; to ravel out the elemental processes from the tangle of consciousness[15], or (if we may change the metaphor) to isolate the constituents in the given conscious formation. His task is a vivisection, but a vivisection which shall yield structural, not functional results. He tries to discover, first of all, what is there and in what quantity, not what it is there for. Indeed, this work of analysis bulks so largely in the literature of experimental psychology that a recent writer has questioned the right of the science to its adjective, declaring that an experiment is something more than a measurement made by the help of delicate instruments[16]. And there can be no doubt that much of the criticism passed upon the new psychology depends on the critic's failure to recognize its morphological character. We are often told that our treatment of feeling and emotion, of reasoning, of the self is inadequate; that the experimental method is valuable for the investigation of sensation and idea, but can carry us no farther. The answer is that the results gained by dissection of the 'higher' processes[17] will always be disappointing to those who have not themselves adopted the dissector's standpoint. Protoplasm[18] consists, we are told, of carbon, oxygen, nitrogen, and hydrogen; but this statement would prove exceedingly disappointing to one who had thought to be informed of the phenomena of contractility and metabolism, respira-

tion and reproduction[19]. Taken in its appropriate context, the jejuneness of certain chapters in mental anatomy[20], implying, as it does, the fewness of the mental elements, is a fact of extreme importance.

2. There is, however, a functional psychology[21], over and above this psychology of structure[22]. We may regard mind, on the one hand, as a complex of processes, shaped and moulded under the conditions of the physical organism. We may regard it, on the other hand, as the collective name for a system of functions of the psychophysical organism[23]. The two points of view are not seldom confused. The phrase 'association of ideas', *e.g.*, may denote either the structural complex, the associated sensation group, or the functional process of recognition and recall, the associating of formation to formation. In the former sense it is morphological material, in the latter it belongs to what I must name (the phrase will not be misunderstood) a physiological psychology[24].

Just as experimental psychology is to a large extent concerned with problems of structure, so is 'descriptive' psychology, ancient and modern, chiefly occupied with problems of function. Memory, recognition, imagination, conception, judgment, attention, apperception, volition, and a host of verbal nouns[25], wider or narrower in denotation, connote, in the discussions of descriptive psychology, functions of the total organism. That their underlying processes are psychical in character is, so to speak, an accident; for all practical purposes they stand upon the same level as digestion and locomotion, secretion and excretion. The organism remembers, wills, judges, recognizes, etc., and is assisted in its life-struggle by remembering and willing. Such functions are, however, rightly included in mental science, inasmuch as they constitute, in sum, the actual, working mind of the individual man. They are not functions of the body, but functions of the organism, and they may—nay, they must—be examined by the methods and under the regulative principles of a mental 'physiology'.[25] The adoption of these methods does not at all prejudice the ultimate and extra-psychological problem of the function of mentality at large in the universe of things[27]. Whether consciousness really has a survival-value, as James supposes, or whether it is a mere epiphenomenon, as Ribot[28] teaches, is here an entirely irrelevant question.

It cannot be said that this functional psychology, despite what we may call its greater obviousness to investigation, has been worked out either with as much patient enthusiasm or with as much scientific accuracy as has the psychology of mind structure. It is true, and it is a truth which the experimentalist should be quick to recognize and emphasize, that there is very much of value in 'descriptive' psychology. But it is also true that the methods of descriptive psychology cannot, in the nature of the case, lead to results of scientific finality. The same criticism holds, as things stand, of individual psychology, which is doing excellent pioneer work in the sphere of function[29]. Experimental psychology has added much to our knowledge, functional as well as structural, of memory, attention, imagination, etc., and will, in the future, absorb and quantify the results of these other, new coördinate branches. Still, I do not think that anyone who has followed the course of the experimental method, in its application to the higher processes and states of mind, can doubt that the main interest throughout has lain in morphological analysis, rather than in ascertainment of function[30]. Nor are the reasons far to seek[31]. We must remember that experimental psychology arose by way of reaction against the faculty psychology[32] of the last century. This was a metaphysical, not a scientific, psychology. There is, in reality, a great difference between, say, memory regarded as a function of the psychophysical organism, and memory regarded as a faculty of the substantial mind[33]. At the same time, these two memories are nearer together than are the faculty memory and the memories or memory complexes of psychological anatomy[34]. There is, further, the danger that, if function is studied before structure has been fully elucidated, the student may fall into that acceptance of teleological explanation which is fatal to scientific advance: witness, if witness be necessary, the recrudescence of vitalism in physiology[35]. Psychology might thus put herself for the second time, and no less surely though by different means, under the dominion of philosophy. In a word, the historical conditions of psychology rendered it inevitable that, when the time came for the transformation from philosophy to science, problems should be formulated, explicitly or implicitly, as static rather than dynamic, structural rather than functional. We may notice also the fact that elementary morphology is intrinsically an easier study than elementary physiology, and that scientific men are so far subject to the law of inertia[36], whose effects we see in the conservatism of mankind at large[37], that prefer the continued application of a fruitful method to the adoption of a new standpoint for the standpoint's sake.

I may, perhaps, digress[38] here for a moment, to raise and attempt to answer two questions which naturally suggest themselves: the questions whether this conservatism is wise, and whether it is likely to persist. I believe that both should be answered in the affirmative. As has been indicated above, the morphological study of mind serves, as no other method of study can, to enforce and sustain the thesis that psychology is a science, and not a province of metaphysics[39]; and recent writing shows clearly enough that this truth has need of constant reiteration[40]. Moreover, there is still so much to be done in the field of analysis (not simply analysis of the higher processes, though these will of course benefit in the long run⁴¹, but also analysis of perception and feeling and idea) that a general swing of the laboratories⁴² towards functional work would be most regrettable. It seems probable, if one may presume to read the signs of the times, that experimental psychology has before it a long period of analytical research, whose results, direct and indirect, shall ultimately serve as basis for the psychology of function; unless, indeed, —and this is beyond predicting, —the demands laid upon psychology by the educationalist become so insistent as partially to divert the natural channels of investigation.

The remaining four psychologies may be dismissed with a briefer mention. 3. Ontogenetic psychology, the psychology of individual childhood and adolescence, is now a subject of wide interest, and has a large literature of its own⁴³. 4. Taxonomic psychology⁴⁴ is not yet, and in all likelihood will not be, for some time to come, anything more than an ingredient in 'descriptive', and a portion of individual, psychology. It deals with such topics as the classification of emotions, instincts and impulses, temperaments, etc., the hierarchy of psychological 'selves', ⁴⁵ the typical mind of social classes (artists, soldiers, literary men), and so forth. 5. The functional psychology of the collective mind is, as might be expected, in a very rudimentary condition. We can delimit its sphere and indicate its problems; minor contributions to it may be found here and there in the pages of works upon psychology, logic, ethics, æsthetics, sociology, and anthropology; and a few salient points—the question, e.g., of the part played by the æsthetic sentiment in the make-up of a national mind—have been touched upon⁴⁶ in essays. But we must have an experimental physiology of the individual mind, before there can be any great progress. 6. Lastly, the labors of the evolutionary school have set phylogenetic psychology upon a fairly secure foundation㊼, and the number of workers is a guarantee of rapid advance in our understanding of mental development.

(From *Psychological Review*, 1898,
Vol.7, PP449 – 465)

注　释

① fall into three parts　分成三个部分。
② We may enquire into the structure of an organism, without regard to function. 我们可以探讨机体的结构而不管其机能。
③ by synthesis exhibiting the mode of its formation from the parts　通过综合揭露从各部分形成结构的方式。
④ Biology, the science of living things, comprises the three mutually interdependent sciences of morphology, physiology, and ontogeny. 生物学作为研究生物的科学，包括形态学、生理学和发育学三个相互依赖的科学。
⑤ species life　物种的生命。
⑥ ... we have taxonomy or systematic zoology. 我们有分类学或系统动物学。
⑦ ... and species and sub-species and races.　种和亚种以及种族。
⑧ physiology　生理学。
⑨ it has been termed 'œcology'　被称为生态学。
⑩ the general economy of nature　指一般自然界布局。
⑪ the science of phylogeny　种系发育的科学。
⑫ with its problems of descent and of transmission　包括继承和遗传的问题。
⑬ A little consideration will make this clear.　这里的思考见德国心理学家艾宾浩斯（Hermann Ebbinghaus, 1850 – 1909）的书《心理学纲要》第 161 页。
⑭ a very large portion of 'experimental' psychology　"实验"心理学的极大部分。

⑮ ... to ravel out the elemental processes from the tangle of consciousness 这里的 tangle 指缠结。全句译为：把基本过程从意识的缠结中清理出来。

⑯ ... that an experiment is something more than a measurement made by the help of delicate instruments. 这里强调实验的好处。见伏尔夫(Wolff)《心理学》一书第 12 页。

⑰ ... by dissection of the 'higher' processes 解剖"高级"过程（所得的结果）。

⑱ Protoplasm 原形质。

⑲ the phenomena of contractility and metabolism, respiration and reproduction 收缩、新陈代谢，呼吸和生殖现象。

⑳ ... the jejuneness of certain chapters in mental anatomy 某些章节在心理解剖学方面的空虚。

㉑ a functional psychology 机能主义心理学

㉒ psychology of structure 构造心理学

㉓ a system of functions of the psychophysical organism 心理物理机体的机能体系。

㉔ a physiological psychology 生理心理学。

㉕ a host of verbal nouns 无数动词性名词。

㉖ under the regulative principles of a mental 'physiology' 在心理"生理学"的调节原则下。

㉗ The adoption of these methods does not at all prejudice the ultimate and extra-psychological problem of the function of mentality at large in the universe of things. 采用这种方法，对世界万物中心理机能最终极的和超出心理学以外的问题完全没有成见。

㉘ Ribot(Theodule-Armand Ribot, 1839 – 1916)瑞波是法国心理学的创始人。

㉙ which is doing excellent pioneer work in the sphere of function 在机能范围内正做着出色的先驱工作。

㉚ ascertainment of function 机能的确定。

㉛ Nor are the reasons far to seek. 理由也是不难寻找的。

㉜ the faculty psychology 指官能心理学。它是十八世纪中叶在欧洲出现的心理学,认为人的心理是由许多不同的官能所组成的。这些官能包括注意、记忆、知觉、想象、推理、判断等。

㉝ a faculty of the substantial mind 心理实体的官能。

㉞ ... memory complexes of psychological anatomy 心理解剖学的各种记忆复合体。

㉟ the recrudescence of vitalism in physiology 生理学中生机论的再现。参见布敦·桑德森(Burdon Sanderson)的 Science Progress(1896)一书。

㊱ ... are so far subject to the law of inertia 受惰性定律的支配。

㊲ at large 大体上。

㊳ digress 离题。

㊴ a province of metaphysics 形而上学的一个领域。

㊵ constant reiteration 反复说明。

㊶ in the long run 从长远利益上说。

㊷ a general swing of the laboratories 实验室的普遍转向。

㊸ a large literature of its own 有自己的大批文献。

㊹ taxonomic psychology 分类心理学。

㊺ the hierarchy of psychological 'selves' 心理"自我"的层级结构。

㊻ touch upon (on) 触及,谈及。如 centre on the main problem and touch upon others 集中谈主要问题,也提及其他问题。

㊼ set phylogenetic psychology upon a fairly secure foundation. 把种系发生心理学建立在一个稳固的基础上。

练　习

1. 判断正误

(1) Biology, the science of living things, comprises the three mutually interdependent sciences of morphology, physiology, and

ontogeny.
(2) The task of experimental psychologists is to do a vivisection which produce functional results.
(3) We are often told that our treatment of feeling and emotion, of reasoning, of the self is enough.
(4) The association of ideas, in Titchener's eyes, refers to the structural complex.
(5) The author thinks that anyone who has followed the course of the experimental method can doubt that the main interest has lain in morphological analysis, rather than in ascertainment of sensations.
(6) In a word, the historical conditions of psychology rendered it inevitable that, when the time came for the transformation from philosophy to science, problems should be formulated, explicitly or implicitly, as static rather dynamic, structural rather than functional.
(7) The morphological study of mind serves to enforce and sustain the thesis that psychology is a province of metaphysics.
(8) The labors of the evolutionary school have set phylogenetic psychology upon a fairly secure foundation and the number of workers is a guarantee of rapid advance in our understanding of mental development.

2. 词汇与短语

Fill in the blanks with the proper words or expressions given below:
digress, comprise, touch on, in the long run, the tangle of, prejudice, inquire into, be subject to
(1) In the short term we expect to lose money on this book but ___ _____ we hope to make large profits.
(2) A deer was caught in _____ vines.

(3) He spoke about social conditions, _____ housing and education.
(4) The anthology _____ samples from the works of ten authors.
(5) I ll tell you a funny story, if I may _____ from my subject for a moment.
(6) The trains _____ delay where there is fog.
(7) His attempted escape seriously _____ any hopes for parole.
(8) He frowned and determined to _____ the matter.

3. 句型模拟
(1) Nor...
(2) So far

4. 汉译英
(1) 它们可以很自然地分成三等。(fall into)
(2) 科学家发现探究新的领域。(a province of)
(3) 他是一个安分守己的人。(sphere)
(4) 那个逃犯仍在逍遥法外。(at large)
(5) 如果你继续不顾礼法行事,你就会招来麻烦。(without regard to)

5. 英译汉
(1) Just as experimental psychology is to a large extent concerned with problems of structure, so is "descriptive" psychology, ancient and modern, chiefly occupied with problems of function.
(2) We must remember that experimental psychology arose by way of reaction against the faculty psychology of the last century.
(3) Ontogenetic psychology, the psychology of individual childhood and adolescence, is now a subject of wide interest, and has a large literature of its own.

7. The Reflex Arc Concept in Psychology

John Dewey

约翰·杜威(John Dewey, 1859—1952)是美国机能主义心理学家。他的主要思想是反对把心理分析成各个元素,或分解为各个部分的做法,他认为心理活动是一个连续的整体,反射弧概念中刺激与反应之间,感觉与运动之间并不存在一条鸿沟。同时他认为人的活动与社会是一个整体,个人与集体不能互相脱离。

《心理学中的反射弧概念》(The Reflex Arc Concept in Psychology, 1896)节选自《心理学评论》(1896)第三卷第357—370页。美国心理学的总倾向是机能主义,但是机能主义在美国作为一个自觉的学派,则起源于十九世纪九十年代的芝加哥大学。这一学派是由于不满意构造主义学派而产生的。创始人为杜威。詹姆斯的实用主义哲学是机能主义心理学的哲学基础。

That the greater demand for a unifying principle and controlling working hypothesis[①] in psychology should come at just the time when all generalizations[②] and classifications are most questioned and questionable is natural enough. It is the very cumulation of discrete facts creating the demand for unification[③] that also breaks down previous lines of classification. The material is too great in mass and too varied in style to fit into existing pigeon-holes[④], and the cabinets of science break of their own dead weight[⑤]. The idea of the reflex arc has upon the whole come nearer to meeting this demand for a general working hypothesis than any other single concept. It being admitted that the sensori-motor apparatus[⑥] represents both the unit of nerve structure and the type of nerve function, the image of this relationship passed over into[7] psychology, and became an organizing principle to hold together the multiplicity of fact[8].

In criticising this conception it is not intended to make a plea for the principles of explanation and classification which the reflex arc idea has replaced; but, on the contrary, to urge that they are not sufficiently displaced, and that in the idea of the sensori-motor circuit[9], conceptions of the nature of sensation and of action derived from the nominally displaced psychology are still in control[10].

The older dualism between sensation and idea is repeated in the current dualism of peripheral and central structures and functions[11]; the older dualism of body and soul finds a distinct echo in the current dualism of stimulus and response. Instead of interpreting the character of sensation, idea and action from their place and function in the sensori-motor circuit, we still incline to interpret the latter from our preconceived and preformulated ideas of rigid distinctions between sensations, thoughts and acts. The sensory stimulus[12] is one thing, the central activity[13], standing for the idea, is another thing, and the motor discharge, standing for the act proper, is a third. As a result, the reflex arc is not a comprehensive, or organic unity, but a patchwork of disjointed parts, a mechanical conjunction of unallied processes[14]. What is needed is that the principle underlying the idea of the reflex arc as the fundamental psychical unity shall react into and determine the values of its constitutive factors. More specifically, what is wanted is that sensory stimulus, central connections and motor responses shall be viewed, not as separate and complete entities in themselves, but as divisions of labor, functioning factors, within the single concrete whole, now designated the reflex arc.

What is the reality so designated? What shall we term that which is not sensation-followed-by-idea-followed-by-movement, but which is primary[15], which is, as it were, the psychical organism of which sensation, idea and movement are the chief organs? Stated on the physiological side, this reality may most conveniently be termed coördination[16]. This is the essence of the facts held together by and subsumed under the reflex arc concept. Let us take, for our example, the familiar child-candle instance. (James, Psychology, Vol. I, p.25.) The ordinary interpretation would say the sensation of light is a stimulus to the grasping as a response, the burn resulting is a stimulus to withdrawing the hand as response[17] and so on. There is, of course, no doubt that is a rough practical way of representing the process. But when we ask for its psychological adequacy, the case is quite different. Upon analysis, we find that we begin not with a sensory stimulus, but with a sensori-motor coördination, the optical-ocular[18], and that in a certain sense it is the movement which is primary, and the sensation which is secondary, the movement of body, head and eye muscles determining the quality of what is experienced[19]. In other words, the real beginning is with the act of seeing; it is looking, and not a sensation of light. The sensory quale gives the value of the act[20], just as the movement furnishes its mechanism and control, but both sensation and movement lie inside, not outside the act.

Now if this act, the seeing, stimulates another act, the reaching, it is because both of these acts fall within a larger coördination; because seeing and grasping have been so often bound together to reinforce each other, to help each other out, that each may be considered practically a subordinate member of a bigger coördination. More specifically, the ability of the hand to do its work will depend, either directly or indirectly, upon its control, as well as its stimulation, by the act of vision. If the sight did not inhibit as well as excite the reaching, the latter would be purely indeterminate, it would be for anything or nothing, not for the particular object seen. The reaching, in turn, must both stimulate and control the seeing. The eye must be kept upon the candle if the arm is to do its work; let it wander and the arm takes up another task. In other words, we now have an enlarged and transformed coördination[21]; the act is seeing no less than before, but it is now seeing-for-reaching purposes. There is still a sensori-motor circuit, one with more content or value, not a substitution of a motor response for a sensory stimulus[22].

Now take the affairs at its next stage, that in which the child gets burned. It is hardly necessary to point out again that this is also a sensori-motor coördination and not a mere sensation. It is worth while, however, to note especially the fact that it is simply the completion, or fulfillment, of the previous eye-arm-hand coördination and not an entirely new occurrence[23]. Only because the heat-pain quale enters into the same circuit of experience with the optical-ocular and muscular quales[24], does the child learn from the experience and get the ability to avoid the experience in the future.

More technically stated, the so-called response is not merely *to* the stimulus; it is *into* it. The burn is the original seeing, the original optical-ocular experience enlarged and transformed in its value. It is no longer mere seeing; it is seeing-of-a-light-that-means-pain-when-contact-occurs. The ordinary reflex arc theory proceeds upon the more or less tacit assumption that the outcome of the response is a totally new experience; that it is, say, the substitution of a burn sensation for a light sensation through the intervention of motion. The fact is that the sole meaning of the intervening movement is to maintain, reinforce or transform (as the case may be) the original quale; that we do not have the replacing of one sort of experience by another, but the development (or as it seems convenient to term it, the mediation) of an experience[25], The seeing, in a word, remains to control the reaching, and is, in turn, interpreted by the burning㉖.

The discussion up to this point may be summarized by saying that the reflex arc idea, as commonly employed, is defective in that it assumes sensory stimulus and motor response as distinct psychical existences㉗, while in reality they are always inside a coördination and have their significance purely from the part played in maintaining or reconstituting the coördination; and (secondly) in assuming that the quale of experience which precedes the 'motor' phase and that which succeeds it are two different states, instead of the last being always the first reconstituted, the motor phase coming in only for the sake of such mediation. The result is that the reflex arc idea leaves us with a disjointed psychology, whether viewed from the standpoint of development in the individual or in the race, or from that of the analysis of the mature consciousness. As to the former, in its failure to see that the arc of which it talks is virtually a circuit, a continual reconstitution, it breaks continuity and leaves us nothing but a series of jerks㉘, the origin of each jerk to be sought outside the process of experience itself, in either an external pressure of 'environment ' or else in an unaccountable spontaneous variation㉙ from within the 'soul' or the 'organism'. As to the latter, failing to see the unity of activity, no matter how much it may prate of unity㉚, it still leaves us with sensation or peripheral stimulus; idea, or central process (the equivalent of attention); and motor response, or act, as three disconnected existences, having to be somehow adjusted to each other, whether through the intervention of an extra-experimental soul, or by mechanical push and pull.

Before proceeding to a consideration of the general meaning for psychology of the summary, it may be well to give another descriptive analysis, as the value of the statement depends entirely upon the universality of its range of application. For such an instance we may conveniently take Baldwin's analysis of the reactive consciousness. In this there are, he says (Feeling and Will, p. 60), "three elements corresponding to the three elements of the nervous arc[㉛]. First, the receiving consciousness, the stimulus—say a loud, unexpected sound; second, the attention involuntarily drawn, the registering element[㉜]; and, third, the muscular reaction following upon the sound—say flight from fancied danger." Now, in the first place, such an analysis is incomplete; it ignores the status prior to[㉝] sound. Of course, if this status is irrelevant to what happens afterwards, such ignoring is quite legitimate. But is it irrelevant either to the quantity or the quality of the stimulus?

If one is reading a book , if one is hunting, if one is watching in a dark place on a lonely night, if one is performing a chemical experiment, in each case, the noise has a very different psychical value; it is a different experience. In any case, what proceeds the 'stimulus' is a whole act, a sensori-motor coördination. What is more to the point, the 'stimulus' emerges out of this coördination; it is born from it as its matrix; it represents as it were an escape from it. I might here fall back upon authority, and refer to the widely accepted sensation continuum theory, according to which the sound cannot be absolutely *ex abrupto*[㉞] from the outside, but is simply a shifting of focus of emphasis, a redistribution of tensions within the former act[㉟]; and declare that unless the sound activity had been present to some extent in the prior coördination, it would be impossible for it now to come to prominence[㊱] in consciousness. And such a reference[㊲] would be only an amplification of what has already been said concerning the way in which the prior activity influences the value of the sound sensation. Or, we might point to cases of hypnotism, mono-ideaism and absent-mindedness, like that of Archimedes[㊳], as evidences that if the previous coördination is such as rigidly to lock the door, the auditory disturbance will knock in vain for admission to consciousness. Or, to speak more truly in the metaphor, the auditory activity must already have one foot over the threshold, if it is ever to gain admittance.

But it will be more satisfactory, probably, to refer to the biological side of the case, and point out that as the ear activity has been evolved on account of the advantage gained by the whole organism, it must stand in the strictest histological and physiological connection with the eye, or hand, or leg, or whatever other organ has been the overt center of action. It is absolutely impossible to think of the eye center as monopolizing consciousness and the ear apparatus as wholly quiescent[39]. What happens is a certain relative prominence and subsidence[40] as between the various organs which maintain the organic equilibrium.

Furthermore, the sound is not a mere stimulus, or mere sensation; it again is an act, that of hearing. The muscular response is involved in this as well as sensory stimulus; that is, there is a certain definite set of the motor apparatus involved in hearing just as much as there is in subsequent running away. The movement and posture of the head, the tension of the ear muscles, are required for the 'reception' of the sound. It is just as true to say that the sensation of sound arises from a motor response as that the running away is a response to the sound. This may be brought out by reference to the fact[41] that Professor Baldwin, in the passage quoted, has inverted the real order as between his first and second elements. We do not have first a sound and then activity of attention, unless sound is taken as mere nervous shock or physical event, not as conscious value. The conscious sensation of sound depends upon the motor response having already taken place; or, in terms of the previous statement (if stimulus is used as a conscious fact, and not as a mere physical event) it is the motor response or attention which constitutes that, which finally becomes the stimulus to another act. Once more, the final 'element', the running away, is not merely motor, but is sensori-motor, having its sensory value and its muscular mechanism[42]. It is also a coördination. And, finally, this sensori-motor coördination is not a new act, supervening upon what preceded[43]. Just as the 'response' is necessary to constitute the stimulus, to determine it as sound and as this kind of sound, of wild beast or robber, so the sound experience must persist as a value in the running, to keep it up, to control it.

(From *Psychological Review*, 1896, Vol. 3, PP357 – 370)

注 释

① a unifying principle and controlling working hypothesis 一个统一原则和支配研究工作的假设。
② generalization 概括
③ the cumulation of discrete facts creating the demand for unification 个别事实累积引起统一的要求
④ pigeon-hole. 分界的格局。
⑤ ... the cabinets of science break of their own dead weight. 此句中 cabinet 指框架, dead weight 指重负。全句译为科学界限打破了他们自身的负荷。
⑥ the sensori-motor apparatus 感觉—运动装置
⑦ pass over into 指(印象)传入到……
⑧ the multiplicity of fact 多种事实
⑨ sensori-motor circuit 感觉运动回路(的观念)。
⑩ in control. 处在支配地位。
⑪ The older dualism between sensation and idea is repeated in current dualism of peripheral and central structures and functions. 在现代关于外围和中枢的构造和功能的二元论中重复了过去感

觉与观念之间的二元论。

⑫ the sensory stimulus 感觉刺激。

⑬ the central activity （观念的）中枢活动。

⑭ As a result, the reflex arc is not a comprehensive, or organic unity but a patch-work of disjoined parts, a mechanical conjunction of unallied processes. 此句中 disjointed parts 指一个缀合体。全句译为：结果，反射弧并不是一个综合有机的统一单元，而是零散部分的缀合体或不相类同的过程的机械结合。

⑮ What shall we term that which is not sensation-followed-by-idea-followed-by-movement, but which is primary. 在此句中，sensation-followed-by-idea-followed-by-movement 是一个复合形容词。指感觉继之以观念，再继之以运动。比如 Women have outgrown the jumping-on-a-chair-at-the-sight-of-a-mouse era. 女人已经摆脱那种一见老鼠就跳到椅子上的时代了。

⑯ coordination 协调一致。

⑰ ... the burning resulting is a stimulus to withdrawing the hand as response... 灼烧是作为缩手反应的刺激

⑱ the optical-ocular 视觉与眼动（的协调）

⑲ ... head and eye muscles determining the quality of what is experienced 头和眼球肌肉的运动决定着所经验到的性质

⑳ The sensory quale gives the value of the act. 感觉的性质提供动作的意义。

㉑ ... an enlarged and transformed coordination 一个扩大的和变化了的协调。

㉒ ... not a substitution of a motor response for a sensory stimulus. 而不是以一个运动反应代替一个感觉刺激。对于刺激的相关关系的解释见《心理学评论》1896 年第五期第 253 页。

㉓ not an entirely new occurrence 不是一个全新的事件。

㉔ with the optical-ocular and muscular quales 带着视觉以及肌肉的感觉

㉕ The ordinary reflex arc theory proceeds upon the more or less tacit assumption that the outcome of the response is a totally new experience. 通常的反射弧理论或多或少在默认的假定下进行，这个假定认为反应的结果是一个全新的经验。

㉖ the mediation of an experience　经验的中介。

㉗ The seeing, in a word, remains to control the reaching, and is, in turn, interpreted by the burning. 总之，看见仍然控制着抓，并且被灼烧所解释。对默认假定的进一步说明见杜威《伦理学大纲》。

㉘ distinct psychical existences　完全不同的心理状态。

㉙ a series of jerks　一系列的惊跳。

㉚ an unaccountable spontaneous variation　一个不可解的自发变异

㉛ prate of unity　谈及统一性

㉜ three elements of the nervous arc　指神经弧的三元素。

㉝ the registering element　登记的元素。

㉞ prior to　在……之前。

㉟ *ex abrupto*　突然出现(拉丁文)。

㊱ a redistribution of tensions within the former act　前面一个动作内部紧张力的再分布。

㊲ come to prominence　突出。

㊳ such a reference　这样一个引证。

㊴ Or, we might point to cases of hypnotism, mono-ideaism and absent-mindedness, like that of Archimedes　或者，我们可以举出催眠状态，或像阿基米德那样专心致志或出神的状态等例子。

㊵ ... think of the eye center as monopolizing consciousness and the ear apparatus as wholly quiescent　想象眼中枢垄断了意识，而耳装置则完全缄默。

㊶ What happens is a certain relative prominence and subsidence. 所发生的一切是某种相对意义的主导和从属。

㊷ This may be brought out by reference to the fact... 这一情况可根据这一事实搞清楚……
㊸ muscular mechanism 肌肉机制。
㊹ ... supervening upon what preceded 外加于前面的……

练　习

1. 回答问题
(1) According to Dewey, what is the reflex arc?
(2) Dewey mentioned the example of the sensation of light as a stimulus in this essay. What did the example suggest?
(3) According to Baldwin, what are three elements corresponding to the three elements of the nervous arc?
(4) Why is the response necessary to constitute the stimulus?

2. 判断正误
(1) The older dualism between sensation and idea is repeated in the current dualism of peripheral and central structure and functions.
(2) There are a sensori-motor circuit and a substitution of a motor response for a sensory stimulus.
(3) The so-called response should be into the stimulus.
(4) The result is that the reflex arc idea leaves us with a disjointed psychology, whether viewed from the standpoint of development in the individual or in the race, or from that of the analysis of the mature consciousness.
(5) The sound is only a mere stimulus.
(6) The sensation of sound arises from a motor response as that the running away is a response to the stimulus.

3. 词汇与短语

Fill in the blanks with the proper words given below:
organic, monopolize, comprehensive, conjunction, unification, occurrence, tacit, spontaneous, stimulus, term(v.)

(1) He has no right to _____ himself a professor.
(2) By sitting quietly at the meeting, he gave his _____ approval to the plan.
(3) Many Christians claim that they are seeking the _____ of the church.
(4) Her remarks were _____ and obviously not planned.
(5) The patient has an _____ malfunction.
(6) They will take measures to guarantee against the _____ of similar incidents in the future.
(7) The government gave a very _____ explanation of its plans for industry development.
(8) The _____ of heavy rains and high winds caused flooding.
(9) The hostess thoroughly _____ the guest's time.
(10) Reduced tariffs were a _____ to foreign trade.

4. 句型模拟

(1) ...may be brought out by ...
(2) on the contrary

5. 汉译英

(1) 他的死因是流感和肺炎的并发。(supervene upon)
(2) 但是他马上就控制住了自己。(in control)
(3) 我母亲结婚前是个护士。(prior to)
(4) 在任何调查中,应注意按照正确的原则出发。(proceed upon)

8. General Characteristics of Original Tendencies

Edward Lee Thorndike

爱德沃德·李·桑代克(Edward Lee Thorndike, 1874—1949)是美国心理学家、动物心理实验的首创者,教育心理学体系和联结主义心理学的创始人。主要著作有:《心理学纲要》(1905)、《动物智慧》(1911)、《成人的学习》(1928)、《人类的学习》(1931)及《学习要义》(1932)。

《原本趋向的普遍特征》(General Characteristics of Original Tendencies, 1974)选自桑代克的《教育心理学》。桑代克1899年任哥伦比亚大学师范学院的教授,在这个学院教学四十年,对美国的心理学,特别是教育心理学,影响很大。他的《教育心理学》一书的出版,使教育心理学在1903年从教育学和心理学中分化出来,成为独立学科,教育心理学体系包括人之本性,学习心理学和个体差异三个部分。桑代克的教育心理学利用了达尔文的进化论问世以来的生物科学成就并由他自己对于动物学习的创造性研究成果发展而来。

The arts and sciences serve human welfare[①] by helping man to change the world, including man himself, for the better. The word education refers especially to those elements of science and art which are concerned with changes in man himself. Wisdom and economy in improving man's wants and in making him better able to satisfy them depend upon knowledge—first, of what his nature is, apart from[②] education, and second, of the laws which govern changes in it[③]. It is the province of educational psychology to give such knowledge of the original nature of man and of the laws of modifiability[④] or learning, in the case of intellect, character and skill.

A man's nature and the changes that take place in it may be described in terms of the responses—of thought, feeling, action and attitude—which he makes, and of the bonds[5] by which these are connected with the situations which life offers. Any fact of intellect, character or skill means a tendency to respond in a certain way to a certain situation—involves a *situation* or state of affairs influencing the man, a *response* or state of affairs in the man, and a *connection* or bond whereby the latter is the result of the former[6].

ORIGINAL *versus* LEARNED TENDENCIES

Any man possesses at the very start of his life—that is, at the moment when the ovum and spermatozoon which are to produce him have united[7]—numerous well-defined tendencies to future behavior[8]. Between the situations which he will meet and the responses which he will make to them, pre-formed bonds exist[9]. It is already determined by the constitution of these two germs, that under certain circumstances[10] he will see and hear and feel and act in certain ways. His intellect and morals, as well as his bodily organs and movements, are in part the consequence of the nature of the embryo[11] in the first moment of its life. What a man is and does throughout life is a result of whatever constitution he has at the start and of all the forces that act upon it before and after birth. I shall use the term 'original nature'[12] for the former and 'environment'[13] for the latter.

THE PROBLEMS OF ORIGINAL NATURE

Elementary psychology acquaints us with the fact[14] that men are, apart from education, equipped with tendencies to feel and act in certain ways in certain circumstances—that the response to be made to a situation may be determined by man's inborn organization[15]. It is, in fact, a general law that, other things being equal, the response to any situation will be that which is by original nature connected with that situation, or with some situation like it. Any neurone will[16], when stimulated, transmit the stimulus, other things being equal, to the neurone with which it is by inborn organization most closely connected. The basis of intellect and character is this fund of unlearned tendencies[17], this original arrangement of the neurones in the brain.

The original connections may develop at various dates and may exist for only limited times; their waxing and waning may be sudden or gradual[18]. They are the starting point for all education or other human control. The aim of education is to perpetuate some of them, to eliminate some, and to modify or redirect others. They are perpetuated by providing the stimuli adequate to arouse them[19] and give them exercise, and by associating satisfaction with their action. They are eliminated by withholding these stimuli so that they abort through disuse[20], or by associating discomfort with their action. They are redirected by substituting, in the *situation-connection-response* series, another response instead of the undesirable original one; or by attaching the response to another situation in connection with which it works less or no harm, or even positive good.

It is a first principle of education to utilize any individual's original nature as a means to changing him for the better—to produce in him the information, habits, powers, interests and ideals which are desirable.

The behavior of man in the family, in business, in the state, in religion and in every other affair of life is rooted in his unlearned, original equipment of instincts and capacities. All schemes of improving human life must take account of man's original nature, most of all when their aim is to reverse or counteract it.

THE ORIGINAL NATURE OF MAN
NAMES FOR ORIGINAL TENDENCIES

Three terms, reflexes, instincts, and inborn capacities[2], divide the work of naming these unlearned tendencies. When the tendency concerns a very definite and uniform response to a very simple sensory situation, and when the connection between the situation and the response is very hard to modify and is also very strong so that it is almost inevitable, the connection or response to which it leads is called a reflex. Thus the knee-jerk is a very definite and uniform response to the simple sense-stimulus of sudden hard pressure against a certain spot. It is hard to lessen, to increase, or otherwise control the movement, and, given the situation, the response almost always comes. When the response is more indefinite, the situation more complex, and the connection more modifiable, instinct becomes the customary term. Thus one's misery at being scorned is too indefinite a response to too complex a situation and is too easily modifiable to be called a reflex. When the tendency is to an extremely indefinite response or set of responses to a very complex situation, and when the connection's final degree of strength is commonly due to very large contributions from training, it has seemed more appropriate to replace reflex and instinct by some term like capacity, or tendency, or potentiality. Thus an original tendency to respond to the circumstances of school education by achievement in learning the arts and sciences is called the capacity for scholarship.

There is, of course, no gap between reflexes and instincts, or between instincts and the still less easily describable original tendencies. The fact is that original tendencies range with respect to the nature of the responses from such as are single, simple, definite, uniform within the individual and only slightly variable amongst individuals, to responses that are highly compound, complex, vague, and variable within one individual's life and amongst individuals. They range with respect to the nature of the situation② from simple facts like temperature, oxygen or humidity, to very complex facts like 'meeting suddenly and unexpectedly a large animal when in the dark without human companions', and include extra-bodily, bodily, and what would be commonly called purely mental, situations. They range with respect to the bond or connection from slight modifiability to great modifiability, and from very close likeness amongst individuals to fairly wide variability.

Much labor has been spent in trying to make hard and fast distinctions between reflexes and instincts and between instincts and these vaguer predispositions㉓ which are here called capacities. It is more useful and more scientific to avoid such distinctions in thought, since in fact there is a continuous gradation.

THE COMPONENTS OF AN ORIGINAL TENDENCY

A typical reflex, or instinct, or capacity, as a whole, includes the ability to be sensitive to a certain situation, the ability to make a certain response, and the existence of a bond or connection whereby that response is made to that situation. For instance, the young chick is sensitive to the absence of other members of his species, is able to peep㉔, and is so organized that the absence of other members of the species makes him peep. But the tendency to be sensitive to a certain situation may exist without the existence of a connection therewith of any further exclusive response[25], and the tendency to make a certain response may exist without the existence of a connection limiting that response exclusively to any single situation. The three-year-old child is by inborn nature markedly sensitive to the presence and acts of other human beings[26], but the exact nature of his response varies. The original tendency to cry is very strong, but there is no one situation to which it is exclusively bound.

Original nature seems to decide that the individual will respond somehow to certain situations more often than it decides just what he will do, and to decide that he will make certain responses more often than it decides just when he will make them. So, for convenience in thinking about man's unlearned equipment, this appearance of *multiple response* to one same situation and multiple *causation* of one same response may be taken roughly as the fact.

It must not, however, be taken to mean that the result of an action set up in the sensory neurones by a situation is essentially unpredictable—that, for instance, exactly the same neurone-action (paralleling, let us say, the sight of a dog by a certain two-year-old child) may lead, in the two-year-old, now to the act of crying, at another time to shy retreat, at another to effusive joy, and at still another to curious examination of the newcomer, all regardless of any modification by experience[27]. On the contrary, *in the same organism the same neurone-action will always produce the same result—in the same individual the really same situation will always produce the same response*. The apparent existence of an original sensitivity unconnected with any one particular response, so that apparently the same cause produces different results, is to be explained in one of two ways. First, the apparently same situations may really be different. Thus, the sight of a dog to an infant in its mother's arms is not the same situation as the sight of a dog to an infant alone on the doorstep. Being held in its mother's arms is a part of the situation that may account for the response of mild curiosity in the former case and fear in the latter. Second, if the situations are really identical, the apparently same organism really differs. Thus a dog seen by a child, healthy, rested and calm, may lead to only curiosity, whereas, if seen by the same child, ill, fatigued, and nervously irritable, it may lead to fear.

Similarly, the really same response is never made to different situations by the same organism. When the same response seems to be made to different situations, closer inspection will show that the responses do differ; or that the situations were, in respect to the element that determined the response, unidentical; or that the organism is itself different. Thus, though 'a ball seen', 'a tin soldier seen', and 'a rattle seen' alike provoke 'reaching for', the *total* responses do differ, the central nervous system㉓ being provoked to three different responses manifested as three different sense-impressions㉔—of a ball, of a tin soldier, and of a rattle. Thus, if 'ball grasped', 'tin soldier grasped', and 'rattle grasped' alike provoke 'throwing', it is because only one particular component㉕, common to the three situations, is effective in determining the act. Thus, if a child now weeps whenever spoken to, whereas before he wept only when hurt or scolded, it is because he is now exhausted, or otherwise changed.

The original connections between situation and response are never due to chance in its true sense, but there are many minor coöperating forces㉛ by which a current of conduction㉜ in the same sensory neurones or receptors㉝ may, on different occasions, diverge to produce different results in behavior, and by which very different sensory stimulations may converge to a substantially common consequence㉞.

One may use several useful abstract schemes[35] by which to think of man's original equipment of reflexes, instincts and capacities. Perhaps the most convenient is a series of S-R connections of three types. Some are of the type—S_1 leads to R_1, its peculiar sequent; some are of the type—S_1 leads to R_1 or R_2 or R_3 or R_4 or R_5, etc., according to very minor casual contributory causes; some are of the type—S_1 leads to $R + r_1$, S_2 leads to $R + r_2$, S_3 leads to $R + r_s$ etc., where r_1, r_2 and r_3 are minor results.

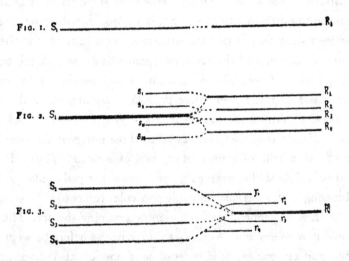

Graphically this scheme is represented by Figs. 1, 2 and 3.

Besides such a system of tendencies deciding which response any given situation will produce, there are certain tendencies that decide the status of features common to all situation-response connections. There is, for example, in man an original tendency whereby any connection once made tends, other things being equal, to persist. There is also a tendency whereby any connection or response may or may not be in readiness to be made—may be excited to action easily or with difficulty. These tendencies toward the presence or absence of a certain feature in all connections or responses will be examined by themselves in due time.

GENERAL CHARACTERISTICS
THE ACTION OF ORIGINAL TENDENCIES

We can imagine a man's life so arranged that one after another original tendency should be called into play[36], each by itself. Let him be in a certain status, and let, successively, the light grow five times as intense[37], snuff be blown up his nostrils[38], a dear friend approach, and the earth quake, without in any case any other changes whatever either in the surroundings or in his internal status[39]. Then the pupils of his eyes would contract, he would sneeze, he would smile, and he would start.

The original tendencies of man, however, rarely act one at a time in isolation one from another. Life apart from learning would not be a simple serial arrangement, over and over, of a hundred or so situations, each a dynamic unit; and of a hundred or so responses, fitted to these situations by a one-to-one correspondence. On the contrary, they coöperate in multitudinous combinations[40]. Their combination may be apparent in behavior, as when the tendencies to look at a bright moving object, to reach for a small object passing a foot away, and to smile at a smiling familiar face combine to make a baby smilingly fixate and reach for the watch which his father swings. Or the combination may take place unobserved in the nervous system, as when a large animal suddenly approaching a solitary child makes him run and hide, though the child in question would neither run nor hide at solitude, at the presence of the animal, or at the sudden approach of objects in general.

It is also the case that any given situation does not act absolutely as a unit, producing either one total response or none at all. Its effect is the total effect of its elements, of which now one, now another may predominate in determining response, according to coöperating forces without and within the man. The action of the situations which move man's original nature is not that of some thousands of keys each of which unlocks one door and does nothing else whatever. Any situation is a complex, producing a complex effect; and so, if attendant circumstances vary, a variable effect. In any case it does, so to speak, what it can.

(From *Educational Psychology*, Vol. I , Chapter I)

注　释

① human welfare 人类幸福。
② apart from 除此以外。
③ the laws which govern changes (人性的)改变依照某种公律。
④ the laws of modifiabililty 改变的公律。
⑤ ... and of the bonds 结合。
⑥ ... and a connection or bond whereby the latter is the result of the former 此句中 whereby 是疑问副词, 指靠什么。比如: Whereby shall we know him? 我们靠什么认出他呢?
⑦ ... at the moment when the ovum and spermatozoon which are to produce him have united 当精子和卵子结合产生人的时候
⑧ ... numerous well-defined tendencies to future behavior. 这里 behavior 是行为的意思, 指人的思想, 感情等活动。
⑨ ... pre-formed bonds exist 存在某种预定的结合。
⑩ under certain circumstances 在某种情形下。
⑪ ... are in part the consequence of the nature of the embryo 在某种程度上是由胚胎的性质决定的。

⑫ ... use the term 'original nature' 使用术语'本性'
⑬ environment 环境
⑭ Elementary psychology acquaints us with the fact that ... 句中 acquaint sb. with sth. 把…通知某人。比如:We acquaint Western readers with the present status of the People's Republic of China. 我们使西方读者了解中华人民共和国的现状。
⑮ by man's inborn organization 人生来的组织
⑯ neurone 神经元
⑰ ... this fund of unlearned tendencies 非习得趋向的资本。
⑱ ... their waxing and waning may be sudden or gradual 它们的消长有时突如其来有时渐渐而起。
⑲ They are perpetuated by providing the stimuli adequate to arouse them. 通过提供足以唤起它们的刺激而使其永久存在。
⑳ they abort through disuse 它们由于使用不当而夭折。
㉑ capacities 能力。
㉒ They range with respect to the nature of the situation. 他们依据环境的性质而改变。
㉓ predispositions 预先倾向。
㉔ ... the young chick is sensitive to the absence of other members of his species, is able to peep 一支小鸡能觉察到它的同类不在它的周围,并能吱吱叫。
㉕ ... without the existence of a connection therewith of any further exclusive response 与其他进一步的某种特殊的反应之间没有联系。
㉖ The three-year-old child is by inborn nature markedly sensitive to the presence and acts of other human beings. 三岁儿童天生就特别能觉察旁人在不在以及他们的动作。
㉗ all regardless of any modification by experience 完全不需要经过经验的改变。
㉘ the central nervous system 中枢神经系统。

㉙ sense-impression 感觉印象。
㉚ one particular component 一个特殊的成分。
㉛ many minor cooperating forces 许多弱小势力的合作。
㉜ a current of conduction 神经电流。
㉝ receptors 感受器官。
㉞ converge to a substantially common consequence 合流到一个实质上相同的归宿。
㉟ abstract schemes 抽象的图式。
㊱ original tendency should be called into play 原本趋向开始出现。
㊲ the light grow five times as intense 光线的强度增加了五倍。
㊳ snuff be blown up his nostrils 鼻烟吹进他的鼻孔。
㊴ in his internal status 他的内部状况。
㊵ multitudinous combinations 指形式多样的组合。

练 习

1. 回答问题
(1) What is the meaning of the word education?
(2) What is the aim of education?
(3) What does a typical reflex, or instinct, or capacity include, as a whole?

2. 判断正误
(1) The arts and sciences serve human welfare by helping man to change the world, including man himself, for the better.
(2) Man's intellect and morals, unlike his bodily organs and movements, are in part the consequence of the nature of the embryo in the first moment of its life.
(3) The basis of intellect and character is this fund of unlearned tendencies, this original arrangement of soul.
(4) It is a first principle of education to utilize any individual's orig-

inal nature as a means to changing him for the better——to produce in him the information, habits, powers, interests and ideals which are not desirable.
(5) According to the author, the sight of a dog to an infant in its mother's arms is not the same situation as the sight of a dog to an infant alone on the doorstep.
(6) The original tendencies of man, however, act one at a time in isolation one from another.

3. 词汇与短语

Fill in the blanks with the proper words given below
govern, perpetuate, abort, modification, component, consequence, intense, status,

(1) The engine has more than 300 _____, made of a number of different materials.
(2) Do you know what the _____ of your action will be?
(3) The Washington Monument was built to _____ the memory of a great man.
(4) In Britain the sovereign reigns but does not _____.
(5) My happiness was so _____, I did not dare to move.
(6) The law, in its present form, is unjust, it needs _____.
(7) Another third of the population had improved its _____ due to better employment opportunities.
(8) The doctor had to _____ the baby.

4. 汉译英
(1) 脱离实践就没有知识。(apart from)
(2) 他的成功在某种程度上是由于幸运。(in part)
(3) 无论到哪儿,他们都想法了解民间音乐。(acquaint with)
(4) 证券交易所对于政治波动很敏感。(sensitive to)

(5) 关于这个小家伙是怎么死的,一点消息也没有。(the absence of)
(6) 让每个孩子阅读根据自己的兴趣爱好选择的书籍。(in terms of)

9. Unlearned Behavior: Emotion

John Broadus Watson

约翰·布诺达斯·华生(John Broadus Watson, 1878—1958)是美国心理学家,行为主义心理学的创建人。主要著作有《行为:比较心理学导论》(1914)、《行为主义》(1925)、《行为主义的方法》和《行为主义的幼稚教育》(1928)。

《非习得的行为:情绪》节选自华生的《从行为主义者的眼光来看心理学》第六章。行为主义的产生有心理学发展史的内部因素,与动物心理学的兴起有密切的关系。动物心理学的兴起直接与生物进化论有关。达尔文在他的《人的宗系》和《人和动物的表情》两本书中提出动物和人的心理有连续性的思想。罗门尼士,摩尔根等关于动物心理学的研究,成了行为主义的先声,也是行为主义产生的重要来源。1913年华生发表《从行为主义者的眼光来看心理学》,里面涉及了动物心理学的研究,同时宣传他关于心理学的主张。华生认为心理学是自然科学,如其他自然科学一样,只应该用客观观察法,从外部观察行为。心理学的目的在于预见并控制人的行为。华生的行为主义思想奠定了行为主义的理论基础,也是对美国机能主义的推广。

Introduction.—In the last three chapters we have been concerned with the details of sensory-motor adjustment. We turn next to man as a reacting organism, and specifically to some of the reactions which belong to his hereditary equipment. Human action as a whole can be divided into *hereditary* modes of response (emotional and instinctive), and *acquired* modes of response (habit)[1]. Each of these two broad divisions is capable of many subdivisions. It is obvious both from the standpoint of common-sense and of laboratory experimentation that the hereditary and acquired forms of activity begin to overlap early in life. Emotional reactions become wholly separated from the stimuli that originally called them out[2], and the instinctive positive reaction tendencies displayed by the child soon become overlaid with the organized habits of the adult. This process of masking or dovetailing of activities is a part of the general process of organization. The separation between hereditary reaction modes and acquired reaction modes can thus never be made absolute. Fortunately in most connections psychology is not called upon to draw a sharp distinction[3] between hereditary and acquired reactions. In making laboratory studies, however, it is sometimes necessary for us to study the details of hereditary response. We find it simpler in such cases to overemphasize for the time the definiteness of the separation. This is unquestionably a legitimate mode of procedure in science. Few biological problems permit of any other treatment. In order to accomplish this at all we have to adopt a genetic method[4]. We have to start with the baby's advent (we would start before if it were not for possible injury to mother and child) and follow his development step by step, noting the first appearance of the hereditary forms of reaction, their course and effect upon the moulding of the child's whole personality; and the early beginnings of acquired modes of response. Undoubtedly learning begins *in utero* (there is no reason to suppose that conditioned reflexes do not begin there), and probably several hereditary modes of action (particular types of reflexes) run their entire course *in utero*. But we are entering here upon a field which just at present is purely speculative[5].

What Is an Emotion? —Hard and fast definitions are not possible in the psychology of emotion, but formulations are possible and sometimes help us to group our facts. A formulation which will fit a part of the emotional group of reactions may be stated as follows: *An emotion is an hereditary " pattern-reaction " involving profound changes of the bodily mechanism as a whole, but particularly of the visceral and glandular systems*[6]. By pattern-reaction we mean that the separate details of response appear with some constancy, with some regularity and in approximately the same sequential order each time the exciting stimulus is presented. It is obvious that if this formulation is to fit the facts, the general condition of the organism must be such that the stimulus can produce its effect. A child alone in a house on a stormy night with only a dim candle burning may display the reaction of fear at the mournful hoot of an owl. If the parents are at hand and the room is well lighted, the stimulus may pass unreacted to. Stimulus then in this sense is used in a broad way to refer not only to the exciting object but also to the general setting. There is implied also the fact that the general state of the organism must be sensitive (capable of being stimulated) to this form of stimulus at the moment. This condition is very important. A young man may be extremely sensitive to the blandishments of every female he meets while in the unmarried state and may show considerable excitement and over-reaction on such occasions. In most cases, he becomes considerably less sensitive after being happily married. This formulation may seem somewhat roundabout— somewhat like saying that a stimulus is an emotional stimulus only when you get the pattern-reaction, but this is very nearly the case. Possibly we can illustrate most easily what we mean by choosing an example from animal life. When the naturalist comes suddenly upon a young sooty tern under four days of age⑦, it lies stock still (it is capable of very rapid locomotion): It can be pushed about or rolled over without explicit forms of response appearing. The moment the intruder moves away, the fledgling may hop to its feet and dash away or give one of its instinctive cries. The pattern-reaction, that is, the explicit observable pattern, is very simple indeed—a death feint⑧ or posture. Such a type of response is quite common in the animal world. In order to bring about⑨ such a tremendous variation in behavior in an animal usually so active there must be a profound modification of the organic processes[10]. We shall see later that the locus of the effect is principally in the visceral system. Often, however, the skeletal musculature is involved in the pattern[11]. A serviceable way to mark off an *emotional* reaction[12] from an *instinctive* reaction is to include in the formulation of emotion a factor which may be stated as follows: The shock of an emotional stimulus throws the organism for the *moment at least* into a chaotic state[13]. When in the first shock of an emotional state, the subject makes few adjustments to objects in his environment[14]. In contrast to this stand the instincts as we shall see farther on[15]. The subject in an instinctive act usually does something: he throws his hand up for defense, blinks his eyes or ducks his head; runs away; he bites, scratches, kicks and grasps whatever his hand touches. We may express our formulation in convenient terms somewhat as follows: when the adjustments called out by the stimulus are internal and confined to the subject's body, we have emotion, for example, blushing; when the stimulus leads to adjustment of the organism as a whole to objects, we have instinct, for example, defense responses, grasping, etc. Emotions seldom appear alone. The stimulus usually calls out emotional instinctive and habit factors simultaneously[16].

Additional Formulation.—The above formulation fits only the more stereotyped forms[17] of emotional response as seen, for example, in the states popularly called blushing, anger, fear and shame. When we take into account the whole group of phenomena in which we see emotional manifestations in adults, a pronounced modification is necessary. Apparently the hereditary pattern as a whole gets broken up. At any rate it largely disappears (the parts never wholly disappear) except under unusual conditions, and there *can be noted only a reinforcement or inhibition of the habit and instinctive (ex-*

aggerated and depressed reflexes, for example) *activities taking place at the moment*. We mean to imply here only the generally observed facts typified by such popular expressions as "He is working at a low ebb today", ⑱ "His tone is low", "He's a gloom"; in psychopathology when this phase is more marked, *depressions* are spoken of. The opposite picture is popularly portrayed by such expressions as "Jones is full of pep today", ⑲ "he is excited", "happy", "he is working with a punch"⑳; in psychopathology, the exaggerated type of this behavior is termed *manic*㉑. It will be noted that these expressions refer to the activity level㉒ at which all of an individual's acts are accomplished, that is, they do not refer to the pattern type of emotion. Only in pathological cases, or in the case of normals in periods of a cataclysmic nature㉓, such as war, earthquake, and the sudden death of loved ones, do we get a complete return to the original and more infantile type㉔ of emotional response.

Observation would seem to suggest the following formulation: Organized activity (hereditary and acquired) may go on and usually does go on at a given level. We may call the most usual *the normal level* or level of equilibrium㉕. It varies with different individuals and one can determine it even with respect to a single individual only after observing him for a considerable time. We may note further that an individual at one time may exhibit more energy, push or pep than normal, for example, during and immediately after a cold shower; we may call this the excited level㉖. Again at times he works at a level lower than normal, for example, when in trouble, after money losses or illness; we may call this the *depressed level*㉗.

Without neurologizing too much㉘, we may venture the assumption that in adults environmental factors have brought about the partial inhibition of the more external features of the primitive pattern types of emotion. The implicit, mainly glandular and smooth muscular side of the pattern, remains. The emotionally exciting object releases important internal secretions[29] which, without initiation new (part) reactions, reinforce or inhibit those actually in progress[30]. This hypothesis would account for changes in level. Only in rare cases do we see mere changes in level. Usually when such changes occur, certain auxiliary or additional part reactions appear, such as we see in whistling while at work, keeping time with the feet, drumming on the table, biting the finger nails. These types of reaction are singled out[31] and spoken of in some detail under the head *Emotional Outlets*.

The Genetic Study of Emotion in the Child.—Unfortunately for the subject of psychology, few experiments have been made upon the emotional life of the child under anything like as favorable conditions as obtain in the study of animals[32]. Our observations upon the child are similar to those which were made upon animals before Thorndike[33] and Lloyd Morgan[34] introduced the experimental method. Until very recently, in spite of volumes written upon it, discussion has been of the armchair variety. The superstition that the human infant is too fragile for study is giving way to a more sensible viewpoint. It has proven practicable in some laboratories to take infants from birth and to study them from the same point of view that animals are studied, giving due consideration to those factors in behavior which do not appear in animal response. But unfortunately this work is handicapped because there are no facilities in maternity wards[35] for keeping the mother and child under close observation for years, a condition which is indispensable for real systematic work.

(Form *Psychology from the Standpoint of
a Behaviorist*, Chapter VI)

注 释

① hereditary modes of response (emotional and instinctive) and acquired modes of response (habit). 遗传的反应模式(情绪的与本能的)和习得的反应模式(习惯)。

② Emotional reactions become wholly separated from the stimuli that originally called them out. call out:引发出来。They called out both military and police forces to suppress the strikers. 他们把军队和警察调来镇压罢工者。原句译为:情绪的反应与原来引起它们的刺激可以完全分离。

③ Fortunately in most connections psychology is not called upon to draw a sharp distinction... call upon (on) 原意是号召,这里指需要。此句译为:幸而心理学通常用不着在二者之间作严格的区别。

④ a genetic method. 发生的研究法。

⑤ But we are entering here upon a field which just at present is purely speculative. enter upon (on):着手开始。比如:He is entering on his second year of office as Primer on October 1. 10月1日他进入了首相任期的第二个年头。原句译为:不过这种说法现在还纯粹是推想而已。

⑥ ...but particularly of the visceral and glandular system. 这里指最显著的是内脏和腺体的变化。

⑦ ...come suddenly upon a young sooty tern under four days of age. sooty tern 指黑鸥,come upon 是抓住的意思。全句译为:突然抓住刚生下来四天的黑鸥。

⑧ a death feint 装死。

⑨ bring about 找到或造成。

⑩ a profound modification of the organic processes 其有机过程的深刻改变。

⑪ the skeletal musculature is involved in the pattern 骨骼肌肉加

111

入这种反应的模式。

⑫ A serviceable way to mark off an emotional reaction 把情绪反应与本能的反应分清楚的有用的方法。

⑬ The shock of an emotional stimulus throws the organism for the moment at least into a chaotic state. 情绪刺激的震动至少在那个时候把机体置于混乱状态中。

⑭ ... the subject makes few adjustments to objects in his environment. 机体对于他所处的环境中的事物产生不了什么反应。

⑮ In contrast to this stand the instincts as we shall see farther on. 本能与此相反,讲到以后章节我们便知道。

⑯ The stimulus usually calls out emotional instinctive and habit factors simultaneously. 刺激通常把情绪性的本能因素及习惯因素同时激发起来。

⑰ stereotyped forms. 刻板形式。

⑱ He is working at a low ebb today. 他今天工作不带劲。

⑲ John is full of pep today. 约翰今天很起劲。

⑳ He is working with a punch. 他工作真带劲。

㉑ manic 疯狂。

㉒ the activity level 活动水平。

㉓ Only in pathological cases, or in the case of normals in periods of a cataclysmic nature. 只有在病人中,或正常人处于激情变化的时期。

㉔ infantile type 婴孩式。

㉕ the normal level or level of equilibrium 正常水平或平衡水平。

㉖ excited level 兴奋水平。

㉗ depressed level 抑郁水平。

㉘ without neurologizing too much... 不必多用神经作用来作依据。

㉙ The emotionally exciting object releases important internal secretions. 激动情绪的事物释放出重要的内分泌物。

㉚ reinforce or inhibit those actually in progress 强化或抑制那些正在进行的动作。
㉛ These types of reaction are singled out 把这些类型反应单独提出来。
㉜ ... the emotional life of the child under anything like as favourable conditions as obtain in the study of animals 这里指对孩子情绪生活所作的实验,所处的情境很少像研究动物所考虑的情境那么有利。
㉝ Thorndike 桑代克。
㉞ Lloyd Morgan (1852—1936)摩尔根。1894年主张根据动物的行为推断它的心理活动。他提出"节约律"。主要著作:《比较心理学导论》。
㉟ maternity wards 妇产医院。

练 习

1. 回答问题
(1) What are the two parts, according to Watson, of human actions as a whole divided into?
(2) According to the author, in the psychology of emotion, what are possible and sometimes can help us to group our facts?
(3) What is an emotion?
(4) How do you explain this phenomenon: a young man may be extremely sensitive to the blandishments of every female he meets while in the unmarried state?

2. 判断正误
(1) The process of masking or dovetailing of activities is a part of the general process of organization.
(2) A child alone in a house on a stormy night with only a dim candle burning may display the reaction of fear at the mournful

hoot of an owl. If the parents are at hand and the room is well lighted, the stimulus may be strong.

(3) Emotions never appear alone.

(4) The stimulus usually calls out emotional instinctive and habit factors simultaneously.

(5) Many psychological experiments have been made upon the emotional life of the child under anything like as favorable conditions as obtain in the study of animals.

3. 词汇与短语

Fill in the blanks with the proper words given below

instinctive, speculative, simultaneously, stereotype, reinforce, inhibit, inhabit, involve

(1) The _____ act of a frightened person is to run away.

(2) No one has _____ that island for over 100 years.

(3) The medicine _____ the spread of the disease.

(4) His philosophical system also _____ a belief in reincarnation.

(5) That concrete is _____ with steel beams.

(6) She believes that she is not a good mother because she does not fit the _____ of a woman who spends all her time with her children.

(7) Reports about his retirement from active politics are largely _____.

(8) I made two copies of this poem, and posted them _____ to different publishers.

4. 汉译英

(1) 和他弟弟相反,他总是能体谅人。(in contrast to)

(2) 我们的国家进入了一个新时代。(enter upon)

(3) 我们用木桩为我们的地划界。(mark off)
(4) 这些研究都是关于阿尔法射线的。(be concerned with)

10. The Principal Instincts and the Primary Emotion of Man

William McDougall

威廉姆·麦独孤(William McDougall, 1871—1938)是美国心理学家,原籍英国,策动心理学的创建人。他对生理心理学、实验心理学、普通心理学、社会心理学和变态心理学都有独创性的研究和见解。主要著作有:《生理心理学入门》(1905)、《社会心理学导论》(1908)、《身与心》(1911)、《心理学:行为的研究》(1922)等。

《人类的主要本能和原始情绪》(1908)节选自《社会心理学引论》(1913)第三章,麦独孤在这篇文章中阐明本能的观点,他认为本能不是一个或一串机械的反射,而是一种动力,一种原始的完整的心理过程,他对本能加以分类,总结出人的十二种主要本能。麦独孤的本能论企图说明行为的目的性,找到行为后面的动力,也叫动力心理学或策动心理学(Hormic Psychology)。这种心理学受到了瓦德和司托特注重心的主动性倾向的影响。

Before we can make any solid progress in the understanding of the complex emotions and impulses that are the forces underlying the thoughts and actions of men and of societies, we must be able to distinguish and describe each of the principal human instincts[①] and the emotional and conative tendencies[②] characteristic of each one of them.

In the foregoing chapter it was said that the instinctive mental process that results from the excitement of any instinct has always an affective aspect, the nature of which depends upon the constitution of that most stable and unchanging of the three parts of the instinctive disposition, namely the central part[③]. In the case of the simpler instincts, this affective aspect of the instinctive process is not prominent; and though, no doubt, the quality of it is peculiar in each case, yet we cannot readily distinguish these qualities and we have no special names for them. But, in the case of the principal powerful instincts, the affective quality④ of each instinctive process and the sum of visceral and bodily changes in which it expresses itself are peculiar and distinct; hence language provides special names for such modes of affective experience, names such as anger, fear, curiosity; and the generic name for them is "emotion".

Each of the principal instincts conditions, then, some one kind of emotional excitement whose quality is specific or peculiar to it; and the emotional excitement of specific quality that is the affective aspect of the operation of any one of the principal instincts may be called a primary emotion⑤. This principle, which was enunciated in my little work on physiological psychology⑥, proves to be of very great value when we seek to analyse the complex emotions into their primary constituents.

In adapting to scientific use a word from popular speech, it is inevitable that some violence should be done to common usage; and, in adopting this rigid definition of emotion, we shall have to do such violence in refusing to admit joy, sorrow, and surprise (which are often regarded, even by write on psychology, as the very types of emotions) to our list whether of simple and primary or of complex emotions. Some arguments in justification of this exclusion will be adduced later. At this stage I will only point out that joy and sorrow are not emotional states that can be experienced independently of the true emotions, that in every case they are qualifications of the emotions they accompany⑦, and that in strictness we ought rather to speak always of a joyful or sorrowful emotion—*e.g.*, a joyful wonder or gratitude, a sorrowful anger or pity.

In considering the claim of any human emotion or impulse to rank as a primary emotion or simple instinctive impulse, we shall find two principles of great assistance[8]. First, if a similar emotion and impulse are clearly displayed in the instinctive activities of the higher animals, that fact will afford a strong presumption[9] that the emotion and impulse in question are primary and simple; on the other hand, if no such instinctive activity occurs among the higher animals, we must suspect the affective state in question of being either a complex composite emotion or no true emotion. Secondly, we must inquire in each case whether the emotion and impulse in question occasionally appear in human beings with morbidly exaggerated intensity[10], apart from such general hyper-excitability as is displayed in mania[11]. For it would seem that each instinctive disposition, being a relatively independent functional unit in the constitution of the mind[12], is capable of morbid hypertrophy[13] or of becoming abnormally excitable, independently of the rest of the mental dispositions and functions. That is to say, we must look to comparative psychology and to mental pathology[14] for confirmation of the primary character of those of our emotions that appear to be simple and unanalysable.

The Instinct of Flight and the Emotion of Fear

The instinct to flee from danger is necessary for the survival of almost all species of animals, and in most of the higher animals the instinct is one of the most powerful. Upon its excitement the locomotory apparatus is impelled to its utmost exertions[15], and sometimes the intensity and long duration of these exertions is more than the visceral organs[16] can support, so that they are terminated by utter exhaustion or death. Men also have been known to achieve extraordinary feats of running and leaping under this impulse; there is a well-known story of a great athlete who, when pursued as a boy by a savage animal, leaped over a wall which he could not again "clear" until he attained his full stature and strength[17]. These locomotory activities are accompanied by a characteristic complex of symptoms, which in its main features is common to man and to many of the higher animals, and which, in conjunction with[18] the violent efforts to escape, constitutes so unmistakable an expression of the emotion of fear that no one hesitates to interpret it as such[19]; hence popular speech recognises the connection of the emotion with the instinct that determines the movements of flight in giving them the one name *fear*. Terror, the most intense degree of this emotion, may involve so great a nervous disturbance, both in men and animals, as to defeat the ends of the instinct by inducing general convulsions or even death[20]. In certain cases of mental disease the patient's disorder seems to consist essentially in an abnormal excitability of this instinct and a consequent undue frequency and intensity of its operation[21]; the patient lives perpetually in fear, shrinking in terror from the most harmless animal or at the least unusual sound, and surrounds himself with safeguards against impossible dangers.

In most animals this instinct may be excited by a variety of objects and sense-impressions prior to all experience of hurt or danger; that is to say, the innate disposition has several afferent inlets[22]. In some of the more timid creatures it would seem that every unfamiliar sound or sight is capable of exciting it. In civilised man, whose life for so many generations has been more or less sheltered from the dangers peculiar to the natural state, the instinct exhibits (like all complex organs and functions that are not kept true to the specific type by rigid selection) considerable individual differences, especially on its receptive side[24]. Hence it is difficult to discover what objects and impressions were its natural excitants in primitive man[24].

In most animals instinctive flight is followed by equally instinctive concealment as soon as cover is reached[25], and there can be little doubt that in primitive man the instinct had this double tendency. As soon as the little child can run, his fear expresses itself in concealment following on flight[26], and the many adult persons who seek refuge from the strange noises of dark nights, or from a thunderstorm, by covering their heads with the bed-clothe, and who find a quite irrational comfort in so doing, illustrate the persistence of this tendency[27]. It is, perhaps, in the opposed characters of these two tendencies, both of which are bound up with the emotion of fear, that we may find an explanation of the great variety of, and variability of, the symptoms of fear. The sudden stopping of heart-beat and respiration, and the paralysis of movement in which it sometimes finds expression, are due to the impulse to concealment; the hurried respiration and pulse, and the frantic bodily efforts[28], by which it is more commonly expressed, are due to the impulse to flight.

That the excitement of fear is not necessarily, or indeed usually, the effect of an intelligent appreciation or anticipation[29] of danger, is especially well shown by children of four or five years of age, in whom it may be induced by the facial contortions or playful roarings of a familiar friend[30]. Under these circumstances, a child may exhibit every symptom of fear even while he sits upon his tormentor's lap and, with arms about his neck, beseeches him to cease or to promise not to do it again. And many a child has been thrown into a paroxysm of terror[31] by the approach of some hideous figure that he knew to be but one of his playfellows in disguise.

Of all the excitants of this instinct the most interesting, and the most difficult to understand as regards its mode of operation, is the unfamiliar or strange as such. Whatever is totally strange, whatever is violently opposed to the accustomed and familiar, is apt to excite fear both in men and animals, if only it is capable of attracting their attention. It is, I think, doubtful whether an eclipse of the moon has ever excited the fear of animals, for the moon is not an object of their attention; but for savage men it has always been an occasion of fear. The well-known case of the dog described by Romanes, that was terrified by the movements of an object jerked forward by an invisible thread, illustrates the fear-exciting powers of the unfamiliar in the animal world. The following incident is instructive in this respect: A courageous child of five years, sitting alone in a sunlit room, suddenly screams in terror, and, on her father hastening to her, can only explain that she saw something move. The discovery of a mouse in the corner of the room at once explains and banishes her fear, for she is on friendly terms with mice[②]. The mouse must have darted across the peripheral part of her field of vision[③], and this unexpected and unfamiliar appearance of movement sufficed to excite the instinct. This avenue to the instinct, the unfamiliar, becomes in man highly diversified and intellectualised[④], and it is owing to this that he feels fear before the mysterious, the uncanny, and the supernatural, and that fear, entering as an element into the complex emotions of awe and reverence, plays its part in all religions.

Fear, whether its impulse be to flight or to concealment, is characterised by the fact that its excitement, more than that of any other instinct, tends to bring to an end at once all other mental activity, riveting the attention upon its object to the exclusion of all others[⑤]; owing, probably, to this extreme concentration of attention, as well as to the violence of the emotion, the excitement of this instinct makes a deep and lasting impression on the mind. A gust of anger, a wave of pity or of tender emotion, an impulse of curiosity, may co-operate in supporting and re-enforcing mental activities of the most varied kinds, or may dominate the mind for a time and then pass away, leaving but little trace. But fear, once roused, haunts the mind⑯; it comes back alike in dreams and in waking life⑰, bringing with it vivid memories of the terrifying impression. It is thus the great inhibitor of action, both present action and future action, and becomes in primitive human societies the great agent of social discipline⑱ through which men are led to the habit of control of the egoistic impulses⑲.

(From *An Introduction to Social Psychology*, Chapter III)

注　释

① the principal human instincts　人的主要本能。
② conative tendencies　意动趋向。
③ In the foregoing chapter it was said that the instinctive mental process that results from the excitement of any instinct has always an affective aspect, the nature of which depends upon the constitution of that most stable and unchanging of the three parts of the instinctive disposition, namely the central part. 在这长句子中，central part 指中枢部分。全句译为：上文中已叙述了任何本能的激动所引起的本能的心理过程常具有感情的方面。这种感情的性质依赖于本能倾向三个组成部分中最稳固不变的一部分，那就是中枢部分。
④ the affective quality　情感性质。
⑤ a primary emotion　一种原始情绪。
⑥ physiological psychology　生理心理学。
⑦ At this stage I will only point out the joy and sorrow are not emotional states that can be experienced independently of the true e-

motions, that in every case they are qualifications of the emotions they accompany. 在这阶段我要指出的是欢乐和悲伤不是能够独立于真正的情绪而被体验到的情绪状态,在任何时候只能是其所伴随情绪的修饰品。

⑧ ... we shall find two principles of great assistance. 我们会看到两个极其有用的原则。

⑨ afford a strong presumption 提供有力的推断。

⑩ ... we must inquire in each case whether the emotion and impulse in question occasionally appear in human beings with morbidly exaggerated intensity,... 在每一种情况下,我们必须查究情绪和冲动是否偶然会以惊人的过大强度表现在人们身上。

⑪ ... apart from such general hyper-excitability as is displayed in mania. 这个短语指除了表现在狂躁症患者身上的过分激动兴奋。

⑫ ... being a relatively independent functional unit in the constitution of the mind 作为心灵结构中相对独立的机能单位(本能倾向)

⑬ is capable of morbid hypertrophy 能进入过度的病态。

⑭ mental pathology 精神病理学。

⑮ Upon its excitement the locomotory apparatus is impelled to its utmost exertions. 在这本能激动之下,运动器官工作量被推动到顶点。

⑯ the visceral organs 内脏。

⑰ ... leaped over a wall which he could not again "clear" until he attained his full stature and strength. 在他身体发育完全成熟前再无一次能越过这堵墙。

⑱ in conjunction with 相联系。

⑲ ... no one hesitates to interpret it as such. 此句中, as such:按照那样。He is a brilliant scholar and is everywhere recognized as such. 他是一位有才华的学者,到处都公认他当之无愧。

⑳ … by inducing general convulsions or even death　通过引起全身的痉挛甚至死亡

㉑ a consequent undue frequency and intensity of its operation　由之而产生的频繁而剧烈的发作。

㉒ several afferent inlets　几个传入口。

㉓ on its receptive side　在感受方面。

㉔ Hence it is difficult to discover what objects and impressions were its natural excitants in primitive man.　在此句子中，natural excitants 指天然激动物。全句译为：因此很难发现哪种对象和印象是原始人类的天然激动物。

㉕ instinctive flight is followed by equally instinctive concealment as soon as cover is reached　一有躲藏之处，其躲藏本能就随其逃避本能而出现。

㉖ his fear expresses itself in concealment following on flight　他的恐惧就表现为逃跑后的躲藏。

㉗ illustrate the persistence of this tendency　说明（成人也具有）牢固的本能趋向。

㉘ the frantic bodily efforts　身体的极度颤动。

㉙ the effect of an intelligent appreciation or anticipation of danger　对危险物有所鉴别或预见的智力（引起了恐惧）。

㉚ by the facial contortions or playful roarings of a familiar friends　由于熟人的怪脸或开玩笑的吼叫。

㉛ thrown into a paroxysm of terror　陷入突发的恐怖中。

㉜ … for she is on friendly terms with mice.　此句中，on good (friendly) terms with: 友善，要好。全句译为：因为她和老鼠有着友好的关系。

㉝ The mouse must have darted across the peripheral part of her field of vision.　老鼠一定是曾从她的视野边缘直冲过来。

㉞ This avenue to the instinct, the unfamiliar, becomes in man highly diversified and intellectualised.　人的这种由不熟悉事物

引起恐惧本能的通道已变得高度多样化和理智化。
㉟ bring to an end　停止。
㊱ ... upon its object to the exclusion of all others　（把注意力）集中在引起恐惧的对象上而不注意其他的事物。
㊲ haunts the mind　在心中盘旋。
㊳ in waking life　（回到）清醒的生活状态。
㊴ the great agent of social discipline　（遵守）社会纪律的重要动力
㊵ ... the habit of control of the egoistic impulses　习惯于控制自私自利的冲动。

练　　习

1. 回答问题
(1) What is the definition of a primary emotion? What is the significance of carrying out a primary emotion research?
(2) How is fear given?
(3) Of all the excitants of the instinct, what is the most interesting and difficult thing to understand as regards the mode of operation?

2. 判断正误
(1) Language provides special names for such modes of affective experience, names such as anger, fear, curiosity; and the generic name for them is emotion.
(2) If a similar emotion and impulse are clearly displayed in the instinctive activities of the higher animals, that fact will afford a weak presumption that the emotion and impulse in question are primary and simple.
(3) Terror, may exclude so great a nervous disturbance, both in men and animals, as to defeat the ends of the instinct by inducing general convulsions or even death.

(4) The innate disposition has several afferent inlets.
(5) It is difficult to know what objects and impressions were its natural excitants in primitive man.
(6) The hurried respiration and pulse, and the frantic bodily efforts, by which it is more commonly expressed, are due to the impulse to flight.

3. 词汇与短语
Fill in the blanks with the proper verbs below
attain, impel, exaggerate, induce, illustrate, diversify, haunt, dart
(1) Bill _____ back into bed as his father's step was heard on the stairs.
(2) People should _____ their in vestments and not in vest all their money in one company.
(3) She often said that she was never allowed to _____ her one ambition, to sit and read.
(4) If you always _____, people won't believe what you say.
(5) Financial pressures _____ the firm to cut back on spending.
(6) Nothing would _____ Elizabeth to give up the cause of education.
(7) Each verb in this dictionary is _____ with a sentence.
(8) The years of the war still _____ me.

4. 句型模拟
(1) as such
(2) Upon ...

5. 汉译英
(1) 我希望我们之间有关基本原则的争论已经结束。(bring to an end)

(2) 我同那班人没有来往。(on terms with)
(3) 思想必须借助词语媒介来表达。(express ... in)
(4) 这一节应当连同前面 3 节一起研读。(in conjunction with)
(5) 他纵马跃过栅栏。(leap over)

11. The Uses of Intelligence Tests

Lewis Madison Terman

刘易斯·麦迪逊·特曼(Lewis Madison Terman, 1877—1956)是美国心理学家。1905年法国心理学家比纳和西蒙制订的比纳—西蒙智力量表,后来由特曼加以修订,称为"斯坦福—比纳智力量表"。特曼首创用智力测验来鉴别和研究天才儿童。他于1921年用斯坦福—比纳智力量表鉴别出1528名天才儿童,平均智商150,并对他们进行了长期的追踪研究。他著有《天才儿童遗传的研究》5卷。此后在西方约40多年,标准化的智力测验便成了鉴别天才儿童的通用工具。

《智力测验的功用》节选自特曼的《智力测量》(The Measurement of Intelligence)(第一章)(1916)。

Intelligence tests of retarded school children[①]. Numerous studies of the age-grade progress of school children have afforded convincing evidence of the magnitude and seriousness of the retardation problem[②]. Statistics collected in hundreds of cities in the United States show that between a third and a half of the school children fail to progress through the grades at the expected rate[③]; that from 10 to 15 per cent are retarded two years or more; and that from 5 to 8 per cent are retarded at least three years. More than 10 per cent of the $400,000,000 annually expended in the United States for school instruction is devoted to re-teaching children what they have already been taught but have failed to learn.

The first efforts at reform which resulted from these findings were based on the supposition that the evils which had been discovered could be remedied by the individualizing of instruction, by improved methods of promotion④, by increased attention to children's health, and by other reforms in school administration. Although reforms along these lines have been productive of much good⑤, they have nevertheless been in a measure disappointing⑥. The trouble was, they were too often based upon the assumption that under the right conditions all children would be equally, or almost equally, capable of making satisfactory school progress. Psychological studies of school children by means of standardized intelligence tests have shown that this supposition is not in accord with the facts⑦. It has been found that children do not fall into two well-defined groups, the "feeble-minded" and the "normal" Instead, there are many grades of intelligence, ranging from idiocy on the one hand to genius on the other. Among those classed as normal, vast individual differences have been found to exist in original mental endowment, differences which affect profoundly the capacity to profit from school instruction⑧.

We are beginning to realize that the school must take into account⑨, more seriously than it has yet done, the existence and significance of these differences in endowment⑩. Instead of wasting energy in the vain attempt to hold mentally slow and defective children up to a level of progress which is normal to the average child, it will be wiser to take account of the inequalities of children in original endowment and to differentiate the course of study in such a way that each child will be allowed to progress at the rate which is normal to him, whether that rate be rapid or slow.

While we cannot hold all children to the same standard of school progress, we can at least prevent the kind of retardation which involves failure and the repetition of a school grade. It is well enough recognized that children do not enter with very much zest upon school work in which they have once failed. Failure crushes self-confidence and destroys the spirit of work. It is a sad fact that a large proportion of children in the schools are acquiring the habit of failure. The remedy, of course, is to measure out the work for each child in proportion to his mental ability⑪.

Before an engineer constructs a railroad bridge or trestle, he studies the materials to be used, and learns by means of tests exactly the amount of strain per unit of size his materials will be able to withstand⑫. He does not work empirically, and count upon patching up the mistakes⑬ which may later appear under the stress of actual use. The educational engineer should emulate this example. Tests and forethought must take the place of failure and patchwork. Our efforts have been too long directed by "trial and error." It is time to leave off guessing and to acquire a scientific knowledge of the material with which we have to deal. When instruction must be repeated, it means that the school, as well as the pupil, has failed.

Every child who fails in his school work or is in danger of failing should be given a mental examination. The examination takes less than one hour, and the result will contribute more to a real understanding of the case than anything else that could be done. It is necessary to determine whether a given child is unsuccessful in school because of poor native ability, or because of poor instruction, lack of interest, or some other removable cause.

It is not sufficient to establish any number of special classes, if they are to be made the dumping-ground for all kinds of troublesome cases—the feeble-minded, the physically defective, the merely backward, the truants, the incorrigibles, etc. Without scientific diagnosis and classification of these children the educational work of the special class must blunder along in the dark⑭. In such diagnosis and classification our main reliance must always be in mental tests, properly used and properly interpreted.

Intelligence tests of the feeble-minded. Thus far intelligence tests have found their chief application in the identification and grading of the feeble-minded⑮. Their value for this purpose is twofold. In the first place, it is necessary to ascertain the degree of defect⑯ before it is possible to decide intelligently upon either the content or the method of instruction suited to the training of the backward child. In the second place, intelligence tests are rapidly extending our conception of "feeble-mindedness" to include milder degrees of defect than have generally been associated with this term. The earlier methods of diagnosis caused a majority of the higher grade defectives to be overlooked. Previous to⑰ the development of psychological methods the lowgrade moron was about as high a type of defective as most physicians or even psychologists were able to identify as feeble-minded.

Wherever intelligence tests have been made in any considerable number⑱ in the schools, they have shown that not far from 2 per cent of the children enrolled have a grade of intelligence which, however long they live, will never develop beyond the level which is normal to the average child of 11 or 12 years. The large majority of these belong to the moron grade; that is, their mental development will stop somewhere between the 7-year and 12-year level of intelligence, more often between 9 and 12.

The more we learn about such children, the clearer it becomes that they must be looked upon as real defectives. They may be able to drag along to the fourth, fifth, or sixth grades, but even by the age of 16 or 18 years they are never able to cope successfully with the more abstract and difficult parts of the common-school course of study. They may master a certain amount of rote learning, such as that involved in reading and in the manipulation of number combinations⑲, but they cannot be taught to meet new conditions effectively or to think, reason, and judge as normal persons do.

It is safe to predict that in the near future intelligence tests will bring tens of thousands of these high-grade defectives under the surveillance and protection of society[20]. This will ultimately result in curtailing the reproduction of feeble-mindedness and in the elimination of an enormous amount of crime, pauperism, and industrial inefficiency[21]. It is hardly necessary to emphasize that the highgrade cases, of the type now so frequently overlooked, are precisely the ones whose guardianship it is most important for the State to assume.

Intelligence tests of delinquents. One of the most important facts brought to light[22] by the use of intelligence tests is the frequent association of delinquency and mental deficiency[23]. Although it has long been recognized that the proportion of feeble-mindedness among offenders is rather large, the real amount has, until recently, been underestimated even by the most competent students of criminology.

The criminologists have been accustomed to give more attention to the physical than to the mental correlates of crime. Thus, Lombroso and his followers subjected thousands of criminals to observation and measurement with regard to such physical traits[24] as size and shape of the skull, bilateral asymmetries[25], anomalies of the ear, eye, nose, palate, teeth, hands, fingers, hair, dermal sensitivity[26], etc. The search was for physical "stigmata" characteristic of the "criminal type."[27]

Although such studies performed an important service in creating a scientific interest in criminology, the theories of Lombroso have been wholly discredited by the results of intelligence tests. Such tests have demonstrated, beyond any possibility of doubt, that the most important trait of at least 25 per cent of our criminals is mental weakness. The physical abnormalities which have been found so common among prisoners are not the stigmata of criminality, but the physical accompaniments of feeble-mindedness. They have no diagnostic significance except in so far as they are indications of mental deficiency. Without exception, every study which has been made of the intelligence level of delinquents has furnished convincing testimony as to the close relation existing between mental weakness and moral abnormality[28]. Some of these findings are as follows:

Miss Renz tested 100 girls of the Ohio State Reformatory[29] and reported 36 per cent as certainly feeble-minded. In every one of these cases the commitment papers had given the pronouncement "intellect sound ".

Under the direction of Dr. Goddard the Binet tests were given to 100 juvenile court cases, chosen at random, in Newark, New Jersey. Nearly half were classified as feeble-minded. One boy 17 years old had 9-year intelligence; another of 15 1/2 had 8-year intelligence.

Of 56 delinquent girls 14 to 20 years of age tested by Hill and Goddard, almost half belonged either to the 9- or the 10-year level of intelligence.

Dr. G. G. Fernald's tests of 100 prisoners at the Massachusetts State Reformatory showed that at least 25 per cent were feebleminded.

Of 1186 girls tested by Miss Dewson at the State Industrial School for Girls at Lancaster, Pennsylvania, 28 per cent were found to have subnormal intelligence.

Dr. Katherine Bemont Davis's report on 1000 cases entered in the Bedford Home for Women, New York, stated that there was no doubt but that at least 157 were feeble-minded. Recently there has been established at this institution one of the most important research laboratories of the kind in the United States, with a trained psychologist, Dr. Mable Fernald, in charge.

Of 564 prostitutes[20] investigated by Dr. Anna Dwyer in connection with the Municipal Court of Chicago, only 3 per cent had gone beyond the fifth grade in school. Mental tests were not made, but from the data given it is reasonable certain that half or more were feeble-minded.

Tests, by Dr. George Ordahl and Dr. Louise Ellison Ordahl, of cases in the Geneva School for Girls, Geneva, Illinois, showed that, on a conservative basis of classification, at least 18 per cent were feeble-minded. At the Joliet Prison, Illinois, the same authors found 50 per cent of the female prisoners feeble-minded, and 26 per cent of the male prisoners. At the St. Charles School for Boys 26 per cent were feeble-minded.

Tests, by Dr. J. Harold Williams, of 150 delinquents in the Whittier State School for Boys, Whittier, California, gave 28 per cent feeble-minded and 25 per cent at or near the border-line. About 300 other juvenile delinquents tested by Mr. Williams gave approximately the same figures. As a result of these findings a research laboratory has been established at the Whittier School, with Dr. Williams in charge. In the girls' division of the Whittier School, Dr. Grace Fernald collected a large amount of psychological data on more than 100 delinquent girls. The findings of this investigation agree closely with those of Dr. Williams for the boys.

At the State Reformatory, Jeffersonville, Indiana, Dr. von Klein-Schmid, in an unusually thorough psychological study of 1000 young adult prisoners, finds the proportion of feeble-mindedness not far from 50 per cent.

But it is needless to multiply statistics. Those given are but samples. Tests are at present being made in most of the progressive prisons, reform schools, and juvenile courts throughout the country, and while there are minor discrepancies in regard to⑩ the actual percentage who are feeble-minded, there is no investigator who denies the fearful role played by mental deficiency in the production of vice, crime, and delinquency.

(From *The Measurement of Intelligence*, Chapter I)

注　释

① retarded school children. 智力落后的学生。
② ... afford convincing evidence of the magnitude and seriousness of the retardation problem. 提供了富有说服力的关于智力落后问题的强度和严重性的证据。
③ through the grades at the expected rate　以预期的速度升级。
④ by improved methods of promotion　通过改进的提高方法。
⑤ Although reforms along these lines have been productive of much good, ... 虽然这些方面的改革产生了一些好的效果……。
⑥ ... they have nevertheless been in a measure disappointing. 在此句中 in a measure 意为部分地,多少。比如: He is selfish in a measure. 他有几分自私。
⑦ ... this supposition is not in accord with the facts. 短语 in accord with 和……一致: I am glad to find myself in general accord with your views. 我很高兴地发现我的意见与你的看法大体一致。
⑧ ... differences which affect profoundly the capacity to profit from school instruction. 其句中 profit (gain) from: 得益于,得到好处。比如: I hope to profit from your comments. 我希望从你的评语中获益。
⑨ take into account 考虑。

⑩ significance of these differences in endowment　先天差异的影响。
⑪ The remedy, of course, is to measure out the work for each child in proportion to his mental ability.　补救方法当然是对各种心理能力不同的每个孩子因材施教。
⑫ ... the amount of strain per unit of size his materials will be able to withstand.　选择材料时,考察每单位的材料有多大的支持力(以免使用时出危险)。
⑬ count upon patching up the mistakes　不能存有试试不行再改错误的念头。
⑭ blunder along in the dark　在黑暗中犯大错。
⑮ the feeble-minded　低能学生。
⑯ to ascertain the degree of defect　断定不健全的程度。
⑰ previous to　在……之前。
⑱ considerable number　相当大的人数
⑲ such as that involved in reading and in the manipulation of number combinations　动用的机械学习方法,正如在朗诵和数字组合计算中运用的机械学习方法一样。
⑳ under the surveillance and protection of society　在社会对他们的特别监督保护下。
㉑ industrial inefficiency　现代工业社会中的不称职者。
㉒ bring to light　发现　bring to light a relic buried deep under the ground　使深埋在地下的历史遗迹重见天日。
㉓ mental deficiency　心理缺陷者。
㉔ Lombroso and his followers subjected thousands of criminals to observation and measurement with regard to such physical traits　指意大利犯罪学者浪勃露沙和他的同事对上千名罪犯的身体外部特征进行观察和测量。
㉕ bilateral asymmetries　两边不对称。
㉖ dermal sensitivity　皮肤的敏感性。

㉗ The search was for physical "stigmata" characteristic of the "criminal type". 这项研究是要发现"罪犯类型"的体征。
㉘ moral abnormality 道德上的不健全。
㉙ State Reformatory 州感化院。
㉚ prostitutes 娼妓。
㉛ in regard to 对于，关于。

练　习

1. 回答问题
（1）What do the statistics collected in hundreds of cities in the United States show?
（2）Why should the educational engineer emulate the example of an engineer's job?
（3）We cannot hold all children to the same standard of school progress, but what can we at least do?
（4）Why are scientific diagnosis and classification of these children important?

2. 判断正误
（1）Psychological studies of school children by means of standardized intelligence tests have shown that this supposition is not in accord with the facts. It has been found that children do not fall into two well-defined groups, the feeble-minded and the normal.
（2）Failure crushes self-confidence and destroys the spirit of work.
（3）The criminologists have been accustomed to give more attention to the physical than to the mental correlates of crime.
（4）The earlier methods of diagnosis caused a majority of the higher grade defectives to be noticed.
（5）The more we learn about such children, the unclearer it be-

comes that they must be looked upon as real defectives.
(6) One of the most important facts concerning the use of intelligence tests is the frequent association of the feeble-minded.

3. 词汇与短语
Fill in the blanks with the proper words given below
retard, magnitude, endowment, blunder(v.), manipulation, zest, feeble, surveillance
(1) She joined in the game with great _____.
(2) The Oxford and Cambridge colleges have numerous _____.
(3) People had been conscious of the problem before, but the new book made them aware of its _____.
(4) They make a lot of money by clever _____ of the Stock Market.
(5) The old woman is too _____ to do her own shopping.
(6) He blundered away a good chance.
(7) The injury to his head seems to have _____ his thought processes.
(8) The police kept the criminal under strict _____.

4. 汉译英
(1) 尽管他的工资很高,但他在家庭开支上每一块钱都抠得很紧。(measure out)
(2) 他有几分自私。(in a measure)
(3) 发明家从别人的工作中得益。(profit from)
(4) 我们决定消除我们之间的分歧,言归于好。(patch up)
(5) 我很高兴地发现我的意见与你的看法大体一致。(in accord with)

5. 写作指导

In this part, you are allowed to write a composition entitled My Views on School Instruction. The following expressions taken from the article are useful in helping you compile your composition.

——afford convincing evidence of ...
——fail to progress through the grades at the expected rate
——make satisfactory school progress
——fall into two well-defined groups
——profit from school instruction
——Failure crushes self-confidence and destroys the spirit of work.
——acquire the habit of failure
——patch up the mistakes

12. The Interpretation of Dreams

Sigmund Freud

弗洛伊德(Sigmund Freud,1856—1939)是奥地利精神病医生,精神分析学派创始人。他的主要著作有《梦的解析》(1900)、《日常生活的心理病理学》(1901)、《精神分析引论》(1919)等。弗洛伊德创用了一种治疗神经症的方法,也是精神分析学说的重要组成部分。弗洛伊德认为,神经症患者在幼年期性心理发展过程中未能满足的欲望,尤其是恋母情结,被压抑到无意识中形成症结。这种违反道德观念的症结仍要求在意识中表现,与超我构成心理冲突,经过心理防御机制的加工,最后以不带明显性内容的神经症症状表现出来。因此,症状是心理冲突的妥协产物,是无意识症结的象征。使病人无意识的观念意识化,病人知道了症状的真意,症状就失去存在的意义而消失。这就是精神分析疗法的原理。弗洛伊德精神分析疗法的技巧主要是自由联想和梦的解析。分析和摆脱移情是精神分析疗法的重要步骤。

《梦的解析》曾被人誉为"最伟大的著作,大大推进了精神分析"。出版十年后,受到普遍重视。在弗洛伊德全部著作中,此书的地位仅次于他的《精神分析引论》,是研究弗洛伊德理论的必读文献之一。在《梦的解析》中,弗洛伊德创建了他自己的一套系统的梦的理论。这涉及到梦的材料、解析方法、以及围绕它的核心观点而提出来的梦的"改装"、"凝缩作用"、"转移作用"、"较正"、"退化现象"等等许多问题。应该指出,弗洛伊德的《梦的解析》一书是他的精神分析学说的代表作之一。其后的二十年里,他的精神分析学说有了更充分的发展。

THE DREAM-WORK[①]

EVERY attempt that has hitherto been made to solve the problem of dreams has dealt directly with their *manifest* content[②] as it is presented in our memory. All such attempts have endeavoured to arrive at an interpretation of dreams from their manifest content or (if no interpretation was attempted) to form a judgement as to their nature on the basis of that same manifest content. We are alone in taking something else into account[3]. We have introduced a new class of psychical material between the manifest content of dreams and the conclusions of our enquiry: namely, their *latent* content, or (as we say) the 'dream-thoughts', arrived at by means of our procedure[4]. It is from these dream-thoughts and not from a dream's manifest content that we disentangle its meaning. We are thus presented with a new task which had no previous existence: the task, that is, of investigating the relations between the manifest content of dreams and the latent dream-thoughts, and of tracing out the processes by which the latter have been changed into the former[5].

The dream-thoughts and the dream-content are presented to us like two versions of the same subject-matter in two different languages. Or, more properly, the dream-content seems like a transcript of the dream-thoughts into another mode of expression, whose characters and syntactic laws it is our business to discover by comparing the original and the translation. The dream-thoughts are immediately comprehensible, as soon as we have learnt them. The dream-content, on the other hand, is expressed as it were in a pictographic script[6], the characters of which have to be transposed individually into the language of the dream-thoughts. If we attempted to read these characters according to their pictorial value instead of according to their symbolic relation, we should clearly be led into error. Suppose I have a picture-puzzle, a rebus, in front of me. It depicts a house with a boat on its roof, a single letter of the alphabet, the figure of a running man whose head has been conjured away, and so on. Now I might be misled into raising objections and declaring that the picture as a whole and its component parts are nonsensical. A boat has no business to be on the roof of a house, and a headless man cannot run[7]. Moreover, the man is bigger than the house; and if the whole picture is intended to represent a landscape, letters of the alphabet are out of place in it since such objects do not occur in nature. But obviously we can only form a proper judgement of the rebus if we put aside criticisms such as these of the whole composition and its parts and if, instead, we try to replace each separate element by a syllable or word that can be represented by that element in some way or other[8]. The words which are put together in this way are no longer nonsensical but may form a poetical phrase of the greatest beauty and significance. A dream is a picture-puzzle of this sort and our predecessors in the field of dream-interpretation have made the mistake of treating the rebus as a pictorial composition; and as such it has seemed to them nonsensical and worthless[9].

THE WORK OF DISPLACEMENT[10]

In making our collection of instances of condensation in dreams, the existence of another relation, probably of no less importance, had already become evident[11]. It could be seen that the elements which stand out as the principal components of the manifest content of the dream are far from playing the same part in the dream-thoughts. And, as a corollary, the converse of this assertion can be affirmed: What is clearly the essence of the dream-thoughts need not be represented in the dream at all. The dream is, as it were, differently centred from the dream-thoughts—its content has different elements as its central point. Thus in the dream of the botanical monograph[12], for instance, the central point of the dream-content was obviously the element 'botanical'; whereas the dream-thoughts were concerned with the complications and conflicts arising between colleagues from their professional obligations, and further with the charge that I was in the habit of sacrificing too much for the sake of my hobbies[13]. The element 'botanical' had no place whatever in this core of the dream-thoughts, unless it was loosely connected with it by an antithesis—the fact that botany never had a place among my favourite studies. In my patient's *Sappho* dream the central position was occupied by climbing up and down and being up above and down below; the dream-thoughts, however, dealt with the dangers of sexual relations with people of an inferior social class. So that only a single element of the dream-thoughts seems to have found its way into dream-content, though that element was expanded to a disproportionate extent[14]. Similarly, in the dream of the may-beetles, the topic of which was the relations of sexuality to cruelty, it is true that the factor of cruelty emerged in the dream-content; but it did so in another connection and without any mention of sexuality, that is to say, divorced from its context and consequently transformed into something extraneous. Once again, in my dream about my uncle, the fair beard which formed its centre-point seems to have had no connection in its meaning with my ambitious wishes which, as we saw, were the core of the dream thoughts. Dreams such as these give a justifiable impression of 'displacement'. In complete contrast to these examples[15], we can see that in the dream of Irma's injection the different elements were able to retain, during the process of constructing the dream, the approximate place which they occupied in the dream-thoughts. This further relation between the dream-thoughts and the dream-content, wholly variable as it is in its sense or direction, is calculated at first to create astonishment. If we are considering a psychical process[16] in normal life and find that one out of its several component ideas has been picked out and has acquired a special degree of vividness in consciousness, we usually regard this effect as evidence that a specially high amount of psychical value—some particular degree of interest—attaches to this predominant idea. But we now discover that, in the case of the different elements of the dream-thoughts, a value of this kind does not persist or is disregarded in the process of dream-formation. There is never any doubt as to which of the elements of the dream-thoughts have the highest psychical value; we learn that by direct judgement. In the course of the formation of a dream these essential elements, charged, as they are, with intense interest, may be treated as though they were of small value, and their place may be taken in the dream by other elements, of whose small value in the dream-thoughts there can be no question[17]. At first sight it looks as though no attention whatever is paid to the psychical intensity of the various ideas in making the choice among them for the dream, and as though the only thing considered is the greater or less degree of multiplicity of their determination. What appears in dreams, we might suppose, is not what is *important* in the dream-thoughts but what occurs in them several times over. But this hypothesis does not greatly assist our understanding of dream-formation, since from the nature of things it seems clear that the two factors of multiple determination and inherent psychical value must necessarily operate in the same sense. The ideas which are most important among the dream-thoughts will almost certainly be those which occur most often in them, since the different dream-thoughts will, as it were, radiate out from them. Nevertheless a dream can reject elements which are thus both highly stressed in themselves and reinforced from many directions, and can select for its content other elements which possess only the second of these attributes.

In order to solve this difficulty we shall make use of another impression derived from our enquiry [in the previous section] into the overdetermination of the dream-content[18]. Perhaps some of those who have read that enquiry may already have formed an independent conclusion that the overdetermination of the elements of dreams is no very important discovery, since it is a self-evident one. For in analysis we start out from the dream elements and note down all the associations which lead off from them; so that there is nothing surprising in the fact that in the thought-material arrived at in this way we come across these same elements with peculiar frequency. I cannot accept this objection; but I will myself put into words something that sounds not unlike it. Among the thoughts that analysis brings to light are many which are relatively remote from the kernel of the dream and which look like artificial interpolations made for some particular purpose[19]. That purpose is easy to divine. It is precisely *they* that constitute a connection, often a forced and far-fetched one, between the dream-content and the dream-thoughts; and if these elements were weeded out of the analysis the result would often be that the component parts of the dream-content would be left not only without overdetermination but without any satisfactory determination at all[20]. We shall be led to conclude that the multiple determination[21] which decides what shall be included in a dream is not always a primary factor in dream-construction but is often the secondary product of a psychical force which is still unknown to us. Nevertheless multiple determination must be of importance in choosing what particular elements shall enter a dream, since we can see that a considerable expenditure of effort is used to bring it about in cases where it does not arise from the dream-material unassisted.

It thus seems plausible to suppose that in the dream-work a psychical force is operating which on the one hand strips the elements which have a high psychical value of their intensity, and on the other hand, *by means of overdetermination*, creates from elements of low psychical value new values, which afterwards find their way into the dream-content[22]. If that is so, *a transference and displacement of psychical intensities*[23] occurs in the process of dream-formation, and it is as a result of these that the difference between the text of the dream-content and that of the dream-thoughts comes about. The process which we are here presuming is nothing less than the essential portion of the dream-work; and it deserves to be described as 'dream-displacement'. Dream-displacement and dream-condensation are the two governing factors to whose activity we may in essence ascribe the form assumed by dreams[24].

Nor do I think we shall have any difficulty in recognizing the psychical force which manifests itself in the facts of dream-displacement. The consequence of the displacement is that the dream-content no longer resembles the core of the dreamthoughts and that the dream gives no more than a distortion of the dream-wish which exists in the unconscious[25]. But we are already familiar with dream-distortion. We traced it back to the censorship which is exercised by one psychical agency in the mind over another. Dream-displacement is one of the chief methods by which that distortion is achieved. *Is fecit cui profuit*[26]. We may assume, then, that dream-displacement comes about through the influence of the same censorship—that is, the censorship of endopsychic defence[27].

The question of the interplay of these factors—of displacement, condensation and overdetermination—in the construction of dreams, and the question which is a dominant factor and which a subordinate one—all of this we shall leave aside for later investigation. But we can state provisionally a second condition which must be satisfied by those elements of the dream-thoughts which make their way into the dream: *they must escape the censorship imposed by resistance*[28]. And henceforward in interpreting dreams we shall take dream-displacement into account as an undeniable fact.

(From *The Interpretation of Dreams*, Chapter Ⅵ)

注　释

① The Dream Work　《梦的运作》节选于弗洛伊德《梦的解析》的第六章。
② manifest content　梦的显意。
③ We are alone in taking something else into account. 在这方面我们有不同的考虑。
④ ...their latent content, or (as we say) the "dream-thoughts", arrived at by means of our procedure. 通过我们的分析而得到的它们的潜在内容,用我们的话来说就是"梦的思想"。
⑤ ...and of tracing out the processes by which the latter have been changed into the former. 探讨使后者转变为前者的过程。
⑥ a pictographic script　象形文字的原稿。
⑦ A boat has no business to be on the roof of a house, and a headless man cannot run. 一只小船不可能摆放在屋顶上,一个无头的人不可能跑动。have no business to　指无权利做某事。
⑧ But obviously we can only form a proper judgment of the rebus if we put aside criticisms such as these of the whole composition and its parts and if, instead, we try to replace each separate element by a syllable or word that can be represented by that element in some way or other. 想对这幅画谜作出正确解释,只有抛弃这些对其整体和各部分的反对批评,并用每一个成分所象征的音节或词来代替该成分。
⑨ ...and as such it has seemed to them nonsensical and worthless. 也因此才会认为梦是毫无意义、一文不值的。
⑩ The work of displacement　梦的转移作用。
⑪ In making our collection of instances of condensation in dreams, the existence of another relation, probably of no less importance,

⑪ had already become evident. 指的是当我们收集"梦凝缩"的例子时,我们就已注意到了另外一种重要性不亚于凝缩作用的关系。

⑫ Thus in the dream of the botanical monograph 这里指在以前提到过的"植物学专论"的梦里。

⑬ ... the complications and conflicts arising between colleagues from their professional obligations, and further with the charge that I was in the habit of sacrificing too much for the sake of my hobbies. (主要关切的问题是)同事间做事时所发生的冲突与矛盾,以及对我自己消耗太多时间于个人嗜好的不满。

⑭ ... was expanded to a disproportionate extent. 到了过分夸张的程度。

⑮ In complete contrast to these examples. 与此相反的例子。

⑯ a psychical process 心理过程。

⑰ In the course of the formation of a dream these essential elements, charged, as they are, with intense interest, may be treated as though they were of small value, and their place may be taken in the dream by other elements, of whose small value in the dream-thoughts there can be no question 在梦形成时,那些附有强烈兴趣的重要部分往往成了次要部分,反而被某些"梦思"中次要的部分所替代。

⑱ ... the overdetermination of the dream-content "梦的内容"的"过度判断"。

⑲ Among the thoughts that analysis brings to light are many which are relatively remote from the kernel of dream and which look like artificial interpolations made for some particular purpose. 通过梦的分析所找出意念里,有些已与梦的核心相去甚远而变成了似乎是为了某种特定目的而设的人为添加物。

⑳ It is precisely they that constitute a connection, often a forced and far-fetched one, between the dream-content and the dream-thoughts; and if these elements were weeded out of the analysis the result would often be that the component parts of the dream-content would be left only without overdetermination but without any satisfactory determination at all. 正是它们构成了"梦的内容"与"梦思"之间的联系，通常是一种牵强的联系。如果在分析中剔除这些元素，那么，结果通常是梦的内容中的构成部分不只是没有过度判断，连差强人意的判断都做不到。

㉑ the multiple determination　多种判断意义。

㉒ It thus seems plausible to suppose that in the dream-work a psychical force is operating which on the one hand strips the elements which have a high psychical value of their intensity, and on the other hand, by means of overdetermination, creates from elements of low psychical value new values, which afterwards find their way into the dream-content. 大概可以这样假设：在梦的运作下，一种精神力量一方面将其本身精神价值较高的单元所含的精神强度予以降低，而另一方面，利用过度判断的方法，可以从精神价值较低的单元中塑造出新的价值，此后这些新价值在梦的内容中得以表现。

㉓ a transference and displacement of psychical intensities　心理强度的转置作用。

㉔ Dream-displacement and dream-condensation are the two governing factors to whose activity we may in essence ascribe the form assumed by dreams. 从根本上我们可以将梦的形式归因于"梦的转置"和"梦的凝缩"这个主要因素的作用。

㉕ ... a distortion of the dream-wish which exists in the unconscious. 梦只以这改装的面目复现潜意识里的梦愿望。

㉖ Is fecit cui profuit　（拉丁文)果真这种方法能形成梦。

㉗ the censorship of endopsychic defence. 一种内在精神自卫的审查制度。

㉘ ... they must escape the censorship imposed by resistance. 它们

必须免于抗拒机制的审查。

练　习

1. 判断正误
(1) If we attempted to read these characters according to their pictorial value instead of according to their symbolic relation, we should clearly get the real meanings of it.
(2) In the case of different elements of the dream-thoughts, a value does persist in the process of dream-formation.
(3) Multiple determination must be of importance in choosing what particular elements shall enter a dream.
(4) Dream-displacement and dream-condensation are the two governing factors.

2. 将下列句子译成中文
(1) The dream-thoughts and the dream-content are presented to us like two versions of the same subject-matter in two different languages.
(2) Or, more properly, the dream-content seems like a transcript of the dream-thoughts into another mode of expression, whose characters and syntactic laws it is our business to discover by comparing the original and the translation.
(3) It could be seen that the elements which stand out as the principal components of the manifest content of the dream are far from playing the same part in the dream-thoughts.
(4) Dreams such as these give a justifiable impression of "displacement".
(5) Nevertheless a dream can reject elements which are thus both highly stressed in themselves and reinforced from many directions, and can select for its content other elements which possess only the second of these attributes.

(6) The process which we are here presuming is nothing less than the essential portion of the dream-work; and it deserves to be described as "dream-displacement."

3. 词汇与短语

Fill in the blanks with the proper words given below

plausible, impose, resistance, ascribe, replace, represent, condensation, distortion

(1) This resolution _____ the opinion of the overwhelming majority of British trade unionists.
(2) By determined attacks they broke down the enemy's _____.
(3) In both cases the new government _____ years of military government.
(4) Your explanation sounds _____, but I am not sure I believe it.
(5) Medical researchers _____ much of the rise in the incidence of lung cancer to the widespread use of cigarettes.
(6) Her convictions were absolute, yet not once did she attempt to _____ these upon me.
(7) A _____ of that famous book was printed in our magazine last month.
(8) This downright _____ of the standpoint of Marxism has been aided by the antidemocratic propaganda.

4. 句型模拟

(1) to ... extend
(2) on the one hand, ... on the other hand, ...

4. 汉译英

(1) 种族问题在本质上是一个阶级问题。(in essence)

(2) 我习惯每天刷两次牙。(in the habit of)
(3) 在人类历史发展过程,新的艺术不断诞生。(in the course of)
(4) 他威胁要将此事分布于众。(bring to light)
(5) 冬天的气候不该这样暖和。(have no business to)

13. Attention in Cognitive Neuroscience: An Overview

Michael I. Posner

波斯纳(Posner, 1940—)是美国俄勒冈大学认知和决策科学院心理系教授。当代著名的认知心理学家。《认知神经科学中的注意:总论》节选自《认知神经科学》的第十八章。此文简要地考察了心理学与神经科学中注意概念的历史。对以往把注意与脑神经系统结合在一起的研究方法进行评述,以促进定向分析过程、高水平的注意研究和警觉的三个解剖网络研究的发展。文章的最后他对心理学今后的发展以及对注意病理学和其他注意状态的应用知识进行了总结。

History

The problem of selective attention[①] is one of the oldest in psychology. William James[②] (1907) wrote, at the turn of the century, "Everyone knows what attention is. It is the taking possession by the mind in clear and vivid form of one out of what seem several simultaneous objects or trains of thought."[③]

The dominance of behavioral psychology postponed research into the internal mechanisms[④] of selective attention in the first half of this century. The finding that integrity of the brainstem reticular formation was necessary to maintain the alert state provided some anatomical reality to the study of the arousal mechanisms underlying one aspect of attention[⑤] (Moruzzi and Magoun, 1949). This approach has led to many new findings relating individual subcortical transmitter systems of arousal (e.g., dopamine, norepinephrine) to the computations underlying selection of information (see chapter 44).

The quest for information-processing mechànisms to support the more selective aspects of attention began with studies of listening following World War II. A filter was proposed that was limited for information (in the formal sense of information theory) and located between highly parallel sensory systems and a limited-capacity perceptual system[6] (Broadbent, 1958).

Selective listening experiments supported a view of attention that suggested early selection of a relevant message, with nonselective information being lost to conscious processing[7]. Physiological studies (Skinner and Yingling, 1977) suggested that selection of the relevant channels might involve a thalamic gating mechanism[8] using the nucleus reticularis thalami[9] and controlled from prefrontal sites. Peripheral gating mechanisms[10] still represent a potential source of selection that might be especially important in lower mammals. However, in human information-processing studies, it was clear that unattended information often was processed to a high level as evidenced by the fact that an important message on the unattended channel might interfere with the selected channel (Posner, 1978)[11]. This suggested selection at higher cortical levels must be involved. More recent monkey studies suggested that thalamic mechanisms might work in conjunction with extrastriate areas to gate information at cortical levels[12] (Moran and Desimone, 1985; see also chapter 41). The ability to select input channels and the levels at which selection occurs has remained an active feature of current studies of attention (see chapter 40 – 43).

In the 1970s, psychologists began to distinguish between automatic and controlled processes (Posner, 1978). It was found that visual words could activate other words similar in meaning (their semantic associates), even when the person had no awareness of the words' presence. These studies indicated that the parallel organization found for sensory information extended to semantic processing. Thus, selecting a word meaning for active attention appeared to suppress the availability of other word meanings. Attention was viewed less as an early sensory bottleneck and more as a system for providing priority for motor acts, consciousness, and memory[13] (Allport, 1980). These higher-level mechanisms of attention involve frontal areas[14] and provide important means of coordination among cognitive activities (see chapter 45).

Another approach to problems of selectivity arose in work on the orienting reflex[15] (Sokolov, 1963; Kahneman, 1973). The use of slow autonomic systems (e.g., skin conductance as measures of orienting[16]) made it difficult to analyze the cognitive components and neural systems underlying orienting. In the mid-1970s, neurobiologists began to study information processing in alert monkeys (Wurtz, Goldberg, and Robinson, 1980). Because the visual system had been relatively well explored using microelectrodes, much of this work involved the visual system. During the last 15 years, there has been a steady advancement in our understanding of the neural systems related to visual orienting from studies using single-cell recording in alert monkeys. This work showed a relatively restricted number of areas in which the firing rates of neurons were enhanced selectively when monkeys were trained to attend to a location. At the level of the superior colliculus, selective enhancement could be obtained only when eye movement was involved but, in the posterior parietal lobe[17], selective enhancement occurred even when the animal maintained fixation. An area of the thalamus, the lateral pulvinar, was similar to the parietal lobe in containing cells with the property of selective enhancement[18](Colby, 1991). Indeed the thalamic areas relate to the earlier rat models (Skinner and Yingling, 1977) but are believed to perform selection at higher levels of analysis (see chapter 41). Vision remains the central system for the integration of cognitive and neuroscience approaches to selectivity (see chapters 40 - 42, 45, and 46).

Until recently, there has been a separation between human information-processing and neuroscientific approaches to attention using nonhuman animals. The former tended to describe attention either in terms of a bottleneck that protected limited-capacity central systems from overload or as a resource that could be allocated to various processing systems in a way analogous to the use of the term in economics[19]. On the other hand, neuroscientific views emphasized several separate neural mechanisms that might be involved in orienting and maintaining alertness. Currently there is an attempt to integrate these two within a cognitive neuroscience of attention (Posner and Petersen, 1990; Näätänen, 1992). The chapters in part V of this book all take this viewpoint.

Methods

The effort to link attention to specific brain systems depends on having methods available to secure these links (Sejnowski and Churchland, 1989). The basic dimensions for classifying methods are based on their spatial localization and their temporal precision. Major methods used for spatial localization in the studies reported in this section include depth recordings, positron emission tomography (PET), and functional magnetic resonance imaging (MRI)[20]. The postsimulus latency histograms[21] from single or small numbers of cells can provide both temporal and spatial precision but their invasive nature[22] requires a protocol based on either surgical interventions in humans or the use of animal models. Temporal precision with normal human subjects is a feature of various cognitive methods involving reaction time or speed accuracy trade-off measures[23] (Bower, 1989) and is also studied by the use of event-related electrical or magnetic potentials[24] (Näätänen, 1992).

An important aspect of understanding the current developments in this field is to track the convergence of evidence from various methods of study. The chapters in part V of this book have been selected to provide a background in various methods. These include performance studies using reaction time or interference during multiple tasks (chapters 40 and 45), study of changes of attention with development (chapter 46), recording from scalp electrodes (chapter 42), lesions in humans and animals (chapters 40, 43, and 44), and various methods for imaging and recording from restricted brain areas (chapter 41), including individual cells (chapter 43).

Current progress in the anatomy of the attention system rests most heavily on two important methodological developments. First, the use of microelectrodes with alert animals showed that attention altered the activity of individual cells (Colby, 1991). Second, anatomical (e.g., computerized tomography or MRI) and physiological (e.g., PET, functional MRI) methods of studying parts of the brain allowed more meaningful investigations of localization of cognitive functions in normal people (Raichle, 1987).

We can distinguish two different types of anatomy related to attention. By the *source* of attention, we mean those anatomical areas that seem to be specific to attention rather than being primarily involved in other forms of processing. (The three attentional networks discussed next are attentional in this sense.) However, when attention operates during task performance[25], it will operate at the site where the computation involved in the task is usually performed. Thus, when subjects attend to the color, form, or motion of a visual object, they amplify blood flow in various extrastriate areas (Corbetta et al., 1991). These areas are known to be involved in the passive registration of the same information. We will expect that most brain areas, especially cortical areas, will show attention effects in this sense, although they are not part of the brain's attention system.

To move beyond the specification of anatomical areas, it is useful to use methods sensitive to the time dynamics of information processing, which usually requires analysis in the millisecond range㉓. The temporal precision of various methods is changing rapidly, but the imaging methods based on blood flow or volume require changes in blood vessels that limit their temporal precision to hundreds of milliseconds at best. Currently, combined studies using anatomical methods and those sensitive to time-dynamic change provide a convenient way to trace the rapid time-dynamic changes that occur in the course of human information processing㉔ (see chapter 42).

It would be ideal if imaging methods were developed that provided the desired combination of high temporal and spatial resolution. However, all the current technologies have their own limitations: For example, cellular recording is limited to animals and is associated with a host of sampling problems㉕; magnetoencephalography is expensive and, unless many channels are used, must be repositioned for examination of each area; scalp electrical recording suffers from difficulty in localizing the generators directly from scalp distributions; and functional MRI is limited by the time for blood vessels to reflect brain activity. Each of the extant methods will lead to modifications that may address some or all of these problems, and entirely new methods may become available. In the following section, the focus is on issues that will need to be addressed with whatever methods prove most useful.

Networks

Three fundamental working hypotheses characterize the current state of efforts to develop a combined cognitive neuroscience of attention. First, there exists an attentional system of the brain that is at least somewhat anatomically separate from various data-processing systems. *By data-processing systems*, we mean those that can be activated passively by input or output. Second, attention is carried out by networks of anatomical areas. It is neither the property of a single brain area nor is it a collective function of the brain working as a whole (Mesulam, 1981, 1990; Posner and Petersen, 1990). Third, the brain areas involved in attention do not carry out the same function, but specific computations are assigned to different areas (Posner et al., 1988; Mesulam, 1990).

It is not possible to specify the complete attentional system of the brain, but something is known about the areas that carry on three major attentional functions: orienting to sensory stimuli, particularly locations in visual space; detecting target events, whether sensory or from memory; and maintaining the alert state. The authors of the chapters in this section address these functions, but they do so using differing methods, theories, and assumptions. Hillyard and colleagues, Johnson, LaBerge, Rafal and Robertson, and Stein and associates deal with sensory orienting primarily, Robbins and Everitt with arousal and the alert state, and Duncan with detection and higher-level functions. The concentration on sensory orienting reflects the fact that this function has been the one selected for much of the effort to link cognitive and neural functions.

ORIENTING NETWORK Much of the work in orienting has involved orienting to visual locations because of its close connection to shifts in eye position, which can be observed so easily from outside. Usually, we define visual orienting in terms of eye movements that place the stimulus on the fovea. Foveal viewing improves the efficiency of processing targets in terms of acuity, but it also is possible to change the priority, given a stimulus, by attending to its location covertly, without any change in eye or head position[29] (Posner, 1988). When a person or a monkey is cued to attend to a location, events that occur at that location are responded to more rapidly, give rise to enhanced scalp electrical activity, and can be reported at lower threshold. This improvement in efficiency is found within the first 50 – 150 ms after a cue occurs at the target location. Similarly, if people are asked to move their eyes to a target, an improvement in efficiency at the target location[30] begins well before the eyes move. This covert shift of attention appears to function as a way of guiding the eyes to appropriate areas of the visual field. In fact, there is evidence that rapid saccades require a shift of attention to the location before they will occur.

Three areas of the monkey brain have shown selective enhancement when monkeys attend to eccentric visual stimuli (Wurtz, Goldberg, and Robinson, 1980; Colby, 1991). These are the posterior parietal lobe, the superior colliculus, and the pulvinar. Brain injury to any of these three areas that have been found to show selective enhancement of neuronal firing rates also causes a reduction in one's ability to shift attention covertly (Posner, 1988). However, each area seems to produce a somewhat different deficit. This underlies the general principle that individual areas carry out separate operations, even though they serve together to carry out the network's function.

Damage to the posterior parietal lobe has its greatest effect on the ability to disengage from attentional focus to a target located in a direction opposite the side of the lesion[3]. Apparently, this effect is mediated both by hyperattention to the ipsilesional cue and difficulty in the attractive ability of the contralesional targets. The effects of the parietal lobes of the two cerebral hemispheres are not identical (DeRenzi, 1982): Damage to the right parietal lobe has a greater overall effect than does damage to the left parietal lobe. There is dispute about the reasons for the asymmetries. One proposal is that the right parietal lobe is dominant for spatial attention and controls attention to both sides of space, whereas the left parietal lobe plays a subsidiary role. This view has been supported by studies using PET, which show that the right parietal lobe is affected by attention shifts in both visual fields, whereas the left parietal lobe is influenced only by right visual field shifts of attention (Corbetta et al., 1993). According to another account, the right parietal lobe is influenced more by the global aspects of figure, whereas the left parietal lobe is influenced more by local aspect (Robertson, Lamb, and Knight, 1988). A third view attributes the asymmetry to differences in arousal in the two cerebral hemispheres (Posner and Petersen, 1990). These positions are not mutually exclusive and are discussed in more detail by Rafal and Robertson in chapter 40.

Lesions of the superior colliculus and the surrounding midbrain areas also affect the ability to shift attention. However, in this case, the shift is slowed whether or not attention is first engaged elsewhere. This finding suggests that a computation involved in moving to the target is impaired. In addition, patients with damage in this midbrain area also return to former target locations as readily as to fresh locations to which they have never attended (see chapter 40).

Normal subjects and patients with parietal and other cortical lesions show a reduced probability of returning attention to an already examined location.

Patients with lesions of the thalamus and monkeys with chemical lesions of one thalamic nucleus (the pulvinar) also show difficulty in covert orienting㉜. This difficulty appears to be in selective attention to a target on the side opposite the lesion, so as to avoid responding in error to distracting events that occur at other locations. A study of patients with unilateral lesions of this thalamic area showed a slowing of responses to a cued target on the side opposite the lesion, even when the subject had plenty of time to orient there (Posner, 1988). This contrasted with the results found with parietal and midbrain lesions, in which responses are nearly normal on both sides once attention has been cued to the location. Alert monkeys with chemical lesions of this area made faster-than-normal responses when cued to the side opposite the lesion, irrespective of the side of the cue (Petersen, Robinson, and Morris, 1987). Data from normal human subjects, required to filter out irrelevant visual stimuli, showed selective metabolic increases in the pulvinar opposite the stimulus being attended (LaBerge and Buchsbaum, 1990). The role of this area has been subject to detailed anatomical and computational analysis in chapter 41.

These findings make two important points. First, they confirm the idea of anatomical areas carrying out individual cognitive operations. Second, they suggest a particular hypothesis of the circuitry involved in covert attention shifts. The parietal lobe first disengages attention from its present focus; then the midbrain is active to move the index of attention to the area of the target, and the pulvinar is involved in restricting input to the indexed area㉝.

(From *The Cognitive Neurosciences*, Chapter 18)

注释:

① selective attention 选择性注意。
② William James 见《习惯》一文前面的说明。
③ It is the taking possession by the mind in clear and vivid form of one out of what seem several simultaneous objects or trains of thought. 这里的意思是在几个同时出现的客体和一系列思想之中,心理是以一种清晰和鲜明的形式占有一席之地。the taking possession 是占有或拥有的意思。out of 是从……之中的意思。simultaneous objects 是指同时出现的客体。
④ the internal mechanisms 内部机制。
⑤ The finding that integrity of the brainstem reticular formation was necessary to maintain the alert state provided some anatomical reality to the study of the arousal mechanisms underlying one aspect of attention. 这里的定语从句 integrity of the brainstem reticular formation 意思是脑干网状结构的完整的形式。the arousal mechanisms 唤醒机制。anatomical reality 指解剖的现实性。本句意为脑干网状结构的整体在维持觉醒状态中必不可少,这一发现为研究注意中的唤醒机制提供了解剖学根据。underlying 是现在分词短语做定语修饰 mechanisms,指存在于注意中的一个方面的唤醒机制。
⑥ ... located between highly parallel sensory systems and a limited capacity perceptual system. 位于高度并行的感觉系统和容量有限的知觉系统之间。
⑦ ... with nonselective information being lost to conscious processing 未被选择的信息未能得到有意识的加工。
⑧ a thalamic gating mechanism 丘脑闸门机制。
⑨ the nucleus reticularis thalami 丘脑网状核。
⑩ peripheral gating mechanism 外周闸门机制。
⑪ However, in human information-processing studies, it was clear

that unattended information often was processed to a high level as evidenced by the fact that an important message on the unattended channel might interfere with the selected channel. 无论如何，在人类信息加工的研究中，可以明确地看到未被注意的信息常常被加工到一个高级水平上，因为未被注意的通道中的重要信息能干扰被选择的通道。

⑫ More recent monkey studies suggested that thalamic mechanisms might work in conjunction with extrastriate areas to gate information at cortical levels. 对猴子近期较多的研究表明丘脑机制可能与纹状外区协同工作,在皮层水平门控信息。

⑬ ... a system for providing priority for motor acts, consciousness, and memory. 为运动、意识和记忆提供优先性的一个系统。

⑭ frontal areas 额叶。

⑮ the orienting reflex 定向反射。

⑯ ... skin conductance as measures of orienting. 将皮肤导电性作为定向的指标。

⑰ in the posterior parietal lobe 在后顶叶。

⑱ An area of the thalamus, the lateral pulvinar, was similar to the parietal lobe in containing cells with the property of selective enhancement. 丘脑的一个区——外枕核与顶叶类似,也包含具有选择性促进特性的细胞。

⑲ The former tended to describe attention either in terms of a bottleneck that protected limited-capacity central systems from overload or as a resource that could be allocated to various processing systems in a way analogous to the use of the term in economics. 前者倾向于用防止容量有限的中枢系统超载的瓶颈作用来说明注意,或者将注意理解为类似于经济学采用的那种可分配给不同加工系统的资源。

⑳ Major methods used for spatial localization in the studies reported in this section include depth recordings, positron emission tomography (PET), and functional magnetic resonance imaging (MRI). (方法分类的基本维量是这些方法的空间定位和时间精确性。)用于空间定位的主要方法包括深度记录、正电子发射层描技术(PET)和功能磁共振成像(MRI)。

㉑ the postsimulus latency histograms 刺激后的潜伏期直方图。

㉒ their invasive nature 它们损伤的性质。

㉓ speed accuracy trade-off measures 速度正确率权衡测量。

㉔ magnetic potentials 脑磁图。

㉕ during task performance 在完成作业期间。

㉖ in the millisecond range 在毫秒级范围。

㉗ Currently, combined studies using anatomical methods and those sensitive to time-dynamic change provide a convenient way to trace the rapid time-dynamic changes that occur in the course of human information processing. 当前运用解剖学方法和对时间动态变化敏感的方法相结合,提供了方便的手段来追踪在人的信息加工过程中出现的迅速的时间动态变化。

㉘ a host of sampling problems 大量的取样问题。

㉙ Foveal viewing improves the efficiency of processing targets in terms of acuity, but it also is possible to change the priority, given a stimulus, by attending to its location covertly, without any change in eye or head position. 这句话的意思是从视敏度来说,中央凹视觉改善靶子加工的效率,但这也可能是由于隐蔽地注意刺激的位置而改变了对刺激的优先感知,并不需要发生眼睛和头部位置的任何变化。

㉚ at the target location 在靶子位置上。

㉛ ... disengage from attentional focus to a target located in a direction opposite the side of the lesion. 指脱离注意焦点而转向位于与损伤侧方向相反的靶子(的能力)。

㉜ Patients with lesions of the thalamus and monkeys with chemical lesions of one thalamic nucleus (the pulvinar) also show difficulty

in covert orienting. 指丘脑损伤患者以及一个丘脑核(枕核)有化学损伤的猴子在隐蔽定向上也有困难。
㉝ The parietal lobe first disengages attention from its present focus; then the midbrain is active to move the index of attention to the area of the target, and the pulvinar is involved in restricting input to the indexed area. 这句话的意思是顶叶首先使注意脱离现在的焦点，然后中脑把注意的指针移向靶子的区域，并且枕核参与对指向区域的输入实施限制。

练 习

1. 回答问题
(1) What is an important aspect of understanding the current developments in this field?
(2) Current progress in the anatomy of the attention system rests most heavily on two important methodological developments. What are they?
(3) What are three fundamental working hypotheses which characterize the current state of efforts to develop a combined cognitive neuroscience of attention?
(4) Three areas of the monkey brain have shown selective enhancement when monkeys attend to eccentric visual stimuli. What are they?

2. 英译汉
(1) The quest for information-processing mechanisms to support the more selective aspects of attention began with studies of listening following World War II.
(2) These studies indicated that the parallel organization found for sensory information extended to semantic processing.
(3) This work showed a relatively restricted number of areas in

which the firing rates of neurons were enhanced selectively when monkeys were trained to attend to a location.
(4) By the source of attention, we mean those anatomical areas that seem to be specific to attention rather than being primarily involved in other forms of processing.
(5) It is not possible to specify the complete attentional system of the brain, but something is known about the areas that carry on three major attentional functions: orienting to sensory stimuli, particularly locations in visual space; detecting target events, whether sensory or from memory; and maintaining the alert state.
(6) The concentration on sensory orienting reflects the fact that this function has been the one selected for much of the effort to link cognitive and neural functions.

3. 词汇与短语
Fill in the blanks with the proper words given below
capacity, mechanism, priority, parallel, alert, integrity, allocate, underlie
(1) The problems requiring immediate solution will be given _____ at the meeting.
(2) Stamp collecting and coin collecting are _____ hobbies.
(3) The _____ of a building depends upon a sound foundation.
(4) Drug and alcohol are used by many as an escape _____ .
(5) They illustrated the Anglo - Saxon _____ for making the best of things.
(6) She was so _____ that not a single error in the report slopped past her.
(7) Half of the medical supplies have already been _____ to the victims of the earthquake.

(8) Does some personal difficulty underlie his lack of interest in work?

4．句型模拟
(1) Given ...,
(2) be similar to

5．汉译英
(1) 两营敌军在遭到重大伤亡之后撤出了战斗。(disengage from)
(2) 预防和治疗都有了着落。(attend to)
(3) 增建部分可能会有损这座建筑物的对称。(interfere with)
(4) 合同规定屋顶用红瓦，并非石板瓦。(specify)
(5) 与其说他是一个客观作家不如说他是主观作家。(rather than)

14. Attention, Intelligence, and the Frontal Lobes

John Duncan

约翰·敦坎(John Duncan)是英国剑桥大学医学研究委员会应用心理学机构的教授。《注意,智力和额叶》一文讨论的是主动行为与被动行为之间,随意行为与刺激驱动行为之间以及控制行为与自动行为之间的分离和显著差异。这些差异已用来解释额叶损伤的后果以及一般智力或者 Spearman 的 g 因素的正常差异可同时发生的在不同任务间注意分配的障碍。这三个方面是紧密联系的,在新异的情景和对行动的微弱环境线索下,三者都与目标加工和抽象行为的选择有关。一个证据就是目标、任务已被理解,但是目标仍被忽视或者不顾任务的要求。一般智力比较低的正常人,如同典型的额叶损伤病人,也是经常忽略目标,尤其在双任务情景中。另一个证据是额叶损伤病人在液态智力任务中比在晶态智力任务中表现出更差的成绩。经过一系列任务或成绩测量,可以预测,额叶损伤,g 相关和双任务作业成绩低下,三者是一致的。但是仍然存在一个尚未解决的问题,即 g 和双任务作业成绩低下是额叶一些不同功能的综合结果还是反映了特定额叶区,比如背外侧前额叶皮层(dorsolateral prefrontal cortex)和扣带前回(anterior cingulate gyrus)的行为特征。

After damage to the human frontal lobes, there can be a widespread disorganization of behavior, reflected in many different types of errors occurring in many different types of tasks[①]. Disturbances may include disinhibition, impulsivity and distractability, rigidity and perseveration, apathy, and lack of response (Luria, 1966). Such difficulties may be revealed in tasks involving perceptual analysis or classification (Milner, 1963; Luria, 1966), memory (Milner, 1971), simple response selections (Drewe, 1975), spatial or verbal problem solving[2] (Milner, 1965; Luria, 1966), and many others; in daily life, there can be widespread difficulties of planning, self-control, and regard for social conventions[3] (e.g. Eslinger and Damasio, 1985). In general, the normal structure of goal-directed behavior[4] is disturbed, producing activity that seems fragmented, irrelevant, or bizarre (Bianchi, 1922).

In this chapter, I relate these effects of frontal damage to two other phenomena. The first concerns individual differences in the normal population. If a disparate set of tests is administered to a broad sample of people, between-test correlations will be almost universally positive[5]: To some extent at least, a person who performs well in one test will tend also to perform well in others (Spearman, 1927). One possible explanation is that some common factor—conventionally termed general intelligence or Spearman's g—makes a contribution to success in all manner of tasks[6]. For example, g might reflect the efficiency of some particular information-processing system involved in the organization of many different activities. Accepting this interpretation, it is easy to show which tests are best correlated with g, and this is the basis for design of standard intelligence tests such as the Wechsler Adult Intelligence Scale or WAIS (Wechsler, 1955) and Raven's Progressive Matrices (Raven, Court, and Raven, 1988).

The remaining set of findings to be considered concerns the problem of divided attention, or interference between concurrent tasks[7]. In part, such interference depends on task *similarity*: Two visual or two manual tasks, for example, will show stronger interference than tasks with different input and output modalities, suggesting conflicts within special-purpose or modality-specific processing systems (Treisman and Davies, 1973; McLeod, 1978). Even when concurrent tasks have nothing obvious in common, however, some interference between them generally remains (Bourke, Duncan, and Nimmo-Smith, 1993; McLeod and Posner, 1984). Again, this might be taken to reflect conflicts within processing systems whose role in the control of behavior is rather broad[8].

In this chapter, I present the hypothesis that these three sets of phenomena are closely related. All three concern a process of abstract action or goal selection, important especially under conditions of novelty or weak environmental prompts to behavior[9]. Variations in the efficiency of this process are reflected in Spearman's g, and conflicts within it are responsible for many cases of interference between dissimilar, concurrent tasks. Though certainly other brain structures are likely to be involved, the general goal selection function is strongly dependent on the integrity of the frontal lobe and therefore is impaired by frontal lesions. In a final section, I consider the importance of specific frontal regions, in particular dorsolateral prefrontal cortex and anterior cingulate cortex[10].

Attention, practice, and environmental cues to action

By attention, we refer loosely to selectivity in cognitive operations[11]. Such selectivity has many components — at any given time, certain goals are in control of behavior, certain stimulus information is thereby relevant, and so on — and there have been many demonstrations of dissociation among different aspects of attention[12] (e.g., Treisman, 1969; Broadbent, 1971; Allport, 1980; Posner and Petersen, 1990). An obvious link among the three sets of phenomena just described, however, is suggested by attention in the sense of a common distinction between controlled, active, or voluntary, and automatic, passive, or stimulus-driven behavior, applied separately to frontal lobe functions[13] (Bianchi, 1922; Luria, 1966; Fuster,

1980; Norman and Shallice, 1980; Frith et al., 1991),Spearman's g (Snow, 1981; Ackerman, 1988), and dual-task interference (James, 1890; Fitts and Posner, 1967; Schneider and Shiffrin, 1977).

This distinction is most directly motivated by the contrast between novel and practiced or habitual behavior. Novelty in two different senses has often been implicated in frontal dysfunction. The first sense concerns *perseveration*, or difficulty changing some line of behavior in the short term. Many examples have been reported in frontal lobe patients and animals, from simple perseveration of inappropriate motor activity[14] (Bianchi, 1922; Luria, 1966; Diamond and Goldman-Rakic, 1989) to perseveration of higher-order mental sets, classification rules, and so forth (Milner, 1963; Owen et al., 1993). The second sense of novelty concerns logner-term *familiarity*. Familiar or regularly practiced lines of activity[15] may be relatively immune to frontal lesions (Luria and Tsvetkova, 1964; Walsh, 1978); complementarily, novel behavior may be interrupted by familiar but inappropriate intrusions or stereotypes (Luria, 1966). Similarly, novelty has been implicated in g correlations[16]. Practicing simple, consistent perceptual-motor tasks[17] may reduce correlations with g (Fleishman and Hempel, 1954; Ackerman, 1988). Finally, the role of novelty in dual-task interference has been noted since the nineteenth century. Novel behavior is hard to combine with concurrent activities and is experienced as requiring active attention[18]. Habitual behavior, in contrast, may interfere rather little with other activities; it may appear automatic and even involuntary, leaving attention free for other concerns (James, 1890; Bryan and Harter, 1899).

Another relevant variable is the strength of the environmental prompt to action, assumed to distinguish voluntary from stimulus-driven behavior (e.g., Frith et al., 1991). One form of prompt is a direct verbal command or suggestion. It has often been noted that frontal lobe patients may need explicit verbal prompts[19] either to continue with a task or to satisfy some aspect of its requirements (Luria and Tsvetkova, 1964; Hecaen and Albert, 1978). For example, the patient may fail to make progress on some complex problem such as preparing a meal (Penfield and Evans, 1935) or solving a spatial puzzle[20] (Luria and Tsvetkova, 1964), yet may perform perfectly adequately when the problem is broken down into a set of separately specified components[21]. Similarly, explicit verbal instructions detailing a precise strategy or manner of procedure may reduce g correlations in a variety of complex tasks, including classroom learning (e.g., Snow, 1981)[22].

For reasons such as these, both frontal lobe functions (Norman and Shalice, 1980) and Spearman's g (Ackerman, 1988) have previously been related to the problem of dual-task interference and attentional versus automatic control of behavior. Interestingly, though, it has been generally accepted, at least since the work of Hebb and Penfield (1940), that frontal lobe functions are rather unrelated to conventional intelligence (Teuber, 1972). It is my contention, however, that conventional wisdom is incorrect and that frontal lobe functions, Spearman's g, and dual-task interference are indeed closely related through the problem of control of behavior under conditions of novelty and weak environmental prompts.

Goal selection

As an extension to more posterior motor systems, prefrontal cortex[23] is generally considered to be involved in the high-level control of action. Accordingly, it may be useful to relate the effects of novelty and prompts to standard accounts of action control.

For this purpose, I shall adopt the common view that action is represented and controlled as a hierarchy of goals and subgoals[a] (Miller, Galanter, and Pribram, 1960). As an example, consider the action of traveling from Cambridge to Squaw Creek (figure 45.1). In the initial plan, motivated by the invitation to make a presentation, this action is specified abstractly (figure 45.1, top level); it might be realized by flying, sailing, hitchhiking, and the like. Suppose, however, that the decision is to fly; now we may fill in the details of acquiring a passport and tickets, traveling to the airport, and so on (figure 45.1, second level). Each of these components is again specified at some level of abstraction: Traveling to the airport might be satisfied by driving, taking a train, or via some other form of transportation but, if the decision is to drive, further details may again be filled in, as shown at the successive levels of figure 45.1, until a level of actual motor commands is reached (Sacerdoti, 1974). Each entry in figure 45.1 specifies a particular abstract requirement on behavior which is then realized by the details beneath it; in other words, each entry functions as a *goal* to which lower-level actions are directed until it has been achieved.

The advantages of this hierarchical scheme (i.e., of working at successive levels of abstraction) are well-known. Typically, only some abstract description of an action will be directly required or cued at any given stage of a plan: For example, the action of acquiring tickets makes sense providing only that the airport can be reached *somehow*, no matter how; or, as another example, the invitation to make a presentation prompts only the abstract goal of travel to Squaw Creek[b], not the detailed working out of this requirement (e.g., which hand to raise in opening the car door). Selecting the relevant abstraction then serves as a framework that

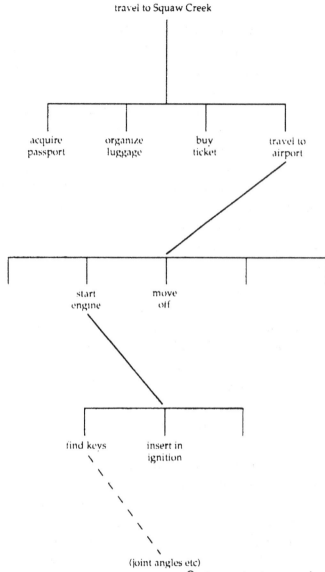

Figure 45.1 Standard hierarchical decomposition of an action into a goal-subgoal tree.

guides the more detailed planning beneath it (Sacerdoti, 1974).

This general idea that actions are planned in a hierarchy of abstractions already raises interesting parallels with the frontal lobe literature. As pointed out by Sacerdoti (1974), planning at a detailed level can be chaotic without guidance from more abstract levels. The problem-solving program is lost in the multitude of detailed response options to consider[7]. Given an adequate abstract framework, however, the lower level functions "just as if (the program) were given (several) small problems to solve consecutively" (Sacerdoti, 1974, page 129). In just the same way, as already noted, frontal lobe patients may make progress on some complex problem such as preparing a meal only when it is broken down into separately prompted components.

Given this hierarchical view of action selection, one may ask how particular goals are selected for control of behavior at any particular time. It has often been noted that two opposite influences must be at work (Duncker, 1945; Reitman, 1965; Anderson, 1983), as shown in figure 45.2. First, new candidate goals arise through working backward from active superordinate goals[8]. For example, the goal of acquiring a passport arises from the supergoal of traveling[9] to Squaw Creek. In figure 45.2, these are called *relevant* next-states; they arise through relevance to an already active goal that the system is working to bring about (Duncan, 1990). Second, new candidate goals arise through working forward from the current world state and, in particular, environmental events. For example, the goal of driving to the airport may be temporarily suspended by the sight of an old friend beckoning in the street. In figure 45.2, these are called *possible* next-states. The set of relevant and possible next-states must somehow be weighted in terms of net importance, leading to a final selection of which goals to pur-

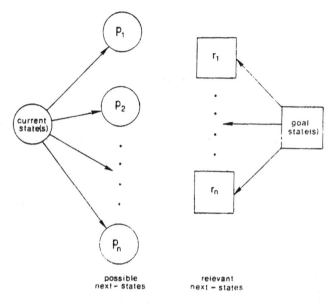

Figure 45.2 Activation of candidate goals. The current state activates possible next-states (p_1, p_2, p_n), Whereas the goal state activates relevant next-states (r_1, r_n). (Reprinted from Duncan, 1990, by permission.)

sue[⑨].

In the context of such a competition among momentary candidate goals, it is easy to see practice and strong environmental prompts as providing one major source of bias[⑩] (cf. Norman and Shallice, 1980). Frequent experience with selecting a particular goal or action in some particular environmental or behavioral context, just like a direct verbal command, may make this goal very easy to select in any given instance. In this case, the efficiency of goal-weighting procedures[⑫] may be relatively unimportant, and behavior may seem automatic or stimulus-driven. Without such a strong bias, however, reductions in the efficiency of goal weighting produce poor choices of behavior. It is under these circumstances that behavior is especially sensitive to frontal lobe impairment, Spearman's g, and dual-task interference.

(From *The Cognitive Neurosciences*, Chapter 24)

注 释

① After damage to the human frontal lobes, there can be a widespread disorganization of behavior, reflected in many different types of error occurring in may different types of task. 人类额叶损伤后,有广泛的无组织行为,在许多不同类型的任务中表现出不同类型的行为偏差。
② spatial or verbal problem solving 空间或言语问题解决。
③ social conventions 社会习俗。
④ goal-directed behavior 以目标为指导的行为。
⑤ If a disparate set of tests is administered to a broad sample of people, between-test correlations will be almost universally positive. 让广泛取样的被试分别做一系列根本不同的测验,那么测验间通常是正相关。
⑥ One possible explanation is that some common factor—conventionally termed general intelligence or Spearman's g—makes a contribution to success in all manner of tasks. 一种可能有的解释是:一些共同因素——我们通常称之为一般智力或 Spearman 的 g 因素——有助于完成不同的任务。in all manner of tasks 指各种不同的任务。
⑦ The remaining set of findings to be considered concerns the problem of divided attention, or interference between concurrent tasks. 剩下的发现与注意的分配或同时发生的任务间的干扰有关。
⑧ Again, this might be taken to reflect conflicts within processing systems whose role in the control of behavior is rather broad. 这

也反映了在行为控制中起着相当广泛作用的加工系统内部冲突。

⑨ ... important especially under conditions of novelty or weak environmental prompts to behavior. 在新异的情景中或环境中只有微弱的行为线索的情况下尤为重要。

⑩ ... dorsolateral prefrontal cortex and anterior cingulate cortex. 背外侧前额叶皮层和扣带前回。

⑪ ... in cognitive operations 认知操作。

⑫ ... many demonstrations of dissociation among different aspects of attention 许多关于注意不同因素间分离的论证。

⑬ ... however, is suggested by attention in the sense of a common distinction between controlled, active, or voluntary, and automatic, passive, or stimulus-driven behavior, applied separately to frontal lobe functions. 就控制行为与自动行为,主动行为与被动行为,随意行为与刺激驱动的行为间的差异而言,也说明额叶的功能。

⑭ simple perseveration of inappropriate motor activity. 对不适当的运动活动的单纯固执。

⑮ Familiar or regularly practiced lines of activity 熟悉的或经常练习的活动模式。

⑯ ... novelty has been implicated in g correlations 在 g 相关中隐含着的新异性。

⑰ consistent perceptual-motor tasks 一致的知觉运动任务。

⑱ requiring active attention 要求积极的注意。

⑲ explicit verbal prompts 明确的言语提示。

⑳ a spatial puzzle 空间迷宫。

㉑ ... when the problem is broken down into a set of separately specified components. 当问题被分解成为一系列不同的独立部分时……

㉒ Similarly, explicit verbal instructions detailing a precise strategy or manner of procedure may reduce g correlations in a variety of complex tasks, including classroom learning. 这句话的意思是，与此类似，指明精确的策略或程序方式的明确言语提示，可以降低不同复杂任务间的 g 相关，包括课堂学习。

㉓ As an extension to more posterior motor systems, prefrontal cortex … 额叶皮质作为后部运动系统概念……。

㉔ … as a hierarchy of goals and subgoals 作为目标和亚目标层次的表征。

㉕ standard hierarchical decomposition 标准的动作层次分解图。

㉖ prompts only the abstract goal of travel to Squaw Creek 促成了到斯考河旅游的抽象目标。

㉗ The problem-solving program is lost in the multitude of detailed response options to consider. 解决问题的方案要迷失在从多数具体反应中做出选择的考虑之中。

㉘ First, new candidate goals arise through working backward from active superordinate goals. 通过返回活跃的上层目标而促生新的备选目标。

㉙ from the supergoal of traveling 来自于旅游的高层目标。

㉚ … be weighted in terms of net importance, leading to a final selection of which goals to pursue. 通过对绝对重要性的权衡，就会得到坚持这一目标的最后决定。

㉛ In the context of such a competition among momentary candidate goals, it is easy to see practice and strong environmental prompts as providing one major source of bias. 在备选目标间时刻存在竞争的背景下，很容易看出练习和明显的环境线索是误差的主要来源。

㉞ the efficiency of goal-weighting procedures 目标评估程序的效率。

练 习

1. 判断正误
(1) Practicing simple, consistent perceptual-motor tasks may reduce correlations with g.
(2) The role of novelty in single-task interference has been noted since the nineteenth century.
(3) Habitual behavior, in contrast, may interfere rather little with other activities; it may appear automatic and even involuntary, leaving attention free for other concerns.
(4) Frequent experience with selecting a particular goal or action in some particular environmental or behavioral context, just like a direct verbal command, may make this goal very easy to select in any given instance.

2. 英译汉
(1) Two visual or two manual tasks, for example, will show stronger interference than tasks with different input and output modalities, suggesting conflicts within special-purpose or modality-specific processing systems.
(2) Another relevant variable is the strength of the environmental prompt to action, assumed to distinguish voluntary from stimulus-driven behavior.
(3) It is my contention, however, that conventional wisdom is incorrect and that frontal lobe functions, Spearman's g, and dual-like interference are indeed closely related through the problem of control of behavior under conditions of novelty and weak environmental prompts.
(4) Accordingly, it may be useful to relate the effects of novelty and prompts to standard accounts of action control.

(5) This general idea that actions are planned in a hierarchy of abstractions already raises interesting parallels with the frontal lobe literature.

(6) Given this hierarchical view of action selection, one may ask how particular goals are selected for control of behavior at any particular time.

3. 词汇与短语

Fill in the blanks with the proper words given below:

damage(n.), convention, demonstration, remaining, conflict(n.), novelty, consistent, explicit, bias, option

(1) If prices rise much higher we shall have to do without our few _____ luxuries.

(2) The _____ of washing dishes soon wore off, and Mary did not want to do it any more.

(3) Additional _____, such as air-conditioning and bucket seats, made it an expensive car.

(4) Some people have a _____ against foreigners.

(5) He reaffirmed his govemment's _____ policy of opposing hegemonism.

(6) No one expected this to be the last _____ between the two countries.

(7) Wearing a coat and tie to a good restaurant is an accepted _____.

(8) The accident did very little _____ to either car.

(9) The lease is _____ in saying the rent must be paid by the 10th of every month.

(10) We attended a _____ of the new manufacturing process.

4. 汉译英

(1) "红皮"这词曾被用来轻蔑地称呼北美印第安人。(apply to)
(2) 经过许多年,岩石风化成泥土。(break down into)
(3) 他因藏有赃物而有参与抢劫的嫌疑。(implicit)
(4) 他谨慎地执行着这个计划。(pursue)
(5) 他承受着许多烦恼的重压。(weight)

15. Implicit Memory: A New Frontier for Cognitive Neuroscience

Daniel L. Schacter

丹尼尔·夏克特(Daniel L. Schacter),美国哈佛大学心理系教授。《内隐记忆:认知神经科学的一个新领域》一文引用了一个新的概念即内隐记忆。内隐记忆指的是先前经验对记忆测验作业的无意识影响,这种记忆测验不需要外显的回忆。在过去的十年中,越来越多的研究表明,可以把记忆的内隐及外显形式加以实验性地分离。本文对内隐记忆研究作了一个总结,同时用从不同领域内得出的证据支持这样的假设,即记忆的内隐与外显形式依赖于不同的记忆系统,而这些记忆系统与大脑的不同区域相联系。

The topic of this chapter—implicit memory—is a relative newcomer to the landscape of memory research. In fact, the term *implicit memory* was first introduced to the field less than a decade ago (Graf and Schacter, 1985; Schacter, 1987). As stated in Schacter (1987, 501), "Implicit memory is revealed when previous experiences facilitate performance on a task that does not require conscious or intentional recollection of those experiences."[①] By contrast, explicit memory[②] "is revealed when performance on a task requires conscious recollection of previous experiences."[③] The relatively recent emergence of the terms *implicit memory* and *explicit memory* is largely attributable to the fact that implicit memory constitutes a novel, if not entirely unprecedented[④], focus for memory research. Most psychological studies of memory have used tasks that involve intentional recollection of previously studied materials, and theoretical accounts have typically focused on data concerning explicit remembering. However, beginning in the 1960s and 1970s, and especially in the early 1980s, evidence began to accumulate indicating that effects of prior experiences could be expressed without, and dissociated from, intentional or conscious recollection[5]. The terms *implicit* and *explicit* memory were put forward in an attempt to capture and describe essential features of the observed dissociations. Related distinctions include declarative versus nondeclarative memory[6] (Squire, 1992), direct versus indirect memory (Johnson and Hasher, 1987), and memory with awareness versus memory without awareness (Jacoby and Witherspoon, 1982).

Despite the recent vintage of the concept, studies of implicit memory have had a profound impact on contemporary research and theorizing. As early as 1988, Richardson-Klavehn and Bjork were able to assert that research on implicit memory constitutes "a revolution in the way that we measure and interpret the influence of past events on current experience and behavior" (1988, 467-477). Since that time interest in the issue has continued and intensified, as studies concerning implicit memory have appeared with astonishing frequency in cognitive, neuropsychological, and even psychiatric journals.

The main purpose of this chapter is to provide an overview of implicit memory research with respect to the concerns of cognitive neuroscience. No attempt is made to provide exhaustive coverage of the area (for recent reviews, see Roediger and McDermott, 1993; Schacter, Chiu, and Ochsner, 1993). Rather, the goal is to acquaint the reader with the major methodological and theoretical issues in contemporary research, and to summarize experimental studies that have examined implicit memory at both the cognitive and neuropsychological levels of analysis. To accomplish this objective, the chapter is divided into four main sections. The first summarizes the historical background of contemporary research, and the seeond considers some basic terminological and methodological issues. The third and major section reviews cognitive and neuropsychological evidence that illuminates the nature and characteristics of implicit memory. The fourth section summarizes contemporary theoretical approaches to relevant phenomena.

Historical background

Although sustained interest in implicit memory has arisen only recently, a variety of clinical, anecdotal, and experimental observations concerning pertinent phenomena have been made during the past several centuries. I have offered a relatively systematic treatment of historical developments elsewhere (Schacter, 1987), and will here only summarize briefly the immediate precursors⑦ to current research.

Contemporary concern with implicit and explicit memory can be traced to two unrelated lines of research that developed during the 1960s and 1970s. First, neuropsychological investigations revealed that densely amnesic patients⑧ could exhibit relatively intact learning abilities⑨ on certain kinds of memory tasks, such as motor skill learning⑩(e.g., Milner, Corkin, and Teuber, 1968), and fragment-cued recall⑪(e.g., Warrington and Weiskrantz, 1974). Second, cognitive psychologists interested in word recognition and lexical access initiated investigations of the phenomenon known as repetition or direct priming, that is, facilitation in the processing or identification of a stimulus as a consequence of prior exposure to it on tests that do not require explicit remembering⑫. For example, several investigators found that performance on a lexical decision test, where subjects judge whether letter strings constitute real words or nonwords, is facilitated significantly by prior exposure to a target word[13] (for historical review, see Schacter, 1987).

By 1980, then, two independent lines of research indicated that effects of past experience could be demonstrated in the absence of, or without the requirement for, conscious recollection. But the possible links between them were not apparent, or at least were not discussed in scientific publications. The situation changed radically during the next few years. Cognitive studies of normal subjects revealed that priming effects on such tasks as word identification and word completion could be dissociated from recall and recognition[14]. (Jacoby and Dallas, 1981; Graf, Mandler, and Haden, 1982; Tulving, Schacter, and Stark, 1982; Graf and Mandler, 1984), and neuropsychological studies of amnesic patients with severe explicit memory deficits demonstrated entirely normal levels of skill learning (Cohen and Squire, 1980; Moscovitch, 1982) and priming (Jacoby and Witherspoon, 1982; Graf, Squire, and Mandler, 1984; Shimamura and Squire, 1984; Schacter, 1985). This convergence of cognitive and neuropsychological evidence provided a basis for the distinction between implicit and explicit memory (Graf and Schacter, 1985; Schacter, 1987).

These developments opened the floodgates for a virtual tidal wave of research. The range of phenomena subsumed under the general label of implicit memory has expanded, theoretical discussion is intense, and the rapid pace of investigation shows no signs of slowing down. Looking back to 1980 from the vantage point of the present, it is no exaggeration to say that we have witnessed the birth and development of a new subfield of memory research. While the vast scope of implicit memory research is in some sense exhilarating, it also means that one cannot hope to cover all of it in a relatively brief chapter. Accordingly, I will focus primarily on studies that have examined phenomena of direct priming, both because more is known about priming than any other implicit memory phenomenon, and because it has played a central role in theoretical discussion and debate. However, an exclusive focus on priming can lead to an overly narrow conception of implicit memory, so I will consider priming in relation to other forms of implicit memory where appropriate.

Methodolgical issues

The terms *implicit* and *explicit* memory were put forward in an attempt to capture salient features[15] of the phenomena described in the preceding section, without implying commitment to a particular theoretical view of the mechanisms underlying the two forms of memory[16]. Thus, Schacter (1987, 501) noted specifically that "the concepts of implicit and explicit memory neither refer to, nor imply the existence of, two independent or separate memory systems." Rather, these concepts "are primarily concerned with a person's psychological experience at the time of retrieval." The terms *implicit memory test* and *explicit memory test* have been used to characterize tasks on which memory performance can be characterized as either implicit (i.e., unintentional, nonconscious) or explicit (i.e., intentional, conscious).

One difficulty that arises when attempting to operationalize and experimentally examine implicit memory is that tasks that are characterized as implicit memory tests can be influenced by explicit memory. Thus, nominally implicit tests are not always functional measures of implicit memory. For example, when a severely amnesic patient exhibits a priming effect on a stem completion test[17], we can be relatively confident that the observed effect reflects the exclusive influence[18] of implicit memory. However, when a college student or any other subject with intact explicit memory exhibits a priming effect, it is always possible that he or she has "caught on" to the fact that test stems can be completed with study list items, and has converted the nominally implicit test into a functionally explicit one[19] (Bowers and Schacter, 1990).

This issue is fundamental to all research on implicit versus explicit memory, and procedures have been developed for confronting the problem. Consider, for example, the *retrieval intentionality criterion*[20] suggested by Schacter, Bowers, and Booker (1989). The criterion consists of two key components: (1) The physical cues on implicit and explicit tests are held constant and only retrieval instructions (implicit or explicit) vary; and (2) an experimental manipulation is identified that affects performance on the two tests differently. The basic argument is that when these conditions are met, we can rule out the possiblility that implicit test performance is contaminated by intentional retrieval strategies. The logic here is straightforward: If subjects are engaging in explicit retrieval on a nominally implicit test, then their performance on implicit and explicit tests that use identical cues should be affected similarly by a given experimental manipulation; thus, dissociations produced under these conditions indicate that the implicit test is not contaminated[21]. And, indeed, a number of studies have produced dissociations that satisfy the retrieval intentionality criterion (e.g., Graf and Mandler, 1984; Hayman and Tulving, 1989; Roediger, Weldon, Stadler, and Riegler, 1992; Schacter and Church, 1992; for a different approach to the "contamination" problem, see Jacoby, 1991).

Characteristics of implicit memory:
Cognitive and neuropsychological research

COGNITIVE STUDIES When contemplating the recent surge of research that constitutes the basis of this chapter, a question that naturally arises concerns the reasons for the intensive scrutiny: Why is implicit memory worth knowing about? One compelling answer to this question is that many situations exist in which implicit memory behaves quite differently from, and independently of, explicit memory. Scientists are naturally curious about surprising phenomena that violate their expectations, and implicit memory is surely one of them. Research with normal subjects has produced two main kinds of evidence for dissociation between implicit and explicit memory: *stochastic independence* and *functional independence*[20].

Stochastic independence Stochastic independence refers to a lack of correlation between two measures of memory at the level of the individual item. To illustrate the concept, consider an early study of priming by Tulving, Schacter, and Stark (1982). Subjects studied a long list of low frequency words[23] (e.g., ASSASSIN), and were later given two successive memory tests: an explicit test of recognition memory in which they indicated via "yes" or "no" responses whether they recollected that a test item had appeared previously on the study list; and an implicit test of fragment completion[24] in which they attempted to complete graphemic fragments of words (e.g., A—A—IN). Priming was observed on the fragment completion test: there was a significantly higher completion rate for fragments that represented previously studied words than for fragments that represented nonstudied words (e.g., -E-S—X for BEESWAX). More importantly, however, a contingency analysis[25] of recognition and fragment completion performance revealed that the probability of producing a studied item on the fragment completion test was uncorrelated with—independent of—the probability of recognizing the same item. This finding of stochastic independence was striking and unexpected, because previous research had indicated that performance on explicit memory tests, such as cued recall[20], is correlated with, or dependent on, recognition memory (see Tulving, 1985).

Stochastic independence between priming and recognition memory has since been observed in a variety of experiments using different kinds of implicit memory tests (see, e.g., Jacoby and Witherspoon, 1982; Hayman and Tulving, 1989; Witherspoon and Moscovitch, 1989; Schacter, Cooper, and Delaney, 1990), and it has been suggested that such evidence is of great theoretical import (Tulving, 1985). But some have contended that findings of stochastic independence are artifacts of either the experimental procedures or the contingency analyses that are used to assess independence (cf. Shimamura, 1985; Hintzman and Hartry, 1990; Ostergaard, 1992). Many of these criticisms, however, have been answered convincingly (see, for example, hayman and Tulving, 1989; Schacter, Cooper, and Delaney, 1990; Tulving and Flexser, 1992).

Functional independence Functional independence between implicit and explicit memory occurs when experimental manipulations affect performance on implicit and explicit tasks in different and even opposite ways. A key source of evidence for functional independence is provided by experiments that manipulate the conditions under which subjects study or encode target items. For instance, a seminal finding from the early 1980s involved experiments that varied the level or depth of encoding during a study task[21]. Research in the levels of processing tradition (e.g., Craik and Tulving, 1975) had already established that explicit recall and recognition performance㉘ are much more accurate following "deep" encoding tasks㉙ that require semantic analysis of target words (e.g., judging the category to which a word belongs) than following "shallow" encoding tasks㉚ that only require analysis of an item's surface features (e.g., judging whether a word has more vowels or consonants). In striking contrast, several studies revealed that the magnitude of priming effects on the word identification task (Jacoby and Dallas, 1981) and stem completion task (Graf, Mandler, and Haden, 1982; Graf and Mandler, 1984) are not significantly influenced by levels of processing manipulations㉛. More recent studies have confirmed and extended this general pattern of results in a variety of experimental paradigms㉜ (e.g., Bowers and Schacter, 1990; Graf and Ryan, 1990; Roediger et al., 1992).

While the foregoing studies used familiar words as target materials, and visual presentation and testing procedures, recent work indicates that the critical dissociation observed in these experiments can be produced with nonverbal figures (e.g., Schacter, Cooper, and Delaney, 1990) and in the auditory modality㉝ (Schacter and Church, 1992). Various other ways of manipulating encoding processes have also produced dissociative effects on implicit and explicit tests (e.g., Jacoby, 1983; Roediger and Challis, 1992)㉞.

Additional evidence is provided by studies that have altered the surface features of target items between study and test. For example, it is well established that priming on identification and completion test is reduced and sometimes eliminated by study-to-test changes in modality of presentation (e.g., Jacoby and Dallas, 1981; Roediger and Blaxton, 1987), even though modality change typically has less impact on explicit memory. In a compelling demonstration, Weldon and Roediger (1987) showed that priming on the word fragment completion test could be eliminated by presenting a picture of a word's referent, rather than the word itself, at the time of study. By contrast, explicit memory was considerably higher following study of the picture than of the word.

(From *The Cognitive Neuroscience*, Chapter 31)

注 释

① Implicit memory is revealed when previous experiences facilitate performance on a task that does not require conscious or intentional recollection of those experiences. 内隐忆记是在这样的情况下显示出来的,即在一个不需要对先前经验进行意识的或有意的回忆任务中,先前经验促进了任务的成绩。
② explicit memory 指外显记忆。
③ is revealed when performance on a task requires conscious recollection of previous experiences. (外显记忆)表现为一个任务的成绩要求有意识地回忆以前的经验。
④ if not entirely unprecedented 即使不是绝无先例的。
⑤ ... indicating that effects of prior experiences could be expressed without, and dissociated from, intentional or conscious recollection. 表明先前经验的效果能够在缺乏有意回忆,或缺乏意识回忆的情况下表现出来,而且还能与它相分离。
⑥ ... declarative versus nondeclarative memory 陈述性的与非陈述性的记忆(之间的差别)。
⑦ the immediate precursors 直接影响。
⑧ densely amnesic patients 严重的失忆症病人
⑨ relatively intact learning abilities 相对完整的学习能力。
⑩ motor skill learning 运动技能的学习。
⑪ fragment-cued recall 补笔线索回忆。
⑫ ... word recognition and lexical access initiated investigations of

⑫ the phenomenon known as repetition or direct priming, that is, facilitation in the processing or identification of a stimulus as a consequence of prior exposure to it on tests that do not require explicit remembering. 对单词再认和词汇通达过程感兴趣的认知心理学家发起了对重复或直接启动现象的研究，即在先前不要求明确记忆的测验中接触过一个刺激，该经验会促进对这个刺激的加工或辨认。

⑬ ... is facilitated significantly by prior exposure to a target work. 对先前呈现过的目标词的辨认显著地加快了。

⑭ ... priming effects on such tasks as word identification and word completion could be dissociated from recall and recognition. 字词辨认、字词补笔等实验中的启动效应能够同回忆及再认分离。

⑮ salient features　显著特征。

⑯ ... without implying commitment to a particular theoretical view of the mechanisms underlying the two forms of memory. 并未暗含赞成关于两种记忆形式的作用机理的某一特定理论观点的意思。

⑰ stem completion test　词干补笔测验。

⑱ exclusive influence　独立影响。

⑲ ... that he or she has "caught on" to the fact that test stems can be completed with study list items, and has converted the nominally implicit test into a functionally explicit one. 可能他或她已经理解测验中的词干可以用学过的项目来填写，并且将名义上的内隐测验转化为功能上的外显测验。

⑳ the retrieval intentionality criterion　有意提取的标准。

㉑ If subjects are engaging in explicit retrieval on a nominally implicit test, then their performance on implicit and explicit tests that use identical cues should be affected similarly by a given experimental manipulation; thus, dissociations produced under these conditions indicate that the implicit test is not contaminated. 如果被试的在内隐测验中使用了外显的提取,那么,他们在用相同线索进行的内隐和外显测验中的成绩受实验操作程序的影响就应该是相似的。因此,在这一条件下产生的分离表明内隐记忆测验未被(外显的意识)混杂。

㉒ stochastic independence and functional independence 随机独立与功能独立。
㉓ a long list of low frequency words 一长串低频词。
㉔ fragment completion 补笔(测验)。
㉕ a contingency analysis (补笔的)列联分析。
㉖ cued recall 线索再现。
㉗ For instance, a seminal finding from the early 1980s involved experiments that varied the level or depth of encoding during a study task. 例如,80年代早期一个创新的发现是在学习任务中改变编码或深度水平。
㉘ recognition performance 再认成绩。
㉙ deep encoding tasks 深层编码加工任务。
㉚ "shallow" encoding tasks 浅层编码加工任务。
㉛ processing manipulations 加工影响。
㉜ in a variety of experimental paradigms 在多种不同的实验范式中。
㉝ the auditory modality 听觉形式。
㉞ Various other ways of manipulating encoding processes have also produced dissociative effects on implicit and explicit tests. 对编码过程进行的其他种不同形式的操作也获得了内隐与外显测验间的分离效应。

练　　习

1. 判断正误
(1) Despite the recent vintage of the concept, studies of implicit memory have had a profound impact on contemporary research

and theorizing.
(2) Looking back to 1980 from the vantage point of the present, we failed to have witnessed the birth and development to a new subfield of memory research.
(3) A number of studies have produced dissociations that dissatisfy the retrieval criterion.
(4) Stochastic independence refers to a lack of correlation between two measures of memory at the level of the individual item.
(5) Stochastic independence between priming and recognition memory has since been observed in a variety of experiments using different kinds of implicit memory tests.

2. 将下列句子翻译成中文
(1) The topic of this chapter—implicit memory—is a relative newcomer to the landscape of memory research.
(2) Despite the recent vintage of the concept, studies of implicit memory have had a profound impact on contemporary research and theorizing.
(3) Contemporary concern with implicit and explicit memory can be traced two unrelated lines of research that developed during the 1960s and 1970s.
(4) This convergence of cognitive and neuropsychological evidence provided a basis for the distinction between implicit and explicit memory.
(5) One difficulty that arises when attempting to operationalize and experimentally examine implicit memory is that tasks that are characterized as implicit memory tests can be influenced by explicit memory.
(6) In a compelling demonstration, Weldon and Roediger showed that priming on the word fragment completion test could be

eliminated by presenting a picture of a work's referent, rather than the word itself, at the time of study.

3. 词汇与短语
Fill in the blanks with the proper words given below
intact, initiate, vary, convert, criterion, contaminate, trace, eliminate
(1) She went through the typescript carefully, to _____ all errors from it.
(2) Several ancient Roman army camps have been _____ with the help of air photographs.
(3) We are thinking of _____ from solid fuel to natural gas before the cool weather sets in.
(4) In Ancient Greece, symmetry and balance were the _____ of artistic beauty.
(5) The museum _____ the fundraising drive with a special exhibition.
(6) The drinking water was _____ with impurities that had got into the reservoir.
(7) Her health _____ from good to rather weak.
(8) The vase that he dropped remained _____.

4. 汉译英
(1) 他们指责不该让儿童接触这类腐蚀心灵的文学。(exposure to)
(2) 当听到那艘船下沉的消息时大家都极为关切。(concern)
(3) 这本书对读者产生了很大影响。(have an impact on)
(4) 一想到这个人,就很难不联想起他的职位。(dissociate from)

16. Mental Models, Deductive Reasoning, and the Brain

Philip N. Johnson-Laird

约翰逊·莱尔德(Philip N. Johnson-Laird)是美国普林斯顿大学心理系教授。《心理模型,演绎推理和脑》一文阐述了演绎推理的两种重要理论:以推理的形式规则为基础的理论主张演绎推理是一种类似逻辑证据的语法过程,心理模型理论则认为演绎是一种类似搜寻反例的语义过程。实验证据则证明了心理模型理论的预测:如果某种园艺推理需要越多的模型,那么这种推理就越难,错误的前提导致错误的结论,一般知识影响搜索加工过程。最近,神经病理学的证据证实了该模型的预测,推理与大脑右半脑具有显著性相关。

> If deduction is a purely verbal process then
> it will not be affected by damage to the right hemisphere.
> It *is* affected by such damage.
> ∴ It is not a purely verbal process.

This argument is an example of a valid deduction: Its conclusion must be true if its premises are true. (They may not be, of course.) Deductive reasoning is under intensive investigation by cognitive scientists, and more is known about it than about any other variety of thinking. The aim of this chapter is to explain its nature and to relate it to the brain. "The cerebral organization of thinking has no history whatsoever," Luria remarked (1973, 323); and Fodor (1983, 119) suggested that nothing can be known about the topic, because thinking does not depend on separate "informationally encapsulated" modules[1] (but cf. Shallice, 1988, 271). Many regions of the brain are likely to underlie it, but as we shall see, a start has been made on the neuropsychology of reasoning.

Many cognitive scientists have argued that deductive reasoning depends on formal rules[2] of inference like those of a logical calculus, and that these unconscious rules are used to derive conclusions from the representations of premises[3]. These "propositional" representations are syntactically structured strings of symbols in a mental language, and the chain of deductive steps is supposedly analogous to a logical proof[4] (see, e.g., the theories of Braine, Reiser, and Rumain, 1984; Osherson, 1974-1976; Rips, 1983). An alternative account postulates a central role for mental models. This account does not reject propositional representations, but it treats them as the input to a process that constructs a mental model corresponding to the situation described by the verbal discourse[5]. The process of deduction—as well as induction and creation (Johnson-Laird, 1993)—is carried out on such models rather than on propositional representations. Models are the natural way in which the human mind constructs reality, conceives alternatives to it[6], and searches out the consequences of assumptions. They are, as Craik (1943) proposed, the medium of thought[7]. But what *is* a mental model?

The underlying idea is that the understanding of discourse leads to a model of the relevant situation akin to one created by perceiving or imagining events instead of merely being told about them (Johnson-Laird, 1970). Experimental studies have indeed found evidence for both initial propositional representations and mental models (see e.g., Johnson-Laird, 1983 van Dijk and Kintsch, 1983; Garnham, 1987). The same idea has led to the model theory of deductive reasoning. The theory was not cut from whole cloth, but was gradually extended from one domain to another. From a logical standpoint, there are at least four main domains of deduction:

1. Relational inferences based on the logical properties of such relations as *greater than*, *on the right of*, and *after*[8].
2. Propositional inferences based on negation and on such connectives as *if*, *or*, and *and*[9].
3. Syllogisms based on pairs of premises that each contain a single quantifier, such as *all* or *some*[10].
4. Multiply quantified inferences based on premises containing more than one quantifier, such as *Some pictures by Turner are more valuable than any by any other English painter*[11].

Logicians have formalized a predicate calculus[12] that covers all four domains and includes the propositional calculus, which deals with inferences based on connectives. The model theory was developed first for relational inferences and syllogisms, and recently for propositional and multiply quantified inferences[13]. In contrast, psychological theories based on formal rules exist for relational and propositional inferences, but not for syllogisms or for multiply quantified inferences.

Theories and evidence have been reviewed in detail elsewhere (Johnson-Laird and Byrne, 1991, 1993; Holyoak and Spellman, 1993). In this chapter, we will stand back from the details and present an integrated account of mental models based on all of this work. We will also bring the story up to date[14] and relate it to the neuropsychology of thinking. The chapter begins with relational inferences and establishes that a model-based system does not require postulates specifying the logical properties of relations. It then shows how models can underlie reasoning with sentential connectives[15], such as *or*, and quantifiers, such as *all*. Next, it shows how certain sorts of diagrams inspired by the model theory can help reasoners to cope with disjunctions. Finally, it considers the neuropsychological findings, and draws some conclusions about the assumptions underlying mental models.

Relational inferences and emergent logical properties

Consider the following simple inference:

The Turner painting is on the right of the Daumier.
The Corot sketch is on the left of the Daumier.
What follows?

A valid answer is that the Turner painting is on the right of the Corot sketch. Psychological theories based on formal rules of inference (e.g., Hagert, 1984; Ohlsson, 1984) explain the derivation of the answer in terms of a formal proof. It depends on the logical properties of the relations: *on the left of* is the converse of *on the right of*[16], and both are transitive relations. These properties have to be added to the premises by stating them in so-called meaning postulates[17], that is, postulates that depend on the meanings of these relations:

For any x, y, if x is on the left of y, then y is on the right of x.
For any x, y, z, if x is on the right of y, and y is on the right of z, then x is on the right of z.

With these postulates the conclusion can be derived:
The Turner painting is on the right of the Corot,

using various rules of inference, including *modus ponens*:

$$\text{if } p \text{ then } q$$
$$p$$
$$\therefore q$$

where p and q denote any propositions whatsoever.

The formal derivation for this simple inference is surprisingly long: It calls for eight steps, but that is the price to be paid for using formal rules[18].

The theory of mental models takes a different approach. It treats propositional representations as instructions for the construction of models[19]. The meaning of, say, *on the right of* consists in the appropriate increments to the Cartesian coordinates of one object, y, in order to locate another object, x, so that: x is on the right of y. Hence, the propositional representation of the assertion[20]:

The Turner painting is on the right of the Daumier

can be used to construct a spatial model[21]:

$$d \quad t$$

where d denotes the Daumier and t denotes the Turner. The information in the second premise:

The Corot sketch is on the left of the Daumier

can be added to yield:

$$c \quad d \quad t$$

This model supports the conclusion:

The Turner painting is on the right of the Corot sketch.

The conclusion is true in the model, but does it follow validly from the premises? The crucial manipulation to test validity is to search for alternative models of the premises that refute the conclusion. In fact, there are no alternative models of the premises in which the conclusion is false, and so it is valid. The model-based method of reasoning accordingly has no need of meaning postulates or formal rules of inference. The logical properties of a relation, such as its transitivity, are not explicitly represented at all, but emerge from the meaning of the relation when it is put to use in the construction of models. The general procedure of searching for alternative models is used to test validity.

The evidence from three-term series problems, such as the example above, does not suffice to decide between formal rules and mental models. However, studies of two-dimensional spatial reasoning[2] have produced more decisive data (Byrne and Johnson-Laird, 1989). We examined problems of the following sort:

> The cup is on the right of the saucer.
> The plate is on the left of the saucer.
> The fork is in front of plate.
> The spoon is in front of the cup.
> What is the relation between the fork and the spoon?

Subjects tend to imagine symmetrical arrangements[3], and so the description corresponds to a single model:

> plate　saucer　cup
> fork　　　　　spoon

It should be relatively easy to answer that the fork is on the left of the spoon. When the second premise of the problem is changed to
　　The plate is on the left of
　the cup the resulting premises are consistent with at least two dis-

tinct models:

>plate saucer cup   saucer plate cup
>fork   spoon   fork   spoon

The same relation holds between the fork and the spoon in both models, but the theory predicts that the task should be harder because both models must be constructed in order to test the validity of the answer. The task should be still harder where the correct response can be made only be constructing both models. The description

> The cup is on the right of the saucer
> The plate is on the left of the cup
> The fork is in front of plate
> The spoon is in front of saucer

is consistent with two distinct models:

> plate saucer cup   saucer plate cup
> fork spoon   spoon fork

that have no relation in common between the fork and the spoon, and so there is no valid answer to the question. Granted that the mind has a limited processing capacity, the model theory predicts the following rank order of increasing difficulty[20]: one-model problems, multiple-model problems with valid answers, and multiple-model problems with no valid answers.

Formal-rule theories need complex meaning postulates to support two-dimensional deductions (Hagert, 1984; Ohlsson, 1984).

Whatever rules a theory uses, however, the one-model problem calls for a longer derivation than the multiple-model problem with a valid answer. It is necessary to infer the relation between the plate and the cup for the one-model problem, but there is no need for such a derivation with the multiple-model problem because the relation is directly asserted by the second premise:

The plate is on the left of the cup.

Hence, formal rule theories predict that the one-model problems should be harder than the multiple-model valid problems, which is exactly the opposite prediction to the one made by the model theory[20].

Our experiments compared the predictions of the two theories (Byrne and Johnson-Laird, 1989). In one experiment, 18 adults carried out four inferences of each of the three sorts, and the percentages of their correct responses were as follows: 70% for the one-model problems, 46% for the multiple-model valid problems, and 8% for the multiple-model problems with no valid conclusion. This robust trend corroborates the model theory runs counter to the formal-rule theories. The same results have been obtained from analogous problems concerning temporal relations (Schaeken and Johnson-Laird, 1993). Subjects also drew correct conclusions to one-model problems reliably faster than to multiple-model problems.

Models for connectives and quantifiers

What remains to be accounted for are the logical constant—sentential connectives and quantifiers. Some psychological theories postulate formal rules of inference for connectives, but no such theories exist for quantifiers. The model theory, however, proposes an account for both. Connectives call for models of alternative possibilities. A conjunction of the form:

$$p \text{ and } q$$

requires only a single model:

$$p \quad q$$

where p and q respectively denote the situations described by the two propositions. But an exclusive disjunction such as⁽²⁶⁾:

$$p \text{ or else } q, \text{ but not both}$$

requires two alternative models, which are shown here on separate lines:

$$p$$
$$q$$

A conditional of the form⁽²⁷⁾:

$$\text{If } p, \text{ then } q$$

calls—at least initially—for one explicit model (of the antecedent and consequent) and one implicit model of an alternative situation:

$$p \quad q$$
$$\ldots$$

The implicit model symbolized by the three dots may subsequently be rendered explicit, but for many inferences the implicit model suffices. We have implemented a computer program (Propsych) that computes the numbers of explicit models required by inferences (see Johnson-Laird, Byrne, and Schaeken, 1992). Consider, for example, the following argument:

Studies have shown that children of people who smoke more than two packs per day have a greater exposure than others to secondhand smoke or a lowered resistance to viral infection[20]. Children exposed to secondhand smoke have an increased risk of lung cancer. Children with lowered resistance to viral infection are harder to treat with chemotherapy. These two factors make for intractable cases of lung cancer. Thus, these children risk contracting untreatable lung cancer.

The first step is to represent the underlying propositional connectives in the premises:

If child of smoker *then* (exposed to smoke *or* lowered resistance).
If exposed to smoke *then* greater risk.
If lowered resistance *then* chemotherapy harder.
If greater risk or chemotherapy harder *then* risk of untreatable cancer.
∴ *If* child of smoker *then* risk of untreatable cancer.

We can then use the Propsych program to work out the total number of explicit models that have to be constructed to carry out the inference. Thus, the first premise calls for two explicit models and one implicit model:

$$\begin{array}{cc} c & s \\ c & l \\ \cdots & \end{array}$$

where c denotes a child of a smoker, s denotes exposure to smoke, and l denotes lowered resistance. The second premise calls for the following models:

$$\begin{array}{cc} s & r \\ \cdots & \end{array}$$

where r denotes a greater risk. The principles for combining sets of models are simple: A new model is made, if possible, from each pairwise combination of a model from one set with a model from the other set, according to the principles in Johnson-Laird, Byrne, and Schaeken (1992, 425):

1. If the model in one set is implicit and the model in the other set is implicit, then the result is an implicit model[29].
2. If the model in one set is implicit but the model in the other set is not, then no new model is formed from them.
3. If the pair of models is inconsistent, that is, one contains the representation of a proposition and the other contains a representation of its negation, then no new model is formed from them.
4. Otherwise the two models are joined together, eliminating any redundancies.

The result of combining the sets of models for the first two premises is, accordingly:

$$
\begin{array}{llll}
c & & s & r \\
c & l & s & r \\
& \cdots & &
\end{array}
$$

Hence, so far, the process of inference has called for the construction of five explicit models. The set of premises as a whole calls for the construction of nine explicit models. Initial models of this sort suffice for all the 61 direct inferences used in a study by Braine, Reiser, and Rumain (1984), and the program was used to count them: They predicted the difficulty of the problems as well as these authors' rule-based theory.

Although many inferences in daily life can be made with such models, sometimes one has to think more carefully and flesh out the models completely. Given the conditional
  If there is a triangle then there is a circle,
could there be a circle without a triangle? Presumably so, given one interpretation of the conditional. Could there be a triangle without a circle? Of course not. That would contravene the meaning of the conditional. Hence, as soon as individuals begin to think more closely about the meaning of the conditional, they realize that the explicit model in the following set:

△ ○
 ...

represents the only possible situation in which a triangle can occur. That is, it must occur with a circle given the truth of the conditional. One way to represent this informations is to use a special annotation:

 ...

where the square brackets⁽ᵂ⁾ indicate that triangles have been exhaustively represented in relation to circles. The procedure for fleshing out models⁽ᵂ⁾ works as follows: When a proposition has been exhaustively represented, its negation is added to any other models; when a proposition has not been exhaustively represented, it and its negation form separate models that replace the implicit model (denoted by three dots). Triangles cannot occur in fleshing out the implicit model above, because they are already exhausted, but their negations can occur with either a circle or its negation. Hence, the result is:

$$\begin{array}{cc} \triangle & \bigcirc \\ \neg\triangle & \bigcirc \\ \neg\triangle & \neg\bigcirc \end{array}$$

Where ¬ is an annotation representing negation. Because there is no longer any implicit model, there is no need for symbols representing exhaustive representations. Exhaustion is thus a device that allows the inferential system to represent certain information implicitly—it can be made explicit, but at the cost of fleshing out the models.

The same principles suffice for the representation of quantifiers. The interpretation of an assertion, such as

All the Frenchmen in the restaurant are gourmets

calls for a model of the following sort, in which each line no longer represents a separate model, but rather a separate individual in one and the same model:

$$\begin{array}{cc} [f] & g \\ [f] & g \\ \cdots & \end{array}$$

where f denotes a Frenchman, g denotes a gourmet, and the three dots represent implicit individuals. As before, the square brackets indicate an exhaustive representation: The tokens denoting Frenchmen exhaust the set in relation to the set of gourmets[20]. The set of gourmets, however, is not exhaustively represented. Hence, if the implicit individuals are fleshed out explicitly, some of them may be gourmets, but none of them can be Frenchmen unless they are also gourmets.

The information from a second premise, say

Some of the gourmets are wine drinkers

can be added to the model

$$\begin{array}{lll} [f] & g & w \\ [f] & g & \\ & & w \\ & \cdots & \end{array}$$

This model supports the believable conclusion:

Some of the Frenchmen in the restaurant are wine drinkers

This conclusion is erroneous, though it is drawn by most subjects (see Oakhill, Johnson-Laird, and Garnham, 1989). It is refuted by an alternative model of the premises:

$$\begin{array}{lll} [f] & g & \\ [f] & g & \\ & g & w \\ & & w \\ & \cdots & \end{array}$$

When the second premise is instead:

Some of the gourmets are Italians

the initial model supports the unbelievable conclusion:

211

Some of the Frenchmen are Italians

and hardly any subjects err now. In other words, reasoners tend to "satisfice" (see Simon, 1959); If they reach a congenial conclusion they tend not to search for alternative models. Satisficing is a frequent cause of everyday disasters, both major and minor. It seems an obvious danger, yet it cannot be predicted by rule theories, which contain no elements corresponding to models of situations.

The model theory generalizes to multiply quantified assertions. For example, the premises:

> None of the Avon letters is in the same place as any of the Bury letters
> All of the Bury letters are in the same place as all of the Caton letters

yield the valid conclusion:

> None of the Avon letters is in the same place as any of the Caton letters.

Granted the following definition of *in the same place as*:

> x is in the same place as $y = x$ is in a place that has the same spatial coordinates as those for y [33]

the premises support a model of the state of affairs:

$$| [a] [a] [a] | [b] [b] [b] [c] [c] [c] |$$

where the vertical barriers demarcate separate places[34], and there are arbitrary numbers of individuals of each sort (*as* denote Avon letters, *bs* denote Bury letters, and *cs* denote Caton letters). This model yields the conclusion:

None of the Avon letters is in the same place as any of the Caton letters.

No alternative model of the premises refutes the conclusion. As the theory predicts, one-model deductions are easier than multiple-model deductions (see Johnson-Laird, Byrne, and Tabossi, 1989).

(From *The Cognative Neurosciences*, Chapter 44)

注 释

① ... because thinking does not depend on separate "informationally encapsulated" modules. 因为思维并不依赖于独立的"信息包装"模块。
② formal rules 形式规则。
③ these unconscious rules are used to derive conclusions from the representations of premises. 人们用这些潜意识的规则从前提表征中推导出结论。
④ These "propositional" representations are syntactically structured strings of symbols in a mental language, and the chain of deductive steps is supposedly analogous to a logical procf. 命题表征是心理语言综合性的，具有结构性的符号串，有人认为演绎推理的方法类似进行逻辑论证的方法。
⑤ ... but it treats them as the input to a process that constructs a mental model corresponding to the situation described by the verbal discourse. 但这种观点将命题表征看成是一个加工过程中的输入，在这个加工过程中(人们)构建起一个与言语描述的情景相符合的心理模型。

⑥ ... conceives alternatives to it. 设想其反例。
⑦ the medium of thought 思维中介。
⑧ Relational inferences based on the logical properties of such relations as *greater than*, *on the right of*, an *after*. 以"大于","在……右边"和"在……之后"等关系的逻辑属性为基础的关系推理。
⑨ Propositional inferences based on negation and on such connectives *as if*, *or*, and *and*. 以否定和诸如"如果","或","和"等连词为基础的命题推理。
⑩ Syllogisms based on pairs of premises that each contain a single quantifier, such as *all* or *some*. 以两个前提,每个前提包含一个单独的量词(如"所有","一些")为基础的三段论推理。
⑪ Multiply quantified inferences based on premises containing more than one quantifier, such as *Some pictures by Turner are more valuable than any by any other English painter*. 以前提包含不止一个量词为基础的多量词推理,如:Turner 所画的一些图比所有其他英国画家所画的所有图都更为有价值。
⑫ a predicate calculus 一种谓词的运算。
⑬ multiply quantified inferences 多量词推理。
⑭ ... bring the story up to date. 也谈到目前研究进展。
⑮ sentential connectives. 句子的连接词。
⑯ ... *on the left of* is the converse of *on the right of*. "在左边"与"在右边"相反。
⑰ ... in so-called meaning postulates 所谓的意义性假设。
⑱ It calls for eight steps, but that is the price to be paid for using formal rules. 要完成这种推理需八个步骤,这就是使用形式规则的代价。
⑲ instructions for the construction of models. 建立模型的指令。
⑳ The meaning of, say, *on the right of* consists in the appropriate increments to the Cartesian coordinates of one object, y, in order

to locate another object, x, so that: x is on the right of y. "在……右边"的意思在于,它作为客体 y 在笛卡尔坐标上的一个合适的增量,用来对另一个客体 x 进行定位,使得 x 在 y 的右边。

㉑ a spatial model　空间模型。
㉒ two-dimensional spatial reasoning　两维空间推理。
㉓ symmetrical arrangements　对称性的分布。
㉔ Granted that the mind has a limited processing capacity, the model theory predicts the following rank order of increasing difficulty. 如果心理加工容量是有限的,那么心理模型理论预测在以下序列中,问题的难度逐渐增加。
㉕ ... which is exactly the opposite prediction to the one made by the model theory. 刚好与模型理论所作的预测相反。
㉖ an exclusive disjunction　一种排他性的析取。
㉗ a conditional of the form　以下形式的条件性判断。
㉘ or a lowered resistance to viral infection　对病毒感染的抵抗力更低。
㉙ If the model in one set is implicit and the model in the other set is implicit, then the result is an implicit model. 如果某集中的模型和另一集中的模型都是内隐的,那么结论是一种内隐的模型。
㉚ the square brackets 方括号。
㉛ The procedure for fleshing out models 使模型运行的程序。
㉜ The tokens denoting Frenchmen exhaust the set in relation to the set of gourmets. 括号表示法国人穷尽了与美食家有关的集。
㉝ x is in the same place as y = x is in a place that has the same spatial coordinates as those for y. x 和 y 在同样的位置等于 x 在一个与 y 有相同空间坐标的位置。
㉞ ... the vertical barriers demarcate separate places. 指竖隔分离出独立的位置。

练 习

1. 判断正误
(1) If deduction is a purely verbal process then it will not be affected by damage to the right hemisphere. It is affected by such damage. It is a verbal process.
(2) The process of deduction— as well as induction and creation— is carried out on such models rather than on propositional representations.
(3) Experimental studies have indeed found evidence for mental model.
(4) The model-based method of reasoning accordingly has no need of meaning postulates or formal rules of inference.
(5) The general procedure of searching for alternative models is used to test reliability.
(6) The model theory generalizes to multiply quantified assertions.

2. 英译汉
(1) Deductive reasoning is under intensive investigation by cognitive scientists, and more is known about it than about any other variety of thinking.
(2) The underlying idea is that the understanding of discourse leads to a model of the relevant situation akin to one created by perceiving or imagining events instead of merely being told about them.
(3) In this chapter, we will stand back from the details and present an integrated account of mental models based on all of this work.
(4) The crucial manipulation to test validity is to search for alternative models of the premises that refute the conclusion.

(5) Satisficing is a frequent cause of everyday disasters, both major and minor.

3. 词汇与短语

Fill in the blanks with the proper words given below

analogous, conceive, denote, exhaust, predict, premise, accordingly, generalize

(1) The two processes of dyeing are not _____ with each other.
(2) When the revolutionary situation changes, revolutionary tactics must change _____ .
(3) The word "dentist" _____ a doctor whose work is the care of teeth.
(4) The coach _____ the strategy that won the game for us.
(5) The soldiers had _____ their supply of ammunition.
(6) It was the lawyer's _____ that his client was innocent.
(7) It is possible to _____ from all the information given to us and to make various decisions.
(8) The surgeon _____ that the patient would be walking again in a week.

4. 句型模拟

(1) Granted that ...
(2) have no need of ...

5. 汉译英

(1) "热"是"冷"的反义词。(the converse of)
(2) 真正的慈善不在于施舍。(consist in)
(3) 西班牙语和拉丁语很相近。(akin to)
(4) 关于那件事,我有很多的话要说。(in relation to)
(5) 美国的国会相当于英国的议会。(correspond to)

17. Models of Consciousness: Serial or Parallel in the Brain?

MARCEL KINSBOURNE

马索·肯斯伯尼(Marcel Kinsbourne)是美国塔福斯大学认知研究中心的教授。《意识的模型:脑内是串行的还是并行的?》一文讨论了传统的以大脑为中心的串行层次模型和现在的研究结果存在的冲突。这些研究发现了大脑结构、生理和病灶损伤对行为的影响。于是,另一模型被提出来,它认为许多表征以行为方式激活,其中一些被激活的表征由于皮层内部的双向相互作用而形成了一个优势兴奋灶。这种兴奋灶不断地形成就决定了意识的内容。盲视和对空间的一侧化忽视症都符合这一模型。

Two problems about consciousness

Brain activity giving rise to conscious experience raises two separable challenges: One is to characterize the neural activity that underlies consciousness in terms of the dynamic properties and topographic distribution of this neural activity[①]. The other is to explain how this neural activity engenders phenomenal experience, relative to which there are two competing positions.

IS NEURAL ACTIVITY TRANSDUCED INTO CONSCIOUSNESS? Some think that awareness is generated by, but different in nature from, neural activity (a distinct "information bearing medium"[②] Mangan, 1993). This putative transformation of neural activity into awareness must involve formidable complexities and even a mathematics or physics that is currently (Penrose, 1989; Searle, 1992) if not permanently (McGinn, 1991) beyond our grasp. This last-frontier mystique of consciousness[3] shows how greatly these theorists value their subjectivity, but it lacks objective support. What form might such support take?

If consciousness is a separate product, it should be separable from the neural activity of the brain. Consciousness should be demonstrable in isolation, and brain activity and information processing should proceed unaltered in the absence of consciousness. But neither phenomenon has been demonstrated. This encourages the more parsimonious view that consciousness is emergent from the neural activity without intervening transduction[4]: It is the subjective aspect of the underlying neuronal activity; subjectivity refers to what it is like for the brain to be in relevant functional states. (Many would find this counterintuitive, but intuitions are data to be explained, not conclusions to be respected. There is no more justification for using intuition to jude theory in behavioral science than in physics; see Dennett, 1991). This directs discussion to the functional states in question. What is the neuropsychology of consciousness?

A_{RE} W_E C_{ONSCIOUS OF} P_{ROCESSING OR OF} R_{EPRESENTATIONS}[5]? It is customary to refer to processing that generates representations of information and of intentions in the brain. Is consciousness the actual functioning of our brains, or only the results of this functioning? Lashley (1958) pointed out that "no activity of mind is ever conscious — experience clearly gives no clue as to the means by which it is organized" (p. 4). Thus conscious contents are the products of preconscious processing. At any time they embody the state changes that have occurred. The processing is opaque to awareness (Prinz, 1992). What, then, are the necessary and sufficient conditions for any item of information that is represented in terms of neuronal activity to contribute to the construction of the phenomenal present?

IS THERE SOMETHING SPECIAL ABOUT CONSCIOUS REPRESENTATIONS? In an information processing sequence, each output serves as input to the next processor. Not all these representations contribute to consciousness. To do so, do the representations have to be of a special kind, enjoy special relationships, or be located in a special place in the brain?

Type of representation An obvious approach to characterizing representations that contribute to consciousness is top-down⑥: Hypothesize the adaptive function of consciousness, and then arrive at the set of representations that would suffice to accomplish that purpose. This tactic usually targets effortful attentional processes, and ends up with far too restricted a set of represented experiences, such as verbalizable features at the focus of attention⑦ (e.g., Johnson-Laird, 1983). It ignores less articulated global feelings⑧ such as pain or panic, and perception in a more dispersed or global mode⑨. An example of the latter is panoramic vision⑩, in which there is immediate (i.e., parallel) acquisition of general textural information⑪, and the observer has a sense of clarity and richness of content, which can only be verbalized after a succession of fixations that enable serial focal analysis. A listing of what *can* enter consciousness might suggest that almost anything that can be represented can be experienced. Conversely, content of which one is usually aware can also control behavior outside awareness (i.e., subliminally).

Because the contents of consciousness are so diverse, they may not all be adapted to the same specific purpose. They may instead characterize a particular stage in the information-processing sequence, or they may share some adaptively important contextual attribute (or both).

Stage of representation Jackendoff (1987) observed that neither the most elementary representations (Marr's primal sketch[12], phonological distinctive features)[13] nor the most abstract (3-D representation, meaning, syntax) contribute their contents to awareness. When viewing a scene, we are not aware of the as-yet-unorganized elements[14] (features) that the brain is extracting from visual input[15]. Nor is speech initially a potpourri of as-yet-unorganized auditory distinctive features[16]. Conversely, when speaking, we do not first represent in awareness the semantic "formal elements" or the syntactic organization of what we intend to say. So, according to Jackendoff, consciousness is embodied in "intermediary representations[17]", not in representations either at the highest abstract level or at the low level of sensory primitives[18].

Are lower-order representations really precluded from awareness[19]? In the unfolding of a percept[20], it is unknown, and probably unknowable, whether early representations were really preconscious, or conscious but already forgotten at the time of report. This problem is pervasive when two or more sensory events occur in very rapid succession (Dennett and Kinsbourne, 1992). As the neural activity "settles", its previous instantiations prove evanescent[21].

Early representations may not be preserved in awareness simply because they are too short-lived, regardless of their stage in processing per se[22]. But if a processing sequence is interrupted by a focal brain lesion, a representation that normally does not access awareness may do so, generating appearances that normal people never experience[23]. For instance, patients recovering from cortical blindness[24] have unusual experiences that could be thus explained (Poppelreuter, 1923). Patients with phantom limbs[25] that they include in intended actions experience the represented intentions as movements in the absent limb, because they are not supplanted by the realized movement[26].

Are higher-order representations really excluded from awareness? The alleged end points of input processing[27] (e.g., 3-D representation) may in fact be fully represented, but implicitly as knowledge about the objects and relationships in the represented scene. Unlike the scene itself, knowledge about it becomes explicit only when called for[28]. But the scene itself is organized by prior knowledge about its constituents, as is the decoding of a verbal utterance[29] (Liberman and Studdert-Kennedy, 1978). This is an interactive (heterarchical) rather than a strictly serial process. The knowledge about the input is not represented separately in awareness, but is inherent in the relationships that form between the input's representation and other representations that coexist (see integrated field model[30], below).

Abstract representations thought to precede speech subdivide into semantic and syntactic categories[31]. The semantics of an utterance may be represented in awareness in the pervasive though unanalyzed feeling that one knows what one is about to say[32]. Again, that ill-differentiated awareness is supplanted by the explicit content of the utterance that follows[33]. If the syntactical elements into which utterances can be analyzed have psychological reality, then again they are supplanted by the elaborated utterance that immediately follows[34], and we cannot know whether they were transiently in consciousness. To be a viable candidate for consciousness, a representation has to persist for a minimum time. Some persisting representations become mutually entrained to give rise to the experience of objects and scenes[35]. Representations are not entrained if they lack intensity (are subthreshold), are incomplete, are too short-lived, or even because they make incompatible demands on output mechanisms.

The field of conscious awareness imposes no restrictions on the types of representations that contribute to it. Probably all categories of representation are sometimes in consciousness and sometimes excluded from it. According to the integrated cortical field model, representations do not change character to become conscious, nor are their contents shuttled to some privileged place[36]. Whether they are conscious depends on their interrelationships.

Integrated field model of awareness

What does distinguish information that is in awareness from the same information when it is not? The integrated field model (Kinsbourne, 1988) supposes that this attribute is contextual, consisting of a relationship to other content that is simultaneously represented in awareness. Conversely, when sensory input is processed outside awareness, it may modify (i.e., prime) response predispositions in interesting ways, but that processing is unrelated to anything else that is currently happening to the individual[37]. It is not incorporated into the phenomenal here-and-now, and therefore cannot be recovered by event memory. Nor can it serve as a cue to what else was happening at the time.

Any experience is inevitably in a context; detailed and rich, or minimal and confined to the fact that it is happening "to me, here and now". It is part of an event, a personal experience, potentially retrieved by event (episodic) memory. This experiential binding[38] gives information acquired in awareness the additional potential to be related to whatever else was happening at the time to or around the observer. The adaptive implications of rare combinations of contingencies can therefore be explored without multitrial learning[39]. Having its contents contribute to awareness does not preclude a representation from modifying response predispositions. But it also enables the individual to evaluate a signal in context, in case its adaptive implication is context dependent.

If awareness stands out not by what it is but by the company it keeps, then we should, in conceptualizing its brain basis, look for corresponding relational design characteristics in the cerebral neuronal architecture[40] that accomodates the neural representations that underlie awareness.

The model of the centered brain

Ever since its mid-nineteenth-century inception, the dominant model in neuropsychology has been the centered brain. Extrapolating the communication channels that converge from the body periphery on the brain, this model postulates continuing convergence within the brain substance, in service of multimodal integration into objects (each uniquely coded by a "grandmother cell")[41]. This hierarchically serial organization culminates in some ill-specified place, the consciousness module, where the by now elaborately preprocessed information purportedly enters consciousness. Suitably informed, the consciousness module arrives at some appropriate decision, which is implemented by the reverse sequence of messages[42], becoming ever more fragmentary and dispersed as they recede from the apex of the hierarchy[43].

As little as the centered brain model has to commend it in any subarea of neuropsychology (Kinsbourne, 1982), it is particularly inadequate as a basis for consciousness. Dennett and Kinsbourne (1992) epitomized the centered brain vis-á-vis consciousness by the metaphorical "Cartesian Theater" along the lines of Descartes's concept of the role of the pineal gland[44]. At some privileged locus, the brain provides a display for the viewing pleasure of a homunculus, who is both experiencer and agent. In that article we examined one consequence — that events should necessarily be experienced in the temporal sequence[45] in which they cross a neural "finish line" for theatric screening[46]— and showed that this conflicts with well-established time related phenomena in perception.

EVIDENCE AGAINST THE CENTERED BRAIN   A centered cortical neuroanatomy, with converging unidirectional channels linking node with node at successively higher levels of integration is not to be found[47]. Instead, there is a diffuse neural network, the neuropil, that is continuous in the cortical gray matter[48]. Many neurons do not fire in the sense of generating action potentials, but instead propagate slow-wave graded potentials[49] (Bullock, 1981). Patches of neuropil are interconnected by corticosubcortical loops or by U-shaped corticocortical connections[50]. No progression in level or hierarchy is indicated by the anatomy, and U-shaped projections are fully reciprocal, with as extensive and specific an innervation in one direction as in the other. There is no point where it all comes together, strategically located at the apex of a hierarchy.

Corresponding to this massively parallel (and heterarchical) anatomy is a parallel neuropsychology. No focal cortical lesion ablates awareness and intention, leaving nonconscious processing intact. Focal cortical lesions impair specific abilities. They do not render a person unconscious. Correspondingly, when either hemisphere is briefly inactivated by intracarotid amobarbital[51], the other suffices to enable the patient to respond to simple verbal commands. Neurophysiology has resoundingly confirmed the long-standing localizationist viewpoint that the cerebral neural network is differentiated in its various parts so as to implement different mental operations[52]. But it has not found that information represented at two (or more) points is integrated at yet another point. Metabolic studies carried out during mental activity reveal a distribution of activation that encompasses the areas that correspond to the ingredients of the task, but no separate area of confluence of these ingredients (Lassen and Roland, 1983). Separate dorsal and ventral "streams" of visual information processing (Ungerleider and Mishkin, 1982) nowhere merge. No centered locus of activation characterizes all tasks that are consciously performed or indicates that consciousness has been entered.

The parallel brain

In contrast to the exclusively connected centered brain, the brain conceptualized as processing in parallel offers scope for the lateral interaction of unrelated processors[53]. In normative studies[54], activating one processor exerts systematic effects (priming or interfering) on other, functionally unrelated systems. These effects are predictable, based on the functional cerebral distance principle[55] (e. g., Kinsbourne, 1970, 1972, 1973, 1975; Kinsbourne and Hicks, 1978; Kinsbourne and Byrd, 1985). This "penetrability" of modules to each others' influences is consistent with a parallel neuronal architecture[56]. According to the centered brain model, different, separately analyzed aspects of a stimulus are bound by conjoint representation at a node downstream[57] in the brain. Abandoning this model implies binding at a distance, probably by repetitive interaction between complementary representations[58]. How this might work is only beginning to be elucidated. Nonetheless, the parallel model, though as yet incompletely specified, does probe brain organization from a more realistic perspective.

How, then, can we arrive at a plausible neural basis for consciousness within the framework of a massively parallel brain, or at least, cerebral cortex?

D_{OMINANT} F_{OCUS}[59] In order to contribute to awareness, representations must be adequately activated. What happens when they are? I have suggested (Kinsbourne, 1988) that at any time in the awake individual's brain there is a dominant focus of patterned neural activity that underlies the phenomenal experience of that moment, the momentarily dominant "draft" of the "multiple drafts" that in rapid succession constitute the ostensibly continuous "stream" of everchanging consciousness[60] (Dennett and Kinsbourne, 1992). Whatever subset of currently active cell assemblies participates in this dominant focus determines what content is represented in awareness and is related to the self (and later available to recollection)[61]. From moment to moment the composition of the dominant focus changes, ad representations become bound to it while others break away. Subsidiary clusters of entrained representations[62] may coexist, candidates for future inclusion in the dominant focus. Thus subjectivity depends on patterned neural activity[63] that is widely and variably dispersed over the cerebral cortex.

M_{ECHANISMS OF} B_{INDING INTO THE} D_{OMINANT} F_{OCUS} One way in which representations might bind is if the respective cell assemblies fire synchronously, or perhaps enter into joint oscillation of firing[64] (von der Malsburg, 1977; Gray and Singer, 1989). This entrainment is perhaps mediated by plastic synapses such as those carrying NMDA receptors (Flohr, 1991). Certain high-frequency rhythms recordable on the EEG may reflect ongoing binding (Loring and Sheer, 1984). This account of binding certainly raises major issues, such as how an attribute can bind simultaneously with other attributes of the same object, with other objects into coordinated displacement[65], with other coexisting objects into a scene, and with the state (physical, emotional, expectancy) of the observer. Does volume oscillation at multiple simultaneous frequencies implement this nested complex of relationships⑥⑥?

Another issue is the representation of temporal order of succession. If simultaneity is applied to the process of binding, the brain cannot at the same time code temporal order in terms of relative time of arrival of stimuli (at least in the microtime of fractions of a second⑥⑦). Dennett and Kinsbourne (1992) suggest that the brain organizes the onrush of inputs by "microtakings", which may violate the strict physical of stimulation in favor of a best-fit organization that takes into account content and experience. Obviously, most of this remains to be worked out. Here I restrict myself to observing that synchronous firing and co-oscillation are consistent with the bidirectionality of corticocortical connections⑥⑧. Any successful account of consciousness must explain how cell assemblies widely scattered in the cerebral cortex can contribute to consciousness.

(From *The Cognitive Neurosciences*, Chapter 50)

注　释

① One is to characterize the neural activity that underlies consciousness in terms of the dynamic properties and topographic distribution of this neural activity. 一个问题是要根据神经活动的动态特征和其在解剖学上的分布,来描述支配意识的神经活动的特点。
② a distinct "information bearing medium" 一种独特的"信息载体"。
③ This last-frontier mystique of consciousness 处在研究最前沿的意识之谜
④ without intervening transduction 不是通过神经活动传递而来的。
⑤ ARE WE CONSCIOUS OF PROCESSING OR OF REPRE-

SENTATIONS? 我们是对过程有意识还是对内部表征有意识？

⑥ An obvious approach to characterizing representations that contribute to consciousness is topdown. 描述表征对意识的作用的一个明显方法是自上而下的。

⑦ This tactic usually targets effortful attentional processes, and ends up with far too restricted a set of represented experiences, such as verbalizable features at the focus of attention. 这种策略主要针对那些需要花费注意的加工，最终可得到一组对经验的有限表征，如处在注意焦点的可用言语描述的特征。

⑧ ...less articulated global feelings 那些较难描述的整体感受。

⑨ perception in a more dispersed or global mode 更为分散或广泛的知觉形式。

⑩ panoramic vision 全景性视觉。

⑪ acquisition of general textural information 获得对整体组织结构的信息。

⑫ primal sketch 初级略图。

⑬ phonological distinctive features 语音的区别特征。

⑭ the as-yet-unorganized elements 尚未组织起来的元素。

⑮ extracting from visual input 从视觉输入中提取。

⑯ Nor is speech initially a potpourri of as-yet-unorganized auditory distinctive features. 言语最初也不是一些未被组织起来的听觉特征的大杂烩。

⑰ intermediary representation 中级表征。

⑱ sensory primitives 原始感觉。

⑲ Are lower-order representations really precluded from awareness? 低层次表征确实处于意识之外吗？

⑳ In the unfolding of a percept 在对意识对象的表述中。

㉑ As the neural activity "settles", its previous instantiations prove evanescent. 当神经激活平息下来时，它先前的具体体验将会消

失。

㉒ regardless of their stage in processing per se　不管早期的表征是在加工的哪个阶段。

㉓ But if a processing sequence is interrupted by a focal brain lesion, a representation that normally does not access awareness may do so, generating appearances that normal people never experience. 但如果脑的局部性病灶将一个加工序列打断，那么正常状态下不能进入意识的表征这时也许可以进入，从而导致出现正常人从未经历过的主观体验。

㉔ cortical blindness　皮层性失明。

㉕ patients with phantom limbs　截肢后的病人。

㉖ supplanted by the realized movement　被实际的运动取代

㉗ ...end points of input processing　输入加工终点。

㉘ ...knowledge about it becomes explicit only when called for　关于它的知识只有在需要的时候才变得明晰起来。

㉙ the decoding of a verbal utterance　对口头语言的解码。

㉚ integrated field model　整合域模型。

㉛ Abstract representations thought to precede speech subdivide into semantic and syntactic categories. 言语之前的抽象表征可分为语义和句法两类。

㉜ The semantics of an utterance may be represented in awareness in the pervasive though unanalyzed feeling that one knows what one is about to say. 话语的语义在意识中以一种泛在的、笼统的形式得以表征，这样，一个人就知道他要说的是什么。

㉝ Again, that ill-differentiated awareness is supplanted by the explicit content of the utterance that follows. 随后，这种未完全分化的意识就被随之而来的话语的外显内容所代替。

㉞ ...supplanted by the elaborated utterance that immediately follows　同样也会被紧随其后的言语的详细内容所替代。

㉟ Some persisting representations become mutually entrained to

give rise to the experience of objects and scenes. 一些持续性表征同时进入意识,形成了对物体和景象的经验。
㊱ ...nor are their contents shuttled to some privileged place. 表征的内容不会涉及到某些特定的地方。
㊲ Conversely, when sensory input is processed outside awareness, it may modify (i.e., prime) response predispositions in interesting ways, but that processing is unrelated to anything else that is currently happening to the individual. 相反,当感觉输入在意识之外被加工,它可能以一种有趣的方式改变反应的倾向(如启动),但这个过程与个体当前遇到的任何其他事情无关。
㊳ this experiential binding 综合的经验。
㊴ multitrial learning 多次的学习。
㊵ in the cerebral neuronal architecture 大脑皮层神经元结构。
㊶ Extrapolating the communication channels that converge from the body periphery on the brain, this model postulates continuing convergence within the brain substance, in service of multimodal integration into objects (each uniquely coded by a "grandmother cell"). 这个模型通过推断从躯体外周汇聚到大脑的各种联系通路,并假设在大脑物质中存在连续的汇集,从而使多种感觉形式整合为客体(由一个"老祖母细胞"单独编码)。
㊷ ...which is implemented by the reverse sequence of messages. 由反向的信息序列加以补充。
㊸ the apex of the hierarchy 层次的最高点。
㊹ Dennett and Kinsbourne epitomized the centered brain vis-a-vis consciousness by the metaphorical "cartesian theater" along the lines of Descartes's concept of the role of the pineal gland. Dennett 和 Kinsbourne 沿着笛卡尔对松果腺作用进行概念论述的方法将以大脑为中心的模型与意识的关系比作"笛卡尔剧院。"
㊺ in the temporal sequence 在时间序列上。
㊻ theatric screening 戏剧场景。

㊼ A centered cortical neuroanatomy, with converging unidirectional channels linking node with node at successively higher levels of integration is not to be found. 许多单向通道将结点与结点相继连在一起,并会聚起来,在更高的水平上加以整合,这种中枢神经解剖并未发现。

㊽ ...that is continuous in the cortical gray matter. 在皮层的灰质中是连续扩散的。

㊾ Many neurons do not fire in the sense of generating action potentials, but instead propagate slow-wave graded potentials. 许多神经元不通过产生动作电位而兴奋,它们只是传播渐次变化的慢波电位。

㊿ Patches of neuropil are interconnected by corticosubcortical loops or by U-shaped corticocortical connections. 神经网的区域通过皮层小的回路或皮层间的 U 型连结联系起来。

㉑ ...by intracarotid amobarbital 在颈动脉注射阿米妥。

㉒ Neurophysiology has resoundingly confirmed the long-standing localizationist viewpoint that the cerebral neural network is differentiated in its various parts so as to implement different mental operations. 神经生理学一再维护长期以来的定位观点,认为皮层的神经网络的各个部分是分化的,以便执行不同的心理操作。

㉓ the lateral interaction of unrelated processors 无关加工器之间的侧向交互作用。

㉔ in normative studies 在标准的研究中。

㉕ the functional cerebral distance principle 功能性皮层距离原则。

㉖ This "penetrability" of modules to each others' influences is consistent with a parallel neuronal architecture. 这种模块间相互的渗透性影响和神经元的并行结构是一致的。

㉗ at a node downstream (在大脑)一个最终结点上。

㉘ Abandoning this model implies binding at a distance, probably by repetitive interaction between complementary representation. 放弃这种模型意味着在各种辅助表征之间可能要通过反复的相互作用来实现远距离的结合。

(59) dominant focus　优势灶。

(60) I have suggested that at any time in the awake individual's brain there is a dominant focus of patterned neural activity that underlies the phenomenal experience of that moment, the momentarily dominate "draft" of the "multiple drafts" that in rapid succession constitute the ostensibly continuous "stream" of everchanging consciousness. 我认为在一个处于觉醒状态下的个体的大脑中,每时每刻都有一个神经活动模式的优势灶来作为那一时刻体验到的经验的物质基础。许多神经信息中短暂的优势兴奋流快速的相继更替就形成了表面上连续的和不断变化的意识流。

(61) Whatever subset of currently active cell assemblies participates in this dominant focus determines what content is represented in awareness and is related to the self (and later available to recollection). 当前活跃的细胞群中的哪个子细胞群进入优势灶,决定了什么样的内容能够在意识中得到表征,并与自我发生联系(而且以后可被提取出来)。

(62) Subsidiary clusters of entrained representation　与表征有关的许多辅助性群集。

(63) Thus subjectivity depends on patterned neural activity that is widely and variable dispersed over the cerebral cortex. 主观性取决于在大脑皮层广泛传播而不断变化的神经活动模式。

(64) joint oscillation of firing　共同进入兴奋的震荡中。

(65) coordinated displacement　同等的替换。

(66) Does volume oscillation at multiple simultaneous frequencies implement this nested complex of relationships? 是同时在多种频率上的大量振荡形成了这种相互嵌套的复杂联系吗?

㊅⃝ ...in the microtime to fractions of a second 在几亿分之一秒至几分之一秒这样的短暂时间里。

㊆⃝ ...consistent with the bidirectinality of corticocortical connection. 和大脑皮层中联系的双向性相一致。

练 习

1. 判断正误
(1) If consciousness is a separate product, it should be separable from the neural activity of the brain.
(2) In an information-processing sequence, each input serves as output to the next processor.
(3) The adaptive implications of rare combinations of contingencies can therefore be explored without multitrial learning.
(4) Corresponding to this massively parallel anatomy is a parallel neuropsychology.
(5) In order to contribute to awareness, representations must be adequately activated.

2. 英译汉
(1) Consciousness should be demonstrable in isolation, and brain activity and information-processing should proceed unaltered in the absence of consciousness.
(2) What, then, are the necessary and sufficient conditions for any item of information that is represented in terms of neuronal activity to contribute to the construction of the phenomenal present?
(3) They may instead characterize a particular stage in the information-processing sequence, or they may share some adaptively important contextual attribute.
(4) The field of conscious awareness imposes no restrictions on the

types of representations that contribute to it.
(5) Having its contents contribute to awareness does not preclude a representation from modifying response predispositions. But it also enables the individual to evaluate a single in context, in case its adaptive implication is context dependent.

3. 词汇与短语

Fill in the blanks with the proper words given below

characterize, perception, medium, distinct, distinctive, disperse, property, supplant, implement (v.), modify

(1) The mediator attempted to get both sides to _____ their positions.
(2) Television can be an excellent _____ for education.
(3) Donations are needed to _____ our child-care programmes.
(4) These two ideas must be kept _____ one from the other.
(5) Each rank in the army has a _____ sign to wear.
(6) A good driver must have a good _____ of distance.
(7) Groups of police were _____ all along the street where the Queen was to pass.
(8) The new baby _____ his older sister in his mother's affection.
(9) Your work is _____ by lack of attention to detail.
(10) Steel is a metal with the _____ of great strength.

4. 汉译英

(1) 以损人开始,以害己告终。(end up with)
(2) 这样大的喧闹声使人不舒服。(be consistent with)
(3) 他们因为有约在先,不能来了。(preclude from)
(4) 语言教师常从语法书中摘录例子。(extract from)
(5) 只有社会实践能产生人的认识。(give rise to)

词 汇 表

A

ablate [æb'leit] vt. 融化
abort [ə'bɔːt] vi. 异常中断的
adolescence [ˌædou'lesos] n. 青春期
affection [ə'fkeʃ(ə)n] n. 友爱,感情
afferent ['æfərənt] a. 传入的
afflict [ə'flikt] v. 折磨
affront [ə'frʌnt] v. 冒犯
agency ['eidʒənsi] n. 中介
aggregate ['ægrigeit] v. 聚集
agitation [ædʒi'teiʃ(ə)n] n. 兴奋
agnosticism [æg'nɔstisizəm] n. 不可知论
altruism ['æltruiz(ə)m] n. 利他主义
amine ['eimiːn] n. 胺
amenable [ə'miːnəb(ə)l] a. 服从的
amnesic [æm'nizik] a. 健忘的
amplify ['æmplifai] vt. 放大
anemia [ə'niːmiə] n. 贫血
anatomical [ˌænə'tɔmik(ə)l] a. 解剖学的
anatomist [ə'nætəmaiz] n. 解剖师,解剖学家
ancillary [æn'siləri] a. 补助的
anecdotical [ˌænek'dɔtikəl] a. 轶话的

annotation [ˌænouˈteiʃən] *n*. 注解
anon [əˈnɔn] *adv*. 不久
antecedent [ˌæntiˈsiːdənt] *a*. 先前的
antipathy [ænˈtipəθi] *n*. 反感
antithesis [ænˈtiθəsis] *n*. 对立面
apathetic [æpəˈθetik] *a*. 缺乏兴趣的
appellation [æpəˈleiʃ(ə)n] *n*. 名称
apperception [ˌæpə(ː)ˈsepʃən] *n*. 知觉
approximation [əprɔksiˈmeiʃ(ə)n] *n*. 接近
aptitude [ˈæptitjuːd; ˈæptitud] *n*. 学能, 性向
array [əˈrei] *n*. 排列
articulation [ɑːtikjuˈleiʃʌ] *n*. 发音
artifact [ˈɑːtifækt] *n*. 人造物
ascertainment [ˌæsəˈtəinmənt] *n*. 探查
assess [əˈses] *vt*. 评价
atrabiliar *a*. 沉闷
auditory [ˈɔːditəri] *a*. 听觉的
auxiliary [ɔːgˈziliəri] *a*. 辅助的
availability [əˌveləˈbiləti] *n*. 可用性

B

bilateral [baiˈlætərəl] *a*. 双边的, 双侧的
bizarre [biˈzɑː(r)] *a*. 古怪的
blandishment [ˈblændiʃmənt] *n*. 奉承
bluffer [blʌfə] *n*. 虚张声势者
boisterous [ˈbɔistərəs] *a*. 喧闹的
bottleneck [ˈbɔtlnek] *n*. 瓶颈
brainstem [breinˈstem] *n*. 脑干

bravado [brə'vɑːdəu] *n*. 虚张声势
brevity ['breviti] *n*. 简短
burlesqued [bɜːˈlesk] *n*. 可笑的
bulk [bʌlk] *n*. 体积
butt [bʌt] *n*. 笑柄

C

calculus ['kælkjuləs] *n*. 微积分
calenture ['kæləntjuə] *n*. 热病
callow ['kæləu] *a*. 未长成羽毛的
candid ['kændid] *a*. 无偏见的
caricature [kærikə'tjuə] *n*. 漫画
carousal [kə'rɑnzəl] *n*. 喧闹的宴会
casuistry ['kæʒiuistri] *n*. 诡辩
cataclysmic [ˌkætəˈklizmik] *a*. 洪水
cataract ['kætərækt] *n*. 大瀑布
cellular ['seljulə] *a*. 细胞的
centripetal ['sen'tripitəl] *a*. 向心的
cephalad ['sefəlæd] *adv*. 向头部地
cerebral ['seribrəl] *a*. 脑的
chemotherapy [kiːməu'θerəpi] *n*. 化学疗法
chivalry ['ʃiv(ə)lri] *n*. 武士
chronological [krɔnə'lɔdʒik(ə)] *a*. 按年代顺序排列
circuity [səːˈkjuː(ː)iti] *n*. 线路
clinical ['klinik(ə)l] *a*. 临床的
cleavage ['kliːvidʒ] *n*. 分裂
clog [klɔg] *v*. 堵塞
coadjutor [kou'ædʒutə] *n*. 助手

coalesce [kəuə'les] v. 结合
colliculus 丘的
colloquial [kə'ləukwiəl] a. 口语的
congenial [kən'dʒi:niəl] a. 适宜的
connective [kə'nəktiv] n. 连接词
connote [kə'nəut] v. 言外之意, 暗示
consecutive [kən'sekjutiv] a. 连贯的
consensus [kən'sensəs] n. 一致意见
consonant ['kɔnsənənt] n. 辅音
constituent [kən'stitjuənt] n. 选举者
contaminate [kən'tæmineit] v. 污染
contingency [kən'tindʒənsi] n. 可能性
contractility [ˌkɔntræk'tiliti] n. 缩小
contradistinguish [ˌkɔntrədis'tiŋgwiʃ] v. 对照
contralesional a. 损伤对侧的
contrariwise [kən'treəriwaiz; 'kɔntreriwaiz] adv. 反之
contravene [ˌkɔntrə'vi:n] v. 抵触
convivial [kən'viviəl] a. 欢乐
convulsion [kən'vʌkʃ(ə)n] n. 震动
corollary [kə'rɔləri] n. 必然的结果
corroborate [kə'rɔbəreit] vt. 确证
cortex ['kɔ:teks] n. 脑皮层
cortical ['kɔ:tikəl] a. 皮质的
counteract [ˌkauntə'rækt] v. 抵触
covert ['kʌvət; 'kəuvɜ:rt] a. 隐蔽的
counterintuitive a. 违反直觉的
culminate ['kʌlmineit] v. 达到顶点
curb [kɜ:b] n. 控制

D

daunt [dɔːnt] v. 沮丧
dawdle ['dɔːd(ə)l] v. 混日子
decomposable [ˌdiːkəm'pəuzəbl] a. 可分解
decorum [di'kɔːrəm] n. 礼貌
deducible [di'djuːzəbl] a. 可推论的
degradation [ˌdegrə'deiʃən] n. 降级
delimit [di'limit] vt. 划界
delinquent [di'liŋkwənt] a. 有过失的
demarcation [diːmɑː'keiʃ(ə)n] n. 划分
denotation [ˌdinou'teiʃən] n. 指示
denounce [di'nauns] vt. 公开指责
designate ['dezignət] vt. 指明
despondency [dis'pɔndənsi] n. 失望
diagnosis [dziəg'nəusis] n. 诊断
diathesis [dai'æθisis] n. 素质
digestion [di'dʒests(ə)n] n. 消化力
digress [dai'gres] v. 离题
dimension [di'menʃ(ə)n] n. 维度
discrete [di'skriːt] a. 离散的
discredit [dis'kredit] n. 怀疑
disentangle [ˌdisin'tæŋgl] vt. 解脱
dispersed [dis'pəːs] a. 分离的
disphoria n. 不快乐
disposition [dispə'ziʃ(ə)n] n. 部署
dissection [di'sekʃən] n. 解剖
distractability [distræk'biliti] n. 转移注意

divine [di'vain] a. 神的
docility [dou'siliti] n. 顺从
dopamine n. 多巴胺
dorsal ['dɔːs(ə)l] a. 背的
dovetailing ['dʌvteil] vt. 吻合
dualistic [ˌdjuːə'lisik] a. 二元的
dunce [dʌns] n. 傻瓜
dwindle ['dwind(ə)l] v. 缩小
dysfunction [dis'fʌnkʃ(ə)n] n. 功能失调
dysentery ['disəntri; 'disənten] n. 痢疾

E

effusive [i'fjuːsiv] a. 感情流露
effeminate [i'feminət] a. 娇气的
egoist ['eɡouist] a. 自我主义的
elaborate [i'læbərət] a. 精细的
elasticity [ˌilæs'tisiti] n. 弹性
electrode [i'lektrəud] n. 电极
elucidate [j'luːsideit] vt. 说明
emanate ['eməneit] vi. 散发
embryo ['embriəu] n. 胚胎
emulate ['emjuleit] n. 仿效
encroach [in'krəutʃ] vi 侵占
engender [in'dʒendə(r)] v. 造成
enunciate [i'nʌnsieit] v. 阐明
ephebos [i'fiːbəs] n. 古希腊男青年
epidemic [epi'demik] a. 流行的
epiphenomenon [ˌepifi'nɔminən] n. 附带现象

episodic [epi'sɔdik] a. 插话的
epistemology [ipisti'mɔlədʒi] n. 认识论
equipotential n. 等位的
equilibrium [iːkwi'libriəm] n. 平衡
euphoria [juː'fɔriə] n. 欢快
exalt [ig'zɔːlt] v. 普升
excretion [ik'skriːʃ(ə)n] n. 排泄
exempt [ig'zempt] v. 免除
exhilarate [ig'ziləreit] vt. 使高兴
exorbitant [ig'zɔːbitənt] a. 过度的
exuberance [ig'zjuːbərenʃ] n. 丰富

F

fad ['fæd] n. 时尚
filter ['filt,(r)] n. 过滤器
fixate ['fik'set] v. 注视
finality ['fai'næliti] n. 结尾
fledgling ['fledʒliŋ] n. 初具雏形的
floodgate ['flʌdʒeit] n. 水门
forestall [fɔː'stɔːl] v. 抢先说
formidable ['fɔːmidəb(ə)l] a. 可怕的
forte ['fɔːtei] n. 拿手戏
fovea ['fouviə] n. 小凹
frivolity ['fri'vɔliti] n. 轻浮
fuse [fjuːz] v. 融合

G

gainsay [gein'sei] v. 否定

gating [geitiŋ] n. 闸门
glandular ['glændjulə(r)] a. 腺的
giggle ['gig(ə)l] v. 傻笑
gourmet ['guəmei] n. 美食家
graphemic ['græfmik] a. 字形的
gridiron ['gridaiən] n. 烤架
gross [grəus] a. 总的
grovel ['grov(ə)l] vi. 趴
guillotine ['gilətiːn] n. 断头台
gustatory ['gʌstətəri] a. 味觉的

H

hallucination [həluːsi'neiʃ(ə)n] n. 幻觉
haphazard [hæp'hæzəd] n. 偶然的事
havoc ['hævək] n. 大破坏
hemlock ['hemlɔk] n. 毒芹
hemisphere ['hemisfiə(e)] n. 右半脑
heredity [hi'rediti] n. 遗传
heterogenerous ['hetərou'dʒiːnjəs] a. 异质的
hieroglyphic [haiərəglifik] n. 象形文字
hilarious [hi'leəriəs] a. 欢闹的
hitchhiking [hitʃ'haikiŋ] n. 搭乘
homogeneous [hɔməu'daiːniəs] a. 同类的
homunculus [hou'mʌŋkjuləs] n. 侏儒
hoot [huːt] vi. 叫
hop [hɔp] v. 跳
hydrogen ['haidrədʒ(ə)n] n. 氢
hyperemia [haipə'riːmiə] n. 充血

hypertrophy [hai'pɜːtrəfi] a. 过度增大的
hypnotism ['hipnətiz(ə)m] n. 催眠术
hypochondria [haipə'kɔndriə] n. 忧郁证
hypothesis [hai'pɔθəsis] n. 假设

I

impair [im'peə(r)] v. 削弱
implement ['impliment] v. 执行
impudence ['impjudəns] n. 轻率
impuger n. 指示者
inalienable [in'eiliənəb(ə)l] a. 不能剥夺的
inception [in'sepʃ(ə)n] n. 起初
incorrigible [in'kɔridʒib(ə)l; in'kɔːridʒib(əl] a. 无可救药的
induction [in'dʌkʃ(ə)n] n. 感应的
inebriation [iˌniːbri'eiʃən] n. 醉
inert [i'nɜːt] a. 惰性的
infantile ['infəntail] a. 婴儿般的
ingenuity [in'dʒinjuːiti] n. 机灵的
inheritance [in'herit(ə)ns()] n. 遗传
inhibitor [in'hibitə] n. 抑制者
inlet ['inlet] n. 入口
instigate ['instigeit] v. 鼓动的
intermission [ˌintə'miʃ(ə)n] n. 间断
intestine [in'testin] n. 肠
introspection [intrə'spekʃ(ə)n] n. 内省
intoxicant [in'tɔksikənt] a. 使醉的
intractable [in'træktəb(ə)l] a. 难处理的
intrinsic [in'trinsik] a. 固有的

inveterate [in'vetərək] a. 根深的
ipsilesional a. 损伤侧的

J

jejuneness [dʒi'dʒuːnis] n. 幼稚
jerk [dʒɜːk] vt. 急推
jocularity [ˌdʒɔkju'læriti] n. 滑稽
judicious [dʒuː'diʃəs] a. 明智的
juncture ['dʒʌŋktʃə(r)] n. 接合点
juvenile ['dʒuːvənɑil] n. 青少年
juxtaposition [ˌdʒʌkstəpə'ziʃən] n. 并列

K

kaleidoscopic [kəlaidə'skɔpikˌ] a. 万花筒似的
kinship ['kinʃip] n. 血缘关系
kinetic [ki'netik] a. 动力学的
krypton ['kriptɔn] n. 氪

L

languid ['læŋgwid] a. 无力的
languor ['læŋgə(r)] n. 衰弱无力
latch [lætʃ] n. 门栓
latent ['leitənt] a. 潜伏的
lavishly [læviʃli] ad. 浪费
legitimate [li'dʒitimət] a. 合法的
lesion ['liːʒ(ə)n] n. 损害
liability [laiə'biliti] n. 责任
loath [ləuθ] a. 不情愿的

lobe [ləub] *n*. 脑叶
locomotion [ləukə'məuʃ(ə)n] *n*. 运动
locus ['ləukəs] *n*. 地点
loiter ['lɔitə(r)] *v*. 闲荡
lurid ['ljuərid] *a*. 苍白的

M

magnetoencephalography 脑磁图描记
maim [meim] *vt*. 使残废
mania ['meiniə] *n*. 狂躁
manic ['mɔænik] *n*. 躁狂者
maze [meiz] *n*. 迷宫
maternity [mə'tɜːniti] *n*. 母性
mediate ['miːdieit] *v*. 调节
membrane *n*. 膜
menagerie [mi'nædʒəri] *n*. 动物展览
menstruation [menstru'eiʃ(ə)n] *n*. 月经
mesmerism ['mezmərizəm] *n*. 催眠术
metabolic [ˌmetə'bɔlik] *a*. 新陈代谢的
metaphysician [ˌmetəfi'ziʃən] *n*. 形而上学
metaphor ['metəfə(r)] *n*. 暗喻
mimic ['mimik] *v*. 模仿
monopolize [mə'nɔpəlaiz] *vt*. 垄断
momentary ['məuməntəri; 'məumənteri] *a*. 瞬间的
momentum [məu'mentəm] *n*. 动力
morbid ['mɔːbid] *a*. 病态的
morphology [mɔː'fɔlədʒi] *n*. 形态学
mortify ['mɔːtifai] *vt*. 克服

multiplication [mʌltipili'keiʃ(ə)n] n. 增加
multitudinous [mʌlti'tju:dinəs] a. 大量的

N

nativistic ['neitivistik] a. 先天的
nausea ['nɔːsiə;'nɔːʒə] n. 恶心
necropsy ['nekrɔpsi] n. 验尸
nestle ['nes(ə)l] vi. 舒服地坐
neurone ['njuərəun;'njuərənur] n. 神经元
neuropsychological [ˌnjuərou'saiələdʒikəl] n. 神经心理学
norepinephrine ['nɔːˌrepi'nefrin] n. 去甲肾上腺素
normative ['nɔːmətiv] a. 标准化
nostril ['nɔstril] n. 鼻孔
notwithstanding [nɔtwið'stændiŋ] adv. 虽然

O

obituary [ə'bitjuən;ə'bitʃueri] n. 讣告
obscuration [ˌɔbskjuə'reiʃən] n. 昏暗
obstreperous [əb'strepərəs] a. 任性的
obviate ['ɔbvieit] vt. 消除
occipital [ɔk'sipitl] a. 枕部的
octave ['ɔktiv] n. 八度音
onrush ['ɔnrʌʃ] n. 突进
ontogeny [ɔn'tɔdʒəni] n. 个体发生
opaque [əu'peik] a. 不透明的
outcrop ['autkrɔp] n. 露出地面的岩石
outlive [əut'liv] v. 活得长
outstrip [əut'strip] v. 超过

P

palate ['pælət] n. 上腭
paradoxical [ˌpærə'dɔksikəl] a. 荒谬的
paralysis [pə'rælisis] n. 瘫痪
parietal [pə'rait(ə)l] a. 腔壁的
paroxysm ['pærəksiz(ə)m] n. 发作
parsimonious [ˌpɑːsi'məuniəs] a. 节省的
pathological [pæθə'lɔdʒik(ə)l] a. 病理的
pep [pep] n. 活力
perennial [pə'reniəl] a. 终年的
peripherally [pə'rifərəli] ad. 外围的
permeability [ˌpəːmjə'biliti] n. 渗透地
peristaltic [ˌperi'stæltik] a. 蠕动的
pertinent ['pəːtinənt; 'pəːtənənt] a. 有关的
perverted [pəː'vəːtid] a. 不正当的
phylogeny [fai'bdʒini] n. 发展史
polemic [pə'lemik] a. 争论的
posterior [pə'stiəriə(r)] a. 较晚的
preconscious ['priːkɔnʃəs] a. 前意识的
precursor [priː'kəːə(r)] n. 影响
predisposition [ˌpriːdispə'ziʃn] n. 易感体质
predominate [pri'dɔmineit] vt. 控制
prefrontal ['pri'frʌntl] a. 前额的
premises ['premis] n. 前提
prestidigitation ['prestiˌdidʒiteiʃən] n. 变戏法
presumption [pri'zʌmpʃ(ə)n] n. 假定
privation [prai'veiʃ(ə)n] n. 缺乏

priori ['prɑaiəri] n. 先验的
prostitute ['prɔstitjuːt; 'prɔstituːt] n. 妓女
protocol ['prəutəkɔl; 'prəutəkɔːl] n. 协议
provisional [prə'viʒən(ə)l] a. 临时的
proximate ['prɔksimət] a. 最近的
psychogenesis [ˌsaikou'dʒenisis] n. 心理发生
psychotherapy [saikəu'θerəpi; sikəu'θerəpi] n. 心理治疗
puberty ['pjuːbəti] n. 青春期
purportedly ['pəːpətidli] ad. 据称
putative ['pjuːtətiv] a. 推断
psychiatric [saiki'ætrik] a. 精神病的

Q

quale ['kweiliː] n. 可感觉的特征
quibble ['kwib(ə)l] vt. 诡辩
quiescent [kwai'esənt] a. 静止的

R

ravel ['rævəl] vt. 使纠缠
rebus ['riːbəs] n. 猜字画谜
recuperative [ri'kjuːpərətiv] a. 使恢复的
reduplication [riˌdjuːpli'keiʃən] n. 复本
reposition [riːpə'ziʃ(ə)n] n. 重新配价
requisite ['rekwizit] a. 需要的
reside [ri'zəid] vi. 居住
respiration [respə'reiʃ(ə)] n. 呼吸
retarded [ri'tɑːdid] a. 迟钝的
retention [ri'tenʃ(ə)n] n. 保持力

reticular [ri'tikjulə] *a*. 网状的
retina ['retinə;'vetənə] *n*. 视网膜
robust [rəu'bʌst] *a*. 精力充沛的
revoke [ri'vəuk] *vt*. 撤回

S

salient ['seliənt] *a*. 易见的
sanction ['sæɔkʃ(ə)n] *n*. 批准
satirize ['sætiraiz] *v*. 讽刺
scalp [skælp] *v*. 头皮
secretion [si'kri:ʃ(ə)] *n*. 分泌物
semantic [si'mæntik] *a*. 语义的
sensuality [sensju'æliti] *n*. 好色
simultaneous [siməl'teiniəs;saiməl'teiniəs] *a*. 同时的
skeletal ['skelitl] *a*. 骨骼的
sluggishness ['slʌgiʃnis] *n*. 行动迟缓
slumber ['slʌmbə(r)] *n*. 睡眠
snuff [snʌf] *n*. 用鼻子吸
sober ['səubə(r)] *a*. 镇定的
spatial ['speiʃ(ə)l] *a*. 空间的
spermatozoon [spɛːmətə'zəuən] *n*. 精子
spinal ['spain(ə)] *a*. 脊骨的
stagnation [stæg'neiʃən] *n*. 停滞
stigmata *n*. 特征
stint [stint] *v*. 节省
striata *n*. 纹状体
subcortical *a*. 皮层下的
supposition [sʌpə'ziʃ(ə)n] *n*. 假定

supervene [suːpəˈviːn;sjuːpəˈviːn] v. 接着发生
surge [sɛːdʒ] n. 震荡
synapse [ˈsainæps;ˈsinæps] n. 突触
syntax [ˈsintæks] n. 句法的
synthesis [ˈsinθisis] n. 综合

T

tactile [ˈtæktail;ˈtæktəl] n. 触觉
tantamount [ˈtæntəmaunt] a. 等价
taunt [tɔːnt] v. 嘲笑
taxonomy [tækˈsɔnəmi] n. 分类法
teleology [teliˈɔlədʒi] n. 目的论
tern [təːn] n. 三人一组
testimony [ˈtestiməni;ˈtestiməuni] n. 陈述
thalamus [ˈθæləməs] n. 丘脑
thither [ˈðiðə(r)] adv. 到那边
threshold [ˈθreʃəuld] n. 阈限
thrush [θrʌf] n. 鸫
trait [treit] n. 特质
trance [trɑːns;træns] n. 出神
transduced [trænzˈdiusid] a. 传递的
transient [ˈtræsiənt,ˈtrɑːnsiət;trænʃnt] a. 短暂的
transitivity [ˈtrænsitiviti] n. 传递性
transmission [trænzˈmiʃ(ə)n] n. 发放
transmitter [trænzˈmitə(r)] n. 递质
trestle [ˈtres(ə)l] n. 高脚架
treatise [ˈtriːtis] n. 论文
truant [ˈtruːənt] n. 逃避

U

utilitarianism [jutili'teəriənzi(ə)m] *n*. 功利主义

V

vantage ['vɑːntidʒ] *n*. 优势
ventral ['ventr(ə)l] *a*. 腹部的
verdict ['vɜːdikt] *n*. 判断
vermicular [vəˈmikjulə] *a*. 蠕动的
viable ['vaiəb(ə)l] *a*. 可行的
vicious ['viʃəs] *a*. 恶的
vindicate ['vindikeit] *vt*. 维护
vintage ['vintidʒ] *n*. 收获
vitalism ['vaitəlizm] *n*. 生机论，泛灵论
vitality [vai'tæliti] *n*. 活力
vivisection [vivi'sekʃ(ə)nl] *n*. 活体解剖
visceral ['visərəl] *a*. 内脏的
volition [vəˈliʃ(ə)n; vəuˈliʃ(ə)n] *n*. 意志
voluptuous [vəˈlʌptuəs] *a*. 奢侈的
vowel ['vauəl] *n*. 元音

W

waggish ['wægiʃ] *a*. 滑稽的
wan [wɔn] *a*. 苍白的
wane [wein] *vi*. (月亮)亏；减少
wax [wæks] *vi*. (月亮)渐满；增加

练习参考答案

1. Association of Ideas

1. 回答问题
(1) When our senses are awake, we receive sensations of our sense, the eye, the ear, for example. After we have got sensations we might have received the excitement of our former sensations, which is called ideas. If we see a horse, that is a sensation. Immediately we think of his master, that is an idea. The idea of his master makes us think of his office, he is a minister of state: that is another idea. A sensation excites us to think of its idea. Its idea arouses us to think of another idea. Sensations excite ideas and ideas follow ideas incessantly. The process always goes on.
(2) The three characteristics of association: permanent, certainty and facility. The causes of strengh in association are vividness and frequency.
(3) They are the synchronous order and the successive order.
(4) In the successive order of ideas, that which precedes, is called the suggesting idea, and that which succeeds, the suggested idea.

2. 判断正误
(1) F. The synchronous order is the order in space.
(2) T.
(3) F. My idea of a man is the most complex of all, including not

only color, and shape, and voice, but the whole class of events in which I have observed him either the agent or the patient.

(4) T.

(5) T.

3. 选词填空

(1) by analogy

(2) committed

(3) apt

(4) lengthen

(5) with regard to

(6) endeavor

(7) preceding

(8) successive

4. 句型模拟

(1) They are financed to a great extent by advertising revenue.

(2) In consequence of his laziness, he was fired.

5. 英译汉

(1) 感觉的发生是依照我们所谓自然界物体彼此间所具有的顺序，这是容易明白的；要把对于这种顺序的知识，精益求精，那是一切自然科学的任务。

(2) 在某些时候，我们的观念会产生许多联想，而在某些时候就不那么容易。这一点可以在我们运用自如的语言和我们掌握得不熟练的语言这一例子中得到明显的解释。

(3) 联想的出现在一些时候具有更大的确定性，而在另一些时候则具有较少的确定性。

6. 汉译英

(1) The old calendar is still adhered to in many country places.
(2) We will have to adapt this building to the needs of the old people.
(3) I have derived a great deal of benefit from his advice.
(4) Misfortunes came in quick succession.
(5) Weeds were springing up everywhere.

2. The Composition of Mind

1. 回答问题

(1) Feelings and relations between feelings.
(2) The three essential characters are as follows: First, each feeling occupies a large place to give it a perceivable individuality. Secondly, each feeling has its individuality marked off from adjacent portions of consciousness by qualitative contrasts. Lastly, each feeling appears to be homogeneous when introspectively contemplated.
(3) A relational feeling is a portion of consciousness inseparable into parts, and a feeling is a portion of consciousness that admits imaginary division into like parts which are related to one another in sequence or coexistence. A feeling proper is either made up of like parts that occupy time, or it is made up of like parts that occupy space, or both. In any case, a feeling proper is an aggregate of related like parts, while a relational feeling is undecomposable.

2. 判断正误

(1) T.
(2) T.
(3) F. The multitudinous states of consciousness yielded by vision, are above all others sharp in their mutual limitations.

3．选词填空
(1) inseparable
(2) intensity
(3) in common
(4) feeling
(5) sensation
(6) provisional
(7) marked
(8) unite

4．英译汉
(1) 把一个关系所牵连的事项除去,这个关系就没有了。固然,分析到最后一步时,我们所谓的关系本来也就是一种体验——伴随一个显著的体验转移到另一个邻接的显著体验的瞬间体验。
(2) 意识全局有一种相互依赖,使得体验所占据的在意识内看得出的区域,离开牵和它的关系,就不能有个性,也像这些关系离开它所联系的体验也不能有个性一样。
(3) 我们将要看到由于发生感觉的神经分布不同,跟着就有感觉与感觉间的某些性质上的不同;并且这些性质上的不同,是随着这些神经近外面或近内中的程度而定的。
(4) 这样说来,这种变化或震动的程度就是关系彼此的区别的最后基础。这种变化也就是对两相接近的状态间的差异程度的体验。

5. 汉译英

(1) It is absurd to differentiate between pupils according to their family background.
(2) He is cleverer than you in proportion to his years.
(3) The party is moderate in views.
(4) He was silent in default of any excuse.

3. Habit

1. 回答问题

(1) An impulse which originally spread its effects over the whole body, or at least over many of its movable parts, is determined to a single definite organ.
(2) According to Dr. Maudsley, when automatic acts are accomplished with comparatively little weariness, the conscious effort of the will soon produces exhaustion.
(3) The order in which he brushes his hair or teeth has something to do with the muscular contraction. In action grown habitual, what instigates each new muscular contraction to take place in its appointed order is the sensation occasioned by the muscular contraction just finished.

2. 判断正误

(1) T.
(2) F. The impulse is determined to the motion of the hand and of the single finger.

(3) F. It is impossible for an individual to realize how much he owes to its automatic agency until disease has impaired its functions.

(4) T.

(5) F. Our lower centers certainly show knowledge by their "surprise" if the objects are altered so as to oblige the movements to be made in a different way.

3. 选词填空

(1) awakened

(2) diminish

(3) economize

(4) impaired

(5) instigated

(6) occasioned

(7) overflow

(8) rehearse

4. 句型模拟

(1) No sooner had he gone to sleep than the telephone rang once more.

(2) If only she had had more courage!

5. 英译汉

(1) 习惯简化了人为了达到一个特别的结果所要做的动作，而且习惯也使动作更准确、并减少疲劳。

(2) 人类生来有个倾向，就是他想做的事情比他神经中枢已有现成准备的事情还多。

(3) 这个过程很像肠子里从上到下的波浪式的蠕动一样。

6. 汉译英

(1) On account of the weather, the match was postponed.

(2) She is a brilliantly accomplished singer.

(3) The situation was considered with a view to its causes and its effect.

(4) Decision is a quality requisite to a commander.

(5) In case of floods, the wall was built along the river.

4. Adolescence

1. 回答问题

(1) Because the heart and arteries in this stage are rapidly increasing in size. Nutritive activities are greatly increased. The temperature of the body is probably a trifle higher.

(2) Because the teens are at the age of natural inebriation. They are facing a natural impulse to experience hot and perfervid psychic states and they are characterized by emotion.

(3) Because the fluctuations of mood are rapid and incessant. Tears and laughter are in close juxtaposition.

2. 判断正误

(1) F. Although we do not know precisely the relation between blood pressure and the strong instinct to tingle and glow, some correlation may safely be postulated.

(2) T.

(3) T.

(4) T.

(5) F. The fact that elation precedes and depression comes as a reaction in the majority of cases is not yet clear.
(6) F. Youth fear inadequacy of its power to cope with the world.

3. 选词填空
(1) elation
(2) exuberance
(3) prone
(4) despondency
(5) convivial
(6) melancholy
(7) hilarious
(8) factitious

4. 汉译英
(1) Every man is liable to error.
(2) The firm distributes its salary on the principle of equal pay for equal work.
(3) The contract specifies red tiles, not slates, for the roof.
(4) Acquaintance has developed into friendship.
(5) I am provoked at his impudence.

5. Early Empiricism, Naturalism, Materialism

1. 回答问题
(1) He used the method of observation and induction.
(2) The primary qualities are those which reproduce essentially external conditions — extension, resistance, movement. These are the qualities by reason of which the external object is what it

is as independent of perception. The secondary qualities are those in which the process of perception itself has a part — such as color, taste, position.

(3) To Locke, reflection is largely a passive power; it was reflection upon the course or flow of our ideas, not reflection as itself determining this flow or course to be what it is.

(4) Locke first used the term, and what's more he thought that the actual flow of ideas is due to the laws of association.

(5) First, the distinction between sensation and reflection, sense and reason, was abolished, even in the functional form of it that Lock's theory of mental "power" had retained. Second, a thorough-going "associationism", essentially mechanical in character, took the place of Locke's Cartesian theory of self-consciousness. The synthetic activity of the mind was replaced by the association of ideas.

(6) By inner impressions, the author refers to those of the inner sphere itself, such as pleasures, pains, efforts, etc., and outer impressions were those received by the senses and having the imprint of externality.

2. 判断正误

(1) F. It was Locke, not Hume that distinguishes the two terms.
(2) T.
(3) F. The ideas of reflection are not innate.
(4) F. The course of ideas — their flow, connection, composition — was ruled by the principle of association.
(5) F. It was Hume, not Locke that raised the idea.

3. 选词填空

(1) vindicate
(2) slumbering
(3) abolished
(4) revealed
(5) proceeded
(6) pursued
(7) transferred
(8) substituted

4. 句型模拟

(1) It is essential that he should be prepared for this.
(2) Judged by the look on his face, he doesn't think much of our local wine.

5. 汉译英

(1) Each speaker was limited in time — two minutes.
(2) The remark has been ascribed to Confucius.
(3) He persistently asserted his right to a share in the money.
(4) The deaths of both popes were attributed to heart attacks.
(5) It is impossible to conceive of anything better.
(6) I don't wish to reflect on your sincerity.

6. The Postulates of a Structural Psychology

1. 判断正误

(1) T.
(2) F. The task of experimental psychologists is to do a vivisection which produce structural results.

(3) F. We are often told that our treatment of feeling and emotion, of reasoning, of the self is very inadequate.
(4) F. The phrase "association of ideas" denote either the structural complex, the associated sensation group, or the functional process of recognition and recall, the associating of formation to formation.
(5) F. The author doesn't think that anyone who has followed the course of the experimental method can doubt that the main interest has lain in morphological analysis, rather than in ascertainment of function.
(6) T.
(7) F. The morphological study of mind serves to enforce and sustain the thesis that psychology is a science, and not a province of metaphysics.
(8) T.

2. 词汇与短语
(1) in the long run
(2) the tangle of
(3) touching on
(4) comprises
(5) digress
(6) are subject to
(7) prejudiced
(8) inquire into

3. 句型模拟
(1) I don't teach because teaching is easy for me. Nor do I teach be-

cause I think I know answers to many questions.

(2) So far this month we have covered ten lessons in the grammar book.

4. 汉译英

(1) They naturally fall into three classes.

(2) Scientists discover new provinces of inquiry.

(3) He is a person who remains in his proper sphere.

(4) The escaped prisoner is still at large.

(5) You'll get into trouble if you continue to behave without regard to decency.

6. 英译汉

(1) 正如实验心理学大部分关注的是结构问题,而古代和现代的"描述"心理学则主要是致力于机能问题。

(2) 我们一定要记住实验心理学是通过反抗上个世纪的机能心理学才出现的。

(3) 个体发育心理学,是儿童个体及青春期的心理学,目前是一个具有广泛兴趣的科目,而且拥有自己的大量文献资料。

7. The Reflex Arc Concept in Psychology

1. 回答问题

(1) The reflex arc is a patchwork of disjointed parts, a mechanical conjunction of unallied processes. What is needed is that the principle underlying the idea of the reflex arc as the fundamental psychical unity shall react into and determine that values of its constitutive factors.

(2) The example suggests that the sensation of light is a stimulus to

the grasping as a response, the burn resulting is a stimulus to withdrawing the hand as response. It is a rough practical way of representing the process.
(3) First the receiving consciousness, the stimulus for example, a loud, unexpected sound. Second, the attention involuntarily drawn, the registering element and third, the muscular reaction following upon the sound, flight from fancied danger.
(4) Because the response can determine the stimulus as sound and as this kind of sound, of wild beast or robber, so the sound experience must persist as a value in the running, to keep it up, to control it. It is a coordination.

2. 判断正误
(1) T.
(2) F. There is a sensori-motor circuit, one with more content or value, not a substitution of a motor response for a sensory stimulus.
(3) T.
(4) T.
(5) The sound is not a mere stimulus, or mere sensation, and it is also an act, that of hearing.
(6) The sensation of sound arises from a motor response as that the running away is a response to the sound.

3. 词汇与短语
(1) term
(2) tacit
(3) unification

(4) spontaneous
(5) organic
(6) occurrence
(7) comprehensive
(8) conjunction
(9) monopolized
(10) stimulus

4. 句型模拟
(1) The misunderstanding is brought out by what may seem to be a little thing, the fact that different countries use different kinds of medical thermometers.
(2) On the contrary, in the long run it is bound to deepen the eventual economic collapse.

5. 汉译英
(1) The cause of his death was pneumonia supervening on influenza.
(2) But the next moment he had himself in control.
(3) Prior to her marriage, my mother was a nurse.
(4) In any inquiry, be careful to proceed on right principles.

8. General Characteristics of Original Tendencies

1. 回答问题
(1) The word Education refers especially to elements of science and art which are concerned with changes in man himself.
(2) The aim of education is to perpetuate some of the original connections, to eliminate some of them, and to modify or redirect others.

(3) A typical reflex, or instinct, or capacity, as a whole, includes the ability to be sensitive to a certain situation, the ability to make a certain response, and the existence of a bond or connection whereby that response is made to that situation.

2. 判断正误
(1) T.
(2) F. Man's intellect and morals, according to the author, as well as his bodily organs and movements, are in part the consequence of the nature of the embryo in the first moment of its life.
(3) F. The basis of intellect and character is this fund of unlearned tendencies, this original arrangement of the neurones in the brain.
(4) F. It is a first principle of education to utilize any individual's original nature as a means to changing him for the better — to produce in him the information, habits, powers, interests and ideals which are desirable.
(5) T.
(6) F. The original tendencies of man, however, rarely act one at time in isolation one from anther.

3. 词汇与短语
(1) components
(2) consequences
(3) perpetuate
(4) govern
(5) intense
(6) modification
(7) status

(8) abort

4. 汉译英
(1) There can be no knowledge apart from practice.
(2) His success is in part owing to luck.
(3) Wherever they went they tried to acquainted themselves with folk music.
(4) The Stock Exchange is sensitive to political disturbances.
(5) There was a complete absence of information as to how the little fellow met his death.
(6) Let each child read in terms of his own tastes and choices.

9. Unlearned Behavior: Emotion

1. 回答问题
(1) Hereditary modes of response and acquired modes of conducted in different individuals.
(2) Formulation.
(3) An Emotion is an hereditary pattern-reaction involving profound changes of the bodily mechanism as a whole, but particularly of the visceral and glandular system.
(4) There is implied the fact that the general state of the organism must be sensitive (capable of being stimulated) to this form of stimulus at the moment. This young man becomes considerable less sensitive after being happily married. It is the formulation that may seem somewhat roundabout—somewhat like saying that a stimulus is an emotional stimulus only when you get the pattern-reaction.

2. 判断正误

(1) T.

(2) F. When a child may display the reaction of fear, and the parents are at hand, or the room is well lighted, the stimulus may pass unreacted to.

(3) F. Emotions seldom appear alone.

(4) T.

(5) F. Few psychological experiments have been made upon the emotional life of the child under anything like as favorable conditions as obtain in the study of animals.

3. 词汇与短语

(1) instinctive
(2) inhabited
(3) inhibited
(4) involved
(5) reinforced
(6) stereotype
(7) speculative
(8) simultaneously

4. 汉译英

(1) In contrast to his brother, he was always considerate in his treatment of others.
(2) Our country has entered on a new period.
(3) We marked off the limits of our lots with stakes.
(4) The researches are concerned with alpha rays.

10. The Principal Instincts and the Primary Emotion of Man

1. 回答问题

(1) Each of the principal instincts conditions some one kind of emotional excitement whose quality is specific or peculiar to it; and the emotional excitement of specific quality that is the affective aspect of the operation of any one of the principal instincts may be called a primary emotion. This principle, which was enunciated in physiological psychology, proves to be of very great value when we seek to analyze the complex emotions into their primary constituents.

(2) The locomotory activities are accompanied by a characteristic complex of symptoms, which in its main features is common to man and to many of the higher animals, and which, in conjunction with the violent efforts to escape. Popular speech recognizes the connection of the emotion with the instinct that determines the movements of flight in giving them the one name 'fear'.

(3) It is the unfamiliar or strange. Whatever is totally strange, whatever is violently opposed to the accustomed and familiar, is apt to excite fear both in men and animals, if only it is capable of attracting their attention.

2. 判断正误

(1) T.

(2) F. If a similar emotion and impulse are clearly displayed in the instinctive activities of the higher animals, that fact will afford a strong presumption that the emotion and impulse in question

are primary and simple.
(3) F. Terror may involve so great a nervous disturbance, both in men and animals, as to defeat the ends of the instinct by inducing general convulsions or even death.
(4) T.
(5) F. It is easy to discover what objects and impressions were its natural excitants in primitive man.
(6) T.

3. 词汇与短语
(1) darted
(2) diversify
(3) attain
(4) exaggerate
(5) impel
(6) induce
(7) illustrated
(8) haunt

4. 句型模拟
(1) He is a child, and must be treated as such.
(2) Upon seeing her child take his first steps, she was joyful.

5. 汉译英
(1) I hope that we have brought our arguments on fundamentals to and end.
(2) I am not on terms with that set.
(3) Ideas must be expressed in the medium of words.

(4) This section should be studied in conjunction with the preceding three.

(5) He leaps a horse over a hurdle.

11. The Uses of Intelligence Tests

1. 回答问题

(1) Statistics show that between a third and half of the school children fail to progress through the grades at the expected rate.

(2) Because before an engineer constructs a railroad bridge or trestle, he studies the materials to be used, and learns by means of tests exactly the amount of strain per unit of size his materials will be able to withstand. He does not work empirically, and count upon patching up the mistakes which may later appear under the stress of actual use. The educational engineer should emulate this example. Tests and forethought must take the place of failure and patchwork.

(3) We cannot hold all children to the same standard of school progress, but we can at least prevent the kind of retardation which involves failure and the repetition of a school grade.

(4) Because the educational work of the special class must blunder along the dark without scientific diagnosis and classification of these children.

2. 判断正误

(1) T.

(2) T.

(3) T.

(4) F. The earlier methods of diagnosis caused a majority of the

higher grade defectives to be overlooked.
(5) F. The more we learn about such children, the clearer it becomes that they must be looked upon as real defectives.
(6) F. One of the most important facts concerning the use of intelligence tests is the frequent association of delinquency and mental deficiency.

3. 词汇与短语
(1) zest
(2) endowment
(3) magnitude
(4) manipulation
(5) feeble
(6) blundered
(7) retarded
(8) surveillance

4. 汉译英
(1) In spite of his good salary, he measured out every dollar needed for household expenses.
(2) He is selfish in a measure.
(3) One inventor profits from the work of others.
(4) We decided to patch up our differences and become friends again.
(5) I am glad to find myself in general accord with your views.

12. The Interpretation of Dreams

1. 判断正误

(1) F. We should clearly be led into error.
(2) F. In the case of the different elements of the dream-thoughts, a value does not persist or is disregarded in the process of dream-formation.
(3) T.
(4) T.

2．英译汉
(1) 梦的隐意与梦的显意就有如以两种不同的语言所表达的一种内容一样。
(2) 或说的更清楚些，梦的显意就是以另一种表达的形式将梦的隐意传译给我们而所采用的符号及法则，我们只有通过译作与原著的对比才能了解。
(3) 某些在梦内容中占有重要篇幅的部分在梦思中却完全不是那么一回事。
(4) 在这些梦里我们不得不相信转移的存在。
(5) 但梦仍可能排斥这些经过特别地强调并且强烈地增援的单元，而在梦的内容中采纳其他只受到强烈地增援的意念。
(6) 这种我们所假设的心理过程是真正梦的工作当中的最重要的一环，我们称它为梦的转移。

3．词汇与短语
(1) represents
(2) resistance
(3) replaced
(4) plausible
(5) ascribe
(6) impose

(7) condensation
(8) distortion

4. 句型模拟
(1) He himself didn't realize to what extent his point of view had changed.
(2) On the one hand you accept her presents, on the other hand, you are rude to the whole family. What really is your attitude to them?

5. 汉译英
(1) The racial problem is in essence a class problem.
(2) I am in the habit of brushing my teeth twice daily.
(3) New arts have been born in the course of the history of man.
(4) He threatened to bring the matter to light.
(5) The weather has no business to be so warm in winter.

13. Attention in Cognitive Neuroscience: An Overview

1. 回答问题
(1) The important aspect of understanding the current developments is to track the convergence of evidence from various methods of study.
(2) First, the use of microelectrodes with alert animals showed that attention altered the activity of individual cells. Second, anatomical and physiological methods of studying parts of the brain allowed more meaningful investigation of localization of cognitive functions in moral people.
(3) First, there exists an attentional system of the brain that is at

least somewhat anatomically separate from various data-processing systems. Second, attention is carried out by networks of anatomical areas. Third, the brain areas involved in attention do not carry out the same function, but specific computations are assigned to different areas.

(4) They are the posterior parietal lobe, the superior colliculus, and the pulvinar.

2. 英译汉
(1) 信息加工机制探索有助于支持注意的多种选择性的研究开始于二战后的听觉研究。
(2) 这些研究表明,针对感觉信息所发现的平行组织扩展到了语义加工。
(3) 这些工作表明,当猴子受到训练去注意一个地方,神经元发放率得到有选择的提高的区域数目是相对有限的。
(4) 我们用注意的根源来指显得为注意所特有、而非主要参与其他加工形式的那些解剖区域。
(5) 现在不可能详细说明脑的完整注意系统,但已多少知道有关执行下述三项主要注意机能的脑区:对感觉刺激特别是视觉空间中位置的定向,无论感觉的还是来自记忆的靶子事件的觉察;以及维持警觉状态。
(6) 研究集中在感觉定向反映着一个事实,即这个机能在多数尝试中是选来将认知的机能和神经的机能连接起来的一个机能。

3. 词汇与短语
(1) priority
(2) parallel
(3) integrity

(4) mechanism
(5) capacity
(6) alert
(7) allocated
(8) underlie

4. 句型模拟
(1) Given the chance, my parents would like to send me abroad to further my studies.
(2) A gas-stove is similar to an oil-stove.

5. 汉译英
(1) Two enemy battalions were disengaged from the battle after suffering heavy casualties.
(2) Prevention and cure are both attended to.
(3) This addition may interfere with the symmetry of the building.
(4) the contract specifies read tiles, not slates, for the roof.
(5) He was an objective rather than a subjective writer.

14. Attention, Intelligence, and the Frontal Lobes

1. 判断正误
(1) T.
(2) F. The role of novelty in dual-task interference has been noted since the nineteenth century.
(3) T.
(4) T.

2. 英译汉

(1) 例如两个视觉或两个手工任务,将会比不同感觉通道的输入或输出任务表现出更强的干扰,表明在特定目的和感觉通道特异的加工系统内存在着冲突。
(2) 另外一个相关变量是环境线索对行动的作用,它可以把随意行为与刺激驱动行为区别开来。
(3) 然而,我认为习俗所谓聪明与否的观点是不正确的,而且额叶的功能,Spearman 的 g 因素和双重任务干扰确实是紧密联系的,在新异的情境和微弱的环境线索下,通过对行为的控制而相互联系。
(4) 与此相应,把新异性与线索的作用和对行为控制的标准叙述相联系是很有效的。
(5) 行为是由抽象的层次结构支配的观点和有关额叶的文献已经让人们产生了同样的兴趣。
(6) 对于层次的选择行动的观点,有人也许会问特殊的目的是如何在特定时间被选择以控制行动的。

3. 词汇与短语
(1) remaining
(2) novelty
(3) options
(4) bias
(5) consistent
(6) conflict
(7) convention
(8) damage
(9) explicit
(10) demonstration

4. 汉译英

(1) The term "Red Skin" was contemptuously applied to American Indians.

(2) After many years, rocks break down into dirt.

(3) Having the stolen goods in his possession implicated him in the robbery.

(4) He prudently pursued the plan.

(5) He was weighted with troubles.

15. Implicit Memory: A New Frontier for Cognitive Neuroscience

1. 判断正误

(1) T

(2) F. It is no doubt that we have witnessed the birth and development of a new subfield of memory research when we looked back to 1980 from the vantage point of the present.

(3) F. A number of studies have produced dissociations that satisfy the retrieval intentionality criterion.

(4) T.

(5) T.

2. 英译汉

(1) 这一章的标题"内隐记忆"是记忆研究领域中一个相对新颖的领域。

(2) 除了概念上的收获以外,内隐记忆的研究对于近期的研究和理论产生了深远的影响。

(3) 当代有关内隐及外显记忆的研究可以追述到本世纪60年代和70年代发展起来的两条不相关的研究路线上。

(4) 认知的神经心理学的证据的汇合提供了区分内隐和外显记忆

的基础。

(5) 我们所面临的一个困难是:当试图操作和实验性地检验内隐记忆时,内隐记忆测验会受到外显记忆的影响。

(6) 另一个不容辩驳的证据来源于 Weldon 和 Roediger 的研究,他们的结果表明当所呈现的是词义的图片,而不是词本身时,补笔测验中的启动效应就不见了。

3. 词汇与短语
(1) eliminate
(2) traced
(3) converting
(4) criterion
(5) initiated
(6) contaminated
(7) varies
(8) intact

4. 汉译英
(1) They denounced the exposure of children to such corruption literature.
(2) Everybody was filled with concern when news came that the ship was sinking.
(3) The book had a great impact on its readers.
(4) It is difficult to dissociate the man from his position.

16. Mental Models, Deductive Reasoning, and the Brain
1. 判断正误
(1) F. If deduction is a purely verbal process then it will not be af-

fected by damage to the right hemisphere. It is affected by such damage. It is not a purely verbal process.
(2) T.
(3) F. Experimental studies have indeed found evidence for both initial propositional representations and mental models.
(4) T.
(5) F. The general procedure of searching for alternative models are used to test validity.
(6) T.

2. 英译汉
(1) 认知科学家门对演绎推理进行了广泛研究,人们对这种推理的了解也比对其他思维形式的了解更为深入。
(2) 人们在理解言语时,就会产生一种与情景有关的模型,这种模型类似于人们所感知的或想象的某种事件,而非听他人所言。
(3) 本章先阐述这些回顾,然后在众多研究的基础上,对心理模型进行一种完整的解释。
(4) 因此我们可以用寻找另一种模型的一般性程序来检验推理的效度。
(5) 满足感是日常大小灾难的主要原因。

3. 词汇与短语
(1) analogous
(2) accordingly
(3) denotes
(4) conceived
(5) exhausted
(6) promise

(7) generalize
(8) predicted

4. 句型模拟
(1) Granted that he has enough money to buy the house, it doesn't mean he is going to do so.
(2) We have no need of your advice.

5. 汉译英
(1) "Hot" is the converse of "cold".
(2) True charity does not consist in almsgiving.
(3) Spanish is akin to Latin.
(4) I have a lot to say in relation to that affair.
(5) The American Congress corresponds to the British Parliament.

17. Models of Consciousness: Serial or Parallel in the Brain?
1. 判断正误
(1) T.
(2) F. In an information processing sequence, each output serves as input to the next processor.
(3) T.
(4) T.
(5) T.

2. 英译汉
(1) 意识应被证明是独立的,而大脑的神经活动和信息加工在缺乏意识的情况下,也不应有所改变。
(2) 有神经元活动表征的任何信息都对当前意识现象的形成起着

作用,那么这些信息产生的充分和必要条件又是什么呢?
(3) 它们可能反映了信息加工序列中的一个特定阶段,或可能共同具有某些在适应上有重要意义的情景特性。
(4) 意识的知觉范围并不限制那些对它有作用的表征的类型。
(5) 表征的内容对意识有作用并不排除它改变反应的倾向。不过,它也使个体根据情境对信号进行评估,在此情况下,其适应的意义依赖于情境。

3. 词汇与短语

(1) modify
(2) medium
(3) implement
(4) distinct
(5) distinctive
(6) perception
(7) dispersed
(8) supplanted
(9) characterized
(10) property

4. 汉译英

(1) Start with the aim of doing harm to others only to end up with ruining oneself.
(2) So much noise is not consistent with comfort.
(3) A prior engagement will preclude them from coming.
(4) Language teachers often extract examples from grammar books.
(5) Social practice alone gives rise to human knowledge.

参考书目：

1. 德汉词典　上海外语教育出版社　1982
2. 拉丁语汉语词典　上海外语教育出版社　1988
3. 牛津现代高级英汉双解词典　商务印书馆　牛津大学出版社　1988
4. 现代英文实用词组　香港华通编辑部　1977
5. 西方心理学家文选　唐钺译　科学出版社　1959
6. 西方心理学家文选　张述祖等译　人民教育出版社　1983
7. 西方心理学史大纲　唐钺编　北京大学出版社　1982
8. 心理学史——心理学思想的主要趋势　黎黑著　刘恩久等译　上海译文出版社　1990
9. 心理学著作　张人骏等编　天津人民出版社　1983
10. 新英汉词典　上海译文出版社　1979
11. 英语搭配大词典　江苏教育出版社　1988
12. 中国大百科全书心理学卷　大百科全书出版社　1991
13. Michael S. Gazzaniga, The Cognitive Neuroscience. A Bradford Book, The Mit Press, Cambridge, Massachusetts, USA, 1975.